BRADLEY R. SMITH
A Personal History of Moral Decay

NINE-BANDED BOOKS

A Personal History of Moral Decay

Copyright © 2014 Bradley R. Smith

ISBN-10: 0989697282
ISBN-13: 978-0989697286

Nine-Banded Books
PO Box 1862
Charleston, WV 25327
NineBandedBooks.com

Special thanks to:

Jim Crawford, Anita Dalton, Ann Sterzinger, and Tito Perdue

Cover design by Kevin I. Slaughter

Foreword

EVERY LIFE is punctuated with fraught moments, some of them transcendently good, some bad, some ethereal, and some commonplace enough to link whole populations together. What Bradley Smith has done is to call up instances from his own life, and in a calm, even whimsical voice to confide the adventures and sudden elucidations that have been granted him.

Life is a process, not a script, and I am glad to see writers finally turning away from "closure," from denouements designed to bring things to a tidy end. It is as if everything that could be done by humans has been done, and if not by us, by others at least. In *A Personal History of Moral Decay*, Smith seems to have made it his project to gather up a sampling of his own particular moments and then pass them off to us—a generous, lapidary, and much appreciated gift.

Tito Perdue
May, 2014

A Personal History of Moral Decay

Contents

Joseph Conrad and the Monster from the Deep ~ 9

The Daring Young Man Meets William Saroyan ~ 19

Something Wrong in Our House ~ 29

Laughing at the Dead. Not Laughing. ~ 35

The Last of the Romans ~ 47

The Morning the Sun Was a Knockout ~ 61

Saved by the Animals ~ 73

Barney's Beanery ~ 85

Secret Spindles ~ 101

Americans at Sea ~ 143

Sue Ann, Ruby, Jenny and Me ~ 155

Old Manuscripts, Old Lives ~ 167

Waiting for Saigon to Fall ~ 179

Lt. Han's Brother's Throat ~ 199

Che Guevara in Saigon ~ 217

Veil of Maya ~ 231

The Journal ~ 247

Libertarians, Aliens, and Malcontents ~ 267

Love at the Nirvana Arms ~ 279

When Cows Bark ~ 293

"Joseph Conrad and the Monster from the Deep"

(1935 / 1965)

One morning when I was five years old my father rented a black automobile and he drove my aunt and me up the hill to the parking lot behind the county hospital. I watched Father walk across the asphalt into the hospital and after a while when he came out my mother was with him and they each had a baby in their arms. It was all a surprise to me and I didn't know what to think. I hadn't known my mother was pregnant. I didn't know what pregnant was. I noticed that first my aunt Grace was very happy to see them, and when they got to the car both my father and mother were very happy. Father was wearing a snap-brim hat.

Later on I came to love my brothers. Mother and Father named the first-born Ronald, and the second Richard. Ronald was a little larger than Richard. On Saturday mornings Mother would put a white blanket on the rug in the front room and lay the twins on it. The neighbors would come over and my grandfather came on the streetcar from Hollywood to where we lived in South Central in his black suit and vest and white shirt and tie and his white hair and everyone gathered in chairs around the blanket where my brothers were and watched them and laughed and talked.

I was just learning how to play baseball and I got the idea that when my brothers grew up and were my age that I could teach them how to play. It was difficult for me to throw the ball up and hit it at the same time, I remember. Sometimes I would miss the ball and hit the little concrete incinerator with the bat. We lived in a little house then behind a large one and sometimes when I hit the ball into the screened porch on the back of the house in front a woman who rolled her stockings down over her calves would come out and speak to me and I would get angry because she was interfering with my plans for my brothers. Anyhow in the end it did not matter about the baseball because pretty soon Richard died of the whooping cough. He was seven months old. And then a couple months later Ronald died too.

When Richard died I didn't know what to think. I listened to how my mother cried. I heard my aunt say to her that it didn't help to cry and that anyhow Mother still had two sons left and that was a lot. I remembered how my aunt didn't have any children at all. After a while I started crying too and no one could get me to stop.

Later on when Ronald died I cried right from the beginning. Mother sat on a chair beside the sewing machine in the bedroom and cried with my aunt's hand on her shoulder while I cried alone in the big chair in the front room.

The funerals of course were difficult but afterward things got back to normal. We were not a family to make a great fuss over things. We went to the cemetery a few times on Sunday afternoons and then we didn't go anymore. I don't remember Mother crying anymore after that, and she didn't go on about how her sons were dying or how hard life was or anything like that.

Secretly, I thought about my brothers a lot, about how it had been when they were alive and how much I wanted them back. Many times when I thought about them it made me cry. We weren't a family to go on about such things so I was very careful to not let anyone know how I felt. I was only a child perhaps but when the memory of my brothers came over me and it was necessary to cry I understood perfectly well how to go off by myself.

That's how it was for three or four years and then the memories slowed down until they hardly came at all. But one night when I was fifteen years old the memory of my brothers came to me in a dream. I woke up out of a dead sleep crying over my brothers who had been dead now for ten years. I couldn't even remember what they looked like. By then we were living in the big house on the front of the lot and I had my own little bedroom but I had been sobbing so hard in my sleep that it woke my mother and father in their bedroom and they came in to me. They were very concerned and wanted to do something for me or say something but I could not tell them and I could not stop sobbing. Afterward I never forgot that night and how it wrenched me, and many times I tried to figure out what it meant but I could never get a handle on it.

Because I loved my own brothers so much it always made me sad to meet people who resented how their parents had favored one of the other children over themselves. I know from my own experience that the love of one brother for the other could overcome anything like that. But there were always people who insisted that this could not be true absolutely, and that always made me impatient and angry. It came to be a touchy matter with me and I got so I didn't like to discuss it or have it brought up.

Now, here is where this story, which I have tried to keep very simple, begins to slip through my fingers.

When I was twenty-one, for reasons that were not entirely clear to me, I decided to become a writer. Once I began to write I never gave it up. I did a lot of other things in order to make money because it was impossible for me to write without making the money, but all that time I knew I was a writer. I thought I understood that if I tried to be something other than the one thing in me that had a chance to grow large, that thing would not grow and in the end something else would snuff it out.

I worked hard at the writing but it went bad from the beginning. I couldn't put my finger on what the trouble was. One year it seemed to be one thing, the next year something else. Over the years I came to see that I had not found out what my subject was. You can laugh if you want but I worked hard at the writing for fifteen years and I wasn't able to discover what it was I was supposed to write about. I had reached that place with the writing that I no longer made a distinction between the writing and the living out of my life.

It was incredible for me to realize that I was thirty-five years old and had no place to sleep except on the couch of a friend and that I still hadn't published my first book and that other things had started to happen with me that I didn't understand. There were periods when I wasn't able to write at all. I would get very intense. It made me feel unusually intense to see or feel things almost any day that were worth writing and yet not be able to write them. And then oftentimes, when I was unable to write, I would realize that I had started thinking about my brothers. It didn't make sense.

One evening when I was very intense about not being able to write and was thumbing nervously through a magazine, I came across a notice about a new book on Joseph Conrad. I felt a degree of excitement about the notice that seemed pointless. Thought recalled that a few months before I had read some of Conrad's letters. One line from one of the letters popped up in my mind:

"I believe that when I was a boy something came into my life and began eating it up."

When thought recalled that sentence I became so intense that I literally rushed out the door onto the street. I had never felt a higher level of intensity. I hurried aimlessly up one of the back streets in Hollywood. I had learned that during the periods of highest tension the most profitable act is not to think but to focus on the tension itself until something exploded. I wound up on Santa Monica Boulevard and realized I was headed toward

Barney's Beanery near La Cienega. I was walking under great pressure when I found myself opposite the Rosedale cemetery. It was commonplace for me to walk past the cemetery and I had never thought anything about it but that night it came to me that here was where my brothers had been buried thirty years earlier. At that moment I began seeing things from out of that old life.

I saw the inside of the little house we lived in when I was a child. A pale blanket was spread out on the rug in the front room and the neighbors and my grandfather in his black suit were laughing and watching Ronald and Richard scoot around on the blanket on their backs. I watched myself walk into the room, and as I did I saw my head transform into the head of a white wolf. I watched myself grab up one of the babies and eat him. I don't know which one. I was wild. I watched myself grab up the second baby, tear off his arms and legs and eat them. No one there in the room dared to interfere. His head was like thin white jade, and when I shoved it into my jaws and crushed it bitter fluids poured out in my mouth.

Out there on the sidewalk in the dark I was afraid I was going to faint. I stopped in the doorway of a closed storefront and leaned into the corner to keep from falling. When the fluids came out in my mouth I wanted to vomit but I couldn't. I stood in the doorway looking across the street at the tan-colored stucco wall that goes around the cemetery. I wanted to be certain that I was not going to see anymore. I kept seeing the scene where I had become a wolf and had eaten my brothers, but I was not there any longer. After a while I didn't see the scene any more and saw only the street and the cars going by with their headlights on.

As I continued my walk along toward Barney's memory recalled how, when my brothers were still alive, I had come down with the whooping cough. I remembered how Mother explained to me very seriously how I wasn't to go into the bedroom where the twins were because I was sick and they could catch my sickness. Oftentimes however when Mother went outside to hang up the wash say, or out front to get the mail, I went in the bedroom to see how Ronald and Richard were doing. I did tricks with my face to make them laugh, and I kissed them. I would keep one ear cocked and when I heard Mother coming back on the walk I would return to the front room and start playing by myself very quietly on the floor.

After that night across from the Rosedale cemetery where I had been willing to watch myself gorge on my little brothers I thought, okay. It can be argued that it is a good thing to see, finally, what you have done that is not right and get over it. People do argue that when you were very young, and especially if you were only a child and you committed a heinous crime, that you can expiate your guilt by confessing it and by accepting the fact that what you did was shameful, and you can turn a corner with your life. That's probably true for some men, but for me it didn't do the trick.

Afterward I was still unable to write what I should have been able to write, and I still suffered periods of intensity that were hardly bearable. I didn't feel particularly guilty about what I had remembered having done to my brothers. I understood that for years I must have felt guilty, but now that it was out in the open, I found it an interesting and unusual act for a six-year-old child to have knowingly, or even half-knowingly, committed. More than that, the tale was visually absorbing, it was a good story, one that I could tell at Barney's—if I was certain to make clear that the joke was on me.

Originally I had thought that my act of visual confession was the point to this story, but it didn't satisfy me. I kept thinking about it. It seemed that there should be more, or that it should be different. I couldn't figure it out. And then last night I had this dream.

I dreamed that I was on a pier and that a casket had been dredged up from the bottom of the ocean. People were standing around looking at it. The casket contained the body of a man my age. The body was completely rotted away from the waist down.

The rest of him was rotted and pretty much decomposed also. His right arm resembled a big turkey wing that had been cooked and now was laying in a mess of gravy. It was sickening.

I heard one of the onlookers say: "Throw the monster back."

Hearing those words, the rotted face of the corpse took on an expression, something that resembled a smile. With a struggle that appeared to take all its strength, the loathsome thing raised itself up on its one good elbow and, the rotted face smiling sweetly, said:

"I am not a monster."

When I saw how sweetly the thing smiled, my heart melted. My feelings toward it changed from loathing its monstrous ugliness, to feelings of sympathy.

And then I heard another voice say:

"Isn't that incredible? He's been dead for thirty years, and now he's coming back to life."

"The Daring Young Man Meets William Saroyan"

(1953)

That morning in the forest we fell out alongside the trail for a rest and some chow. There was the creek, the trail that followed alongside it, the trees, the bars of slanting sunlight with the specks drifting down, the underbrush and so on. It was a nice spring morning.

I ate a can of C-rations and threw the empty over my shoulder. After a moment it seemed something wasn't right. When I looked back the empty was sitting on the quilted, uniformed chest of a Chinese infantryman.

"Hey, Decker," I said. "Look at that."

Decker looked back. "Shit."

"I threw my empty back there and it fell on the guy's chest. Right side up and everything."

"Shit," Decker said.

"I'm going to get a look at him."

"Say hello for me."

There was the brown leather chest strap, the quilted cotton cap with the ear flaps tied on the top of the head, the serene sickly yellow face. I circled the corpse carefully, my M-1 at ready, though I couldn't have explained why I was being so careful because the corpse was half gone. It was missing from the belly button on down.

"Hey Decker, this guy's only half here."

Decker looked around again. He didn't say anything.

"He's been whacked off clean as a whistle just above his San Brown belt."

"What the fuck are you doing over there?"

"I'm being careful to look at him from the top end, I can tell you that much."

I couldn't see any wires attached to the corpse. I couldn't see his legs or ass anywhere either. I looked around. Nothing. It made me feel funny.

"Decker, don't you have any curiosity?"

"Yeah, I do. I want to know what the fuck you're doing back there."

"The other half must be around here someplace."

"When you find it what are you going to do with it? Save it?"

"It must have been artillery."

"Get the fuck down here before you start tripping off wires or some other goddamn thing."

I looked through the trees and the underbrush but I didn't find anything and then the column started up again and I fell in with my squad.

"Are you satisfied" Decker said?

"I'd like to know the answer to that one."

"The answer to that one is that Chink never had no legs. He never had no ass either. It's the latest thing in Chink infantry. He's probably following us right now."

Decker was always saying something to make me laugh. The image of hundreds, maybe thousands of Chinese infantry gliding through the forest all around us with no legs and no ass was too much.

Decker said: "You won't laugh tonight when you wake up and find that no-ass Chinaman cutting your balls off."

"Will you quit it," I said? "I can't stop laughing."

The corpses were everywhere. In the forests, on the ridgelines, along the trails, in the paddies, in the thatched huts and in the houses with tile roofs. At first they were in the snow and on the ice, later they were in the mud, the swollen creeks, the irrigation ditches. In the end they were in the dirt in the hot summer sunlight covered with flies.

The first corpses were three Chinese machine gunners in a shallow hole on a ridgeline. I stopped in the cold afternoon wind at the edge of the hole and looked down on them. They were charred black, like barbecue left too long on the spit. Grey dirt blew across the top of the hole and settled on the charred heads and hands. I snapped a photograph with my brownie box and hustled on up the ridgeline to my place in the column.

One afternoon in a storm we climbed up on a small plateau where the Chinese had slaughtered a battalion of Englishmen. The English had buried their dead where they died. We stayed on the plateau three days and nights. The first couple days the rain washed out the graves. The Chinese had had time to bury their corpses deeper than the English. It's always better when you win. I didn't have the same interest in American corpses as I did in the Chinese and Korean.

They made a corpse out of O'Neil by shooting him through his radio pack so that he fell face down in three inches of paddy water where no one could get to him. They made a corpse out of Steubbens when they shot his jaw off with a fifty so that he bled to death in the middle of the dirt road. He couldn't have made it without the jaw anyway. Doug Smith became a corpse one black night as the result of a single bullet to his heart from a Chinese officer's pistol while Doug stood at my side on a mountain ledge.

Those things were all right with me. I didn't have bad feelings toward the Chinese for how they made corpses out of us. Fair's fair. We made more corpses out of them then they did of us. When Doug fell across my feet with a single anguished death groan I sat over him all that night and in the dawn light when I saw how yellow he had become I thought: "Well that's all right, they turn pale and we turn yellow." But when the Chinese made Captain Grey into a corpse with a machine gun my feelings began to change, and I didn't look at corpses the same way I had before. They were less interesting than they had been, but more meaningful.

One afternoon when we relieved the Fifth Battalion there were the usual corpses. One Chinese corpse that wasn't dead yet but would be any minute was sitting against an embankment with part of its skull off. A Mexican kid was sitting on the embankment above, his legs dangling down, poking a straw through the open place in the Chinaman's skull. Each time he poked the straw into the open place the Chinese who was becoming a corpse moaned and shrugged its shoulders.

"Don't do that again," I said. "I mean it."

"Oh, man," the kid said. "It's a Chink." He gave another poke with the straw and the corpse moaned and shrugged its shoulders. I started up the embankment. The kid jumped up and stepped back.

"MAN," he yelled, "YOU CRAZY OR WHAT?

"LEAVE IT ALONE."

"IT'S A FUCKING CHINK."

I put the barrel of my M-1 to the soon-to-be corpse's ear. The blast tore off the back of its head. I'd wanted it to go straight through but I hadn't done it right.

"NOW DO WHAT YOU WANT, ASSHOLE."

"Oh, man," the kid said quietly. "You make me feel bad."

When I was a child my ambition had been to go to war and be killed in battle. My greatest hero was Roland. I'd read the Saga of Roland at nine or ten and I wasn't able to get over it. I never wanted to be a fireman or a scientist or president. I wanted to be a great hero like Roland and fight the foreigners to a standstill and be killed at the moment of my greatest feat. I daydreamed about it for years. The important point, the way I looked at it when I was a child, was to remember that if they don't kill you when you are trying, you aren't trying hard enough, or what you are trying isn't important.

After they brought me back from Korea to the hospitals I had time to think about what had happened to me over there and what had happened to the others. I thought about how I hadn't tried to do anything heroic. Real life it seemed had thwarted my ambition. At moments of great danger I had looked to my survival. The rest of the time I had tried to not be too uncomfortable. And I had followed, I hadn't led. And then it wasn't as if there had been some significance to the fighting itself. None of us had thought that. If there had been some significance to it perhaps a lot of us would have behaved differently than how we did. In those days I still didn't understand how important significance is.

One morning in the ward I was sitting cross-legged on the bed remembering. I did that a lot. Remembering. At one point, without any preliminary consideration, I stepped into my slippers and walked through the empty wooden corridors to the Post Exchange and bought a pencil and a fifteen cent notepad and returned to the ward. I got up on the bed again and began writing down how it had been the last day on line. The mountainside, the trees, the Chinese bunkers, the machine guns, the blasts of the hand grenades, the blood bubbling from the hand, the bones gleaming wetly in the sunlight, how I sat beneath the tree and searched through the leaves and pine needles for the missing finger while the air swarmed with bullets and falling branches and the yelling and the noise.

It didn't come out right so the next day I sat at a card table in the little recreation room at the end of the ward with the fog pressing at the windows and wrote it out again. It didn't come out right then either. It never did come out right. But I started writing down the other things I kept remembering all the time. The corpses, the dreaming, the old childhood, the father. The usual stuff. None of it came out right but I began thinking I liked the writing and that I would go on with it.

The hospital lasted ten months then they discharged me from the army. I had no plans. I moved into the front bedroom at my parents' house. I hitchhiked to Mexico City and came back. I took a job loading trucks at a dairy plant. I enrolled in a drawing class. When the dairy plant laid me off I found a job as a brakeman for the Southern Pacific. No matter what I did or what job I worked at, when I got home I would set up the card table in the bedroom and try to write something. It wasn't easy to think up things to write. It was as if I had already written what was important to me and there was nothing left to write about.

One night at Southern Pacific yard I had to jump off a runway tanker and when I hit the ground I crushed the left heel so I had to quit the railroad. When I could move around again I took a job driving an ice cream truck through the neighborhood. There was a loudspeaker on the cab and a musical recording I could switch on to get the attention of the kids as I drove slowly up their block. I didn't mind the job. I didn't really mind anything but oftentimes I felt as if there was something inside me coming up, that something was going to happen.

I wrote to the consul of Vietnam in San Francisco inquiring about the procedure for enlisting in the Vietnamese army. I didn't have anything against the Viet Minh but I was willing to do what was necessary. I felt it was important to start doing something. The Consul responded saying there was no procedure for accepting foreigners into the Vietnamese military.

One quiet, desperate Sunday afternoon I drove to the beach at Playa Del Rey and parked the car at the edge of the road and looked out over the sand and the blue ocean. A breeze was blowing off the water and I rolled down the windows so it could blow through the car. It was a nice afternoon but I could feel it coming up and I didn't know what it was or what to do about it.

I had a couple paperback books with me. I decided to start the one by William Saroyan. The first story was called "The Daring Young Man On The Flying Trapeze." The young man in the story was a writer. He must have been about my own age. The only thing important to him was the writing. He lived alone in a rented room and wrote every day but he couldn't get any money for his stories. He couldn't pay the rent on his room and most of the time he didn't have money for food.

One day after he finished writing he went out walking. After a while he came to a café. He stopped and looked through the window. He looked at the people inside eating food, people who had ordinary jobs and ordinary salaries and could afford to eat food in ordinary cafes. The young writer knew he did not want to be like them but he couldn't stop looking at their food and imagining he had some.

He walked around the neighborhood looking in all the café windows. He was weak and hungry but he was happy because he was living the life of a writer and not the ordinary life of the others. He walked slowly and uncertainly back to his room and collapsed on the bed. He grew delirious with hunger. He had already been delirious with that other hunger, the hunger to be true to himself, and now the room began to whirl in a hunger delirium. It was a wonderful story.

Then the young writer died. I was stunned. He had starved himself to death on principle! He had died for his art! It had never occurred to me it was possible to do that. No one had told me that writing could be that important. Were you supposed to find that out on your own? Everything seemed to be up to the writer himself. You had to decide for yourself. You could take the writing however far you wanted. I knew at that moment that that was what I wanted. I had never thought about it before that moment but I recognized it the moment I saw it. I wanted to risk death for the writing. I wanted to take it all the way.

The wind had come up considerably. It blew off the top of the blue ocean and across the sand and through the rolled down windows of the car. I sat on the front seat behind the steering wheel in a kind of elevated stupor, the Saroyan book still open, its pages fluttering in my hands. I felt the tears going sideways across my face. That's how hard the wind was blowing.

"Something Wrong in Our House"

(1953)

When I came back from Korea I didn't see anything wrong, I thought that everything at our house was okay. The very next day my aunt rang me up and invited me for coffee. My uncle came too and we sat at the counter in a café that was all wrong while they told me about my mother and father.

My aunt said: "After you left for over there they had an argument about you and he knocked her down. Did you know he hasn't spoken to her in all the time you were away?"

"No," I said. "I didn't know."

My aunt said: "Imagine living in the same house and not speaking with someone for eight months. Why, it's just crazy."

I didn't say anything.

"After you went away and they had the fight he wouldn't ride in the same car with her so she's had to take the bus back and forth to work all the time."

I was wishing they hadn't chosen this particular place to tell me about Mother and Father. Anyone could see that it was all wrong with its neon lights and the aluminum cooking area and the white plastic covered stools.

"Your mother cooks breakfast and supper just like always," my aunt was saying, "but he won't eat with her. He walks up to the corner and eats at that Jake's Café. It's nothing but a greasy spoon that place."

My uncle said: "Your father always had an ungovernable temper but now it's worse than ever. No one can talk sense to him."

He paused, for me to say something I believe, but I remained silent.

"Do you remember the time at the supper table when he knocked you out of your chair on the floor because he said you were eating too fast? I don't think you were ten years old."

"I remember that," I said. It made me grin, remembering it. "Wasn't that something? I thought I could get away with it because we had company. It's sort of funny when you look back on it. I mean eating too fast."

"He used to swear at you," my uncle said, "like you were a man."

"I don't remember that."

"He called you names that even now I wouldn't say in front of your aunt."

I waited for him to go on.

"One night I told him: Henry, you're crazy, I said. No one talks to his boy that way. You must be crazy."

My aunt said: "He just wasn't much of a father to you sometimes. I know that must sound like a terrible thing to say."

She put her hand over mine where it rested on the bright white counter alongside my coffee cup. "We've never had children, your uncle and I, but if we had, we couldn't have asked for a son any nicer than you."

I was very careful to make my hand lie absolutely still on the counter underneath my aunt's hand.

My uncle said: "We're telling you this because we were afraid for your mother. We don't know how much longer she's going to be able to go on with him."

My aunt said: "Now that you're back it will be better for her. She'll be able to count on you."

She paused as if she wanted me to say something again, and when I didn't say anything she went on.

"You know, after you left your mother was very sick. The doctor told her she was passing blood, even pus. There wasn't anything he could do to help. It was just worry over what might happen to you. As soon as she got the telegram saying you were in the hospital and out of danger, she got better."

I knew especially I should say something about how Mother had been but I couldn't think of anything to say. What came to my mind just then was how one night when I was a very young child, Mother and Father took me with them to visit my aunt and uncle: "If it wasn't for the kid, I would have left her a long time ago."

I said goodbye to my aunt and uncle and when I got home, Mother was standing at the kitchen sink crying.

"You're the most selfish kid I've ever seen in my life," she said.

"What's the matter, Mother?"

"Where have you been, will you tell me that?"

"Just driving around. I didn't know anything was wrong."

"Why didn't you telephone? You've only been back one day and you can't be home for supper. I don't know how you can be so selfish."

"I didn't think, I guess."

"You didn't think," Mother said. "And now your father has hit me again. I'm not going to take very much more."

"Why did he hit you?"

"It doesn't matter why. If you had been home when you should have been, it wouldn't have happened."

She tried to stop crying but she kept crying and sort of choking. I didn't know what to do. In all my life I had hardly seen her cry. I was very uncomfortable because I could see how she was trying not to but that she couldn't make herself stop.

"Just once in your life," she said, "try to think of someone besides yourself."

"Where's Father now?"

"Oh, I don't know."

"Did he say when he was coming home?"

"No he didn't. And when he comes back I don't want you to say anything to him."

"I don't understand why he should hit you." I felt myself growing angry. Some of my anger came out in my voice.

"Now I'm telling you, Brad. When your father comes in I don't want you to interfere."

I was really angry. I watched television a while then went to bed to wait. Gradually my anger slipped away into darkness. When I had been a child I had hated my father but that had been when I was a child. When you're grown up, it seems, your father is simply your father and there are things you want to talk to him about.

When Father came back I waited half an hour then went to the back bedroom. There was smoke in the air and the glow of a cigarette. At first I thought that perhaps I would hit him, but when I got there I knew for sure I just wanted to talk.

Father said: "What do you want?"

Before I could answer I heard Mother call out from her bedroom: "Brad, I told you I didn't want you to interfere."

"What do you want?" Father said.

Mother said: "Get out of there Brad. Now I mean it."

Father said very quietly: "What were you going to do when you came in here, Brad?"

"Brad," Mother said from her bedroom, "it's none of your business. Get back in your own room."

I went to my room and got back into bed. There had been something wrong in our house all my life. I never knew what it was, but there had always been something. Nobody ever talked about it. There were things tonight that I wanted to say to her as well as to Father. But now I guessed I wasn't going to say them. I guess I suspected all along.

"Laughing at the Dead. Not Laughing."

(1955)

We took the second-class bus from Mexico City to the plaza in Xochimilco, then started walking carrying the bundles with our suits and capes and the swords. The afternoon was sunny and hot. The street was paved with rocks for several blocks, then it was dirt. I hadn't noticed before, but maestro Fijardo walked like a duck. I pointed it out to Sergio.

"Mida. El maestro camine como un pato."

Sergio grinned and shook his head no. He nodded toward Antonio, warning me.

"Camine como un pato," I said. I started walking like a crippled duck. Antonio looked at me suspiciously. Sergio grinned and shook his head no.

Maestro Fijardo turned in through two tall, green wooden doors in an adobe wall and we followed him into an old stock pen. The bullring was a corral built from poles and timbers inside the rectangular stock pen. Spectators would buy their tickets and enter the same doors we had, which is where, during the week, the animals were still driven through.

Inside the pen in one corner was a small modern stuccoed house. We went in the house to the kitchen and stood around, then we went in the bare little bedroom and began changing. I took off my clothes down to my shorts and drew on the long pink stockings. I put on the white shirt, then the green tights I'd rented with the heavy white embroidery and the silver ornaments. The seam on one leg opened up so I took the tights off and got the sewing kit from the maestro and sewed up the tear with green thread. There were four repaired places on the tights, three on the right thigh and one on the left. The repaired place on the left thigh was eight inches long and was on the inside of the thigh but there was no stain.

I drew on the tights again and Sergio and I helped each other draw on our slippers because we couldn't bend over to draw on our own slippers. Sergio used hairpins to fasten my pigtail to my hair. The clerk in the second floor showroom where we had rented the equipment we didn't own hadn't had any blond pigtails so I'd rented a brown one. In the little bedroom there was a full-length mirror leaning against one wall and we inspected ourselves carefully. I tried on my rented cap. It had gotten smaller since I'd rented it.

"Do not worry," Sergio said in Spanish. "You can carry it when we enter. You do not have to wear it."

When we started dressing we'd been alone in the bedroom but by the time we were finished the room and the little hallway outside were full of men drinking and smoking cigars and laughing. The Americans from Mexico City came in the bedroom to wish me well. They had cameras with them.

He said: "How do you feel?"

"I feel all right," I said.

"Are you nervous?"

"No. I'm all right."

"If I were in your shoes, I'd be really scared."

"Well, I'm all right."

"Your first formal fight and all."

"Huh?"

"Your first formal fight. Nobody would blame you if you felt anxious."

"Yes. I'm all right though."

There was a moment when the Americans didn't say anything.

"I'm all right," I almost said.

When it was time we walked through the house out into the stock pen. The spectators had climbed up on the adobe wall and they were sitting on the corral rails and peering through the bars. Some were sitting in the dirt eating lunch. Men were drinking beer and whooping it up. There were a lot of people.

On the west side of the corral there was a raised platform with eight metal folding chairs. The judges were sitting up there with their backs to the sun, along with the two Americans and a couple Mexican spectators who had paid extra. The two judges wore neckties and snap-brimmed felt hats.

The flatbed truck with the three big shipping crates was on the east side of the ring backed up to the corral. Each crate held one small bull of mixed blood, a criollo. We walked through the spectators and climbed through the poles into the ring and when the two men with trumpets began to play we strode across the little ring, saluted the judges who nodded gravely in return, and walked back to our place behind the wooden tabla.

Two men in straw hats were standing on the bed of the truck. Now they climbed up on top of one of the crates and at a signal from the chief judge they yanked up its sliding gate and a strong little animal jumped out onto the ground, stumbled, then got up and charged around the corral blowing and bellowing.

In the first moment it looked like a good animal but when Antonio went out to work it, it chose a territory to defend beneath the judge's stand and Antonio, who was the best of the three of us with a fully developed style who we all believed had a career before him, couldn't draw it out. After fifteen minutes of fruitless drudgery, he killed it.

Sergio killed his animal next, which wasn't much better than

Antonio's had been, and when it was time for my animal the crowd was restless. They tossed beer bottles in the ring and yelled insults. The little animal jumped out of her cage into the ring and charged around the corral. It was a two-year-old becerra. She looked very good. She was clearly the best of the three. I watched her carefully from behind the tabla to determine which horn she favored. I was still studying her when Antonio ran out and called her with his capote. She charged beautifully. Antonio performed three good veronicas and ended with a standing remate. The crowd cheered. I turned to Sergio.

"He should not have done that," I said.

"No," Sergio said.

"It is my animal. "

"Yes. Go to her."

I walked out toward the powerful little animal with my capote. Somebody yelled out in Spanish: "Do not be afraid, gringo. That Indian has already shown you how to do it."

I heard men laughing. I called the animal carefully and thoughtfully with the cape.

"Hey, gringo," someone shouted. "You do not have to be so careful. You weigh more yourself than that calf weighs."

I heard the crowd laughing. I made a few passes with the capote. They weren't very good. I didn't understand why. I positioned the becerra very carefully and made two more. They didn't quite work. I heard the maestro shouting for me to exchange the capote for the smaller muleta. At that moment I heard someone yell in Spanish at the top of his voice:

"GUARD YOURSELF. SHE IS COMING!"

I jumped behind the nearest tabla with the maestro.

"NOT THAT LITTLE CALF," the guy yelled. "MY OLD LADY."

The crowd thought that one was funnier still.

The maestro said: "Do not laugh."

"It is all right," I said.

I saw Sergio and Antonio trying not to laugh. Antonio was not trying as hard to not laugh as Sergio was.

The maestro said to them: "Do not laugh."

I tried a few passes with the muleta. I could pass her high but I couldn't work her low. It wasn't clear to me why. High passes don't mean as much with an animal as low passes do, no matter what size it is. I worked her with the right hand, then the left, but I couldn't get anything going. A half-eaten tamale whizzed past my face. A beer bottle hit the animal on the ass and she gave a start. I heard a man shout:

"Hit the gringo, not the cow."

I could hear the laughing.

I exchanged the wooden sword for the killing sword. I lined up the becerra with great care. I wanted to prepare her perfectly and go in perfectly. It had become necessary for me to do this one thing right. Sergio was nearby with his capote to take care of me if anything went wrong.

"Do not wait," he said

I felt like I was being rushed. The afternoon from beginning to end had gone too fast. The animals had moved faster than I'd expected. Antonio, the bastard, had moved faster than I'd expected. Now I was being rushed into the kill.

"Do not wait," Sergio shouted.

The crowd was yelling and taunting me. I wasn't ready, but I was very close. I drew her toward me with the left hand with the muleta and swept her by and as she passed I went in with the sword over her right horn keeping the right elbow high. The blade entered between her withers at a deep angle just like I had practiced it so many times. It went in her body like a hot knife slipping into butter. The ease of the entry took my breath away. At the same time I heard a gasp escape from the crowd.

And then I was standing alone in utter silence before the swaying animal, my right arm half-raised, aware of the fullness that was somehow in the sudden quiet, aware of the late afternoon sunlight flooding the corral, how the trash littering the ground at that moment was somehow not merely trash, aware of the different textures of the ground through the soles of my slippers. I think I was aware in that moment for the first time of the wonderful purity of silence and light when they are inside you too and not just outside.

I watched the vecerra lower her head, I heard her moan, I saw the blood roll down one whither. Snot poured from her nostrils like long lavender and green jewels and trailed in the dirt. I watched her make one last move toward me then fall on her side. I heard the crowd cheer and then Sergio put his knife through her spinal chord just behind the skull and there was the spasm and then the sudden stiffness of her death and then the afternoon was over and when we went in the little house to change back into street clothes there was blood on my right wrist up under the cuff of the white shirt and I knew it wasn't mine. Later on there would be times when it would be my blood.

There were always those Americans who were against the bulls because of the cruelty of the baiting and who treated toreros contemptuously. It isn't possible to deny that it is cruel to bait and kill bulls in public, but bulls don't whine like mistreated dogs or run from danger. Fighting bulls have a different sense of things and when you're in the ring with one you understand the cruelty intellectually but you understand about the cruelty of the bull too and that neither of you will complain about what happens or have hard feelings afterward. I've met many ex-toreros who have been crippled by a bull, the tendons torn from their legs, their forearms twisted, an ear gone or an eye ripped out or a testicle but I never met one who complained about the bulls or had bad feelings toward them.

Nevertheless it troubled me that I couldn't defend the bulls intellectually. It troubled me that even those who had no experience with bulls could talk against them so successfully. I tried one argument then another to defend what I was doing but finally I always understood I was losing the argument on moral grounds. It was very frustrating and troubling. It surprised me sometimes how angry it made me feel.

In Mexico City I usually trained in the Plaza Monumental. At eight in the morning I'd be at the Plaza with the others at the iron gate beneath the stands with my capes and the training sword and when the watchman unlocked the gate we'd walk through the dark tunnel out into the stands, then down through the stands in the bright morning sunshine to the ring where the sand would still be softly dark with the dampness from the night.

I'd do the track work first, running backwards around the ring for twenty minutes, then I'd work with the capes. By midmorning there would be twenty or thirty of us on the sand. At ten-thirty sharp the gatekeeper would wheel out the killing machine and we'd take turns practicing on it. There was the bull's head mounted on a bicycle wheel, and behind it the chunk of maguey plant wired to the frame and then the two long handles. When the machine was run at you the idea was to go in properly with a little class over the right horn and place the sword in the maguey at the correct angle. The angle is very important because if you enter tendida, at too shallow an angle, you won't go deep into vital organs, which is what kills, and you will have to withdraw the sword and go in again and you will have diminished all the work you have done with the animal up to that moment.

From the beginning I felt a particular interest in the sword and after the first corrida in Xochimilco my interest heightened. At the same time I couldn't get over my uneasiness at the barbarity of the way of life I was entering, because I knew that was what it was. I knew I would never be able to convince myself it was right to perform cruel acts in public for pleasure and money. I was willing to convince myself that it was right, but I couldn't, and every morning at eight I was at the iron gate beneath the Plaza with the others.

One morning after I finished training I walked up through the stands and through the tunnel and out again into the bright sunlight and around the Plaza toward Avenida de los Insurgentes. Ahead I saw a truck parked at the curbing filled with workmen wearing straw hats. They sat quietly in the back of the truck. As I approached the rear of the truck I felt I was being watched. I thought probably the men were curious seeing a gringo carrying capes and a sword.

Then I saw the workman lying on the pavement on his back. With a single glance I knew by the position of his body that he had fallen off the back of the truck. Maybe he'd been sitting on the tailgate, the truck had lurched forward suddenly and there you had it. As I drew near I saw that the back of the man's head was perfectly flat against the pavement and that there was blood and other stuff coming out of it.

I looked up at the workmen in the back of the truck. They had been waiting for the moment when I would understand what had happened, and now as I looked up they looked off into the distance or down at their feet. One of the men in the truck, sitting with his back to the cab, grinned at me. He was wearing a ragged shirt with only one sleeve and some of his teeth were missing.

I didn't mean to but I smiled in return. He shrugged his shoulders and gave a little laugh. I looked away. I walked past the truck and on up the street. Behind, I heard someone in the truck begin to talk. Then there were many different voices and there was someone who laughed. I walked on past the concrete soccer stadium that seats a hundred thousand spectators. The grass in the parking way was very green. There were beds of snapdragons and beds of roses and petunias exploding their colors into the brilliant sunlight.

When the bus came I realized I was still smiling. I dropped the fare in the coin box and moved down the aisle. Thought was saying it was all right to laugh at the dead. Then as I started listening to it and thought said it was all right about the bulls too, that it was all right about a lot of things that appear questionable to decent people but that nevertheless are perfectly all right in the real scheme of things, which isn't very much like very many decent people imagine it to be. It was exciting listening to thought go on like that and I understood why I was still smiling.

I didn't get off the bus at my regular stop but went on downtown to the park at the Alameda where I bought a cone of shaved ice from a man with a pushcart. The man put the ice in a white paper cup and poured strawberry syrup over it and I walked across the park through the green shade to where the display of photographs of the old revolutionaries hanging by their necks and the cadavers of working men thrown into piles in the streets were still being exhibited. I looked at the portraits of Zapata, Villa and Carranza and the other historical and non-historical figures. I looked at their horses.

I'd seen the photographs before but it was good looking at them again because I felt I was going to see them now from a new perspective, with a new understanding. At first it was fine and the photographs were very interesting but after a while I started seeing them like I'd seen them the other times. They fascinated me, but they enraged me too. I wanted to tear them off the walls and destroy them. It wasn't the photographs themselves. It was how they were being exhibited. As if they were art.

"The Last of the Romans"

(1963)

Worthington has agreed to let me sleep in his room for a while, along with him and Marlow. I walked over here a couple days ago with my typewriter and a paper bag with my clothes in it. The room is off Highland Avenue a couple blocks from Hollywood Boulevard with an alley entrance, in the basement of an apartment building.

We've taken the mattress off the single bed and put it on the floor and that's where Worthington sleeps. Marlow sleeps on the springs until five-thirty in the morning, then it's my turn. There's no heat so I sleep with my clothes on. At night the face bowl runs over and pops the linoleum tiles off the bathroom floor. The water seeps out into the room and soaks the rug, which is glued to the cement slab. A damp, mildewed odor pervades the air.

Marlow smokes incessantly but never empties an ashtray. He seldom even sets one down. I watch him frying eggs on the hot plate with one hand while he fondly holds his ashtray in the other. A burning cigarette hangs from his lips. Marlow likes to completely fill an ashtray, then remove the butts by spiking them with a Victorian hat pin and stores the filled trays of pure ash in the cupboard. Once I absentmindedly dropped a prune pit onto one of his mounds of pure ash and he looked at me like I'd peed in his coffee.

At night I sit in the armchair and read until I get drowsy, then I walk around the neighborhood or drink coffee someplace until it's time for Marlow to get up. Last night I did four pages of notes for the journal and finished reading a one-volume edition of the *Goncourt Journals*. The Goncourt book pleased me immensely. At one place it was reported to the Emperor, Napoleon the Third, how it was rumored that his faculties were declining. The Emperor replied: "That is consistent with all the reports I have received."

When Worthington comes in about one in the morning Marlow is usually fast asleep on the springs. He's got a growling, strangulation type snore that prevents Worthington from sleeping. Worthington used to get up and turn Marlow over when the snoring started, or reach up with one foot and kick him on top of the head. When he came in tonight, however, he put a Squibbs multi-vitamin capsule in each ear before he laid down on the mattress and that seemed to do the trick.

I feel perfectly content doing nothing. I sleep, I read a little, I do a page or two in the journal. When I think about how I lost my business, how Pamela is divorcing me, I feel as if my life has been cut in half. I walk to the library and flip absentmindedly through the magazines. I walk to Maurice Sobelman's place and we play chess. I secretly hope that when he asks me to stay to dinner I won't be too embarrassed to accept.

This evening after chess Maurice asked me what I'm going to do about money.

"I don't know," I said. "Nothing at all, I hope."

"Yeah?" he said. He gave me a baleful look. "Are you serious?"

"I've made a pact with myself," I said. "I'm going to write. I'm not going to do anything else. And I'm never going to do another man's work again. I'm going to do my own."

"Yeah?" He started taking things out of the refrigerator. "You're getting pretty idealistic, don't you think?"

"Is that what it is?"

"Help me out with this crap. I don't mind feeding you once in a while. I don't want to have to wait on you too."

I put the stuff he gave me on the little table.

"Well, Kiddo, I understand how you feel about work. Who wants to work, for Christ sake? No man in his right mind, that's who. There's something so dreadful about work that the sociologists won't even study it. Not from the point of view of how much damage it does."

Maurice is in his sixties now so he calls me Kiddo. We cooked pork chops and peas and drank Cokes. I told a funny story about Marlow.

Maurice said: "How can you live that way?"

"It's all right."

"It's not all right. You're living with neurotics. And I use that word only because I can't think of a worse one right now. It's all right if a man lives with a neurotic because he has no choice. But it's another story when he does it because he likes it. You'd better decide if you want to take your life seriously or if you're going to piss it away."

"I have decided. I'm going to do both."

"Eat the pork chop. What the hell are you laughing at?"

When people ask me how I can live the way I do I say I don't know and I laugh, but I know. It's because Worthington and Marlow don't ask anything of me. Nothing. If they ever do I'll look for another place to stay. People see me laughing, I'm a big laugher, and they think I'm on top of things. I'm not on top of anything. I just like to laugh.

This evening I was sitting on the springs with my back to the wall making notes for the journal. Worthington was sitting in the armchair reading *The Sexually Adequate Male*. It was his night off. With one hand he shaded his eyes from the naked light bulb while with the other he held a long, pale green cigarette. Worthington has the angular face and body of the rich society blade who loses his fiancée to the Sicilian truck driver.

"God," he said, looking at me from the corner of his eye and grinning sheepishly. "I wonder if they're reading this book in Elmira? I wonder if my sister has read it? If she's even heard of it."

"Your sister?"

Worthington returned to the book but something was agitating him. "You know," he said, "I came to Hollywood to be an actor. I had a good job working for a publisher in New York, I didn't have to come here, but I couldn't get acting out of my mind. Then I discovered one of my aunts, the one who never married, knew a producer out here. I got her to write me a letter of introduction and I quit my job and caught a bus to Hollywood.

"I called the producer as soon as I got here. On the telephone he was very friendly. He invited me to the studio the next morning to see a private showing of a new film. I can't tell you how fortunate I felt. The film was a stag movie showing Greek whores being screwed by goats. There was some other stuff too but that's what I remember most. I practically went into shock. I'd seen stag films before, but I couldn't understand why I was seeing this one. I mean, why had I been invited? Did my acting career depend on how I reacted to what I was watching? I felt so confused I wished I could just go blind.

"Then I saw that the producer, my aunty's friend, was masturbating. We were in this private little screening room, you know how they have them, and he saw me staring at him. It was the most degrading thing I had ever seen. Here was this big burly man smoking a stogie and masturbating and saying: 'Hey, this is the life, eh, Kid? Wha'cha say?' And it was ten o'clock in the morning."

Worthington laughed and ran his fingers through his lank hair. "I think I'm going to write aunty. I'll thank her for the letter of introduction, then I'll tell her everything that happened. I won't leave out any of the details either."

"That's a good idea," I said.

"It isn't that masturbation is offensive. I've masturbated since I was twelve, a boy scout taught me how, but it isn't something I like to do in company for heaven's sake."

When Worthington went to sleep I went out walking in the dark. It was about three in the morning. I thought about how grateful I am to have Worthington and Marlow for friends. I thought about how I walk mostly at night because I don't want anybody to see me who used to know me. I thought about Pamela. I thought about Mother.

This morning I bought some cheese and bread and walked to my lawyer's office where I read part of the transcript of the trial. The transcript is twelve hundred pages and that's the condensed version. I had no idea there was so much of it. Fleishman's office is well appointed. It was pleasant sitting at the oak table. It was pleasant seeing the bookshelves from floor to ceiling packed with clean heavy law books. I read some of my testimony. I read some by the other witnesses. The others read better, more sincere, even those for the prosecution. It was like they knew what was expected of them.

Thought said: "You have to disown yourself." I didn't know what it meant.

Then I understood it was a reference to my shame, as if that were my self.

When I grew too sleepy to hold my head up I walked over to Maurice's. He wasn't home so I sat on his step and waited. When he came back I beat him three out of four games at chess and that made me laugh so hard I almost fainted. I had to brace myself against the wall to keep from falling over.

"It's not natural to laugh like that," Maurice said. "You ought to look into your reasons for doing it pretty carefully."

Life isn't going well for Maurice. He hasn't sold a television script in twelve months. He has a little income from residuals but he's using up his savings.

"I'm too old to live like this," he said. "I'm almost sixty, for Christ sake. I deserve a steady income and a regular lay. Any man my age deserves that much at least, and any decent society would see that he got it. What the hell are those people in Washington thinking about? It's not like the old days when a man could go out and find a whore when he needed one. Girls don't whore anymore. They can't be bothered with that. Nowadays they just screw. That's fine for young bucks who still have all their hair, but where does it leave an old middle-aged guy like me? Out in the cold, that's where."

He puttered around the apartment emptying ashtrays, squinting through his eyeglasses, clicking his false teeth.

"Well," he said, "have you decided yet what you're going to do about money?"

"I'm going to live on my government pension," I said for the hundredth time.

"You can't live on twenty dollars a month. I don't care what you say. How many times do I have to explain that to you? You're too old for that nonsense. You either have to get a job that'll leave you with enough energy to write in the evenings, or you'll have to move back in with Pamela. If you had any sense, which even on the face of it you don't, you'd go back to Pamela and live like a human being. And you'd stay away from those creeps you live with now. Pamela's a good, steady girl, much better than you deserve. You know she wants you back, so there's no reason to be afraid to ask her."

I walked back to Worthington's and read Boswell until Marlow came in. He took off all his clothes, except for the tennis shoes, and turned on the sun lamp. He appeared to be preoccupied with some important matter. He found the sun lamp the other day in somebody's trash. It doesn't have a stand so he's tied it to a nail in the wall with a shoelace. I watched him lay down naked on the springs under the lamp and begin reading an old copy of *Yachting Magazine*.

"Marlow," I said, "why do you sleep naked but leave your sneakers on?"

He looked up from the magazine and studied my face for a moment. "I'm not sleeping, Mr. Smith. I'm reading *Yachting Magazine*."

"I see."

"You don't just go out and buy a yacht, Mr. Smith. You need to be well informed. A yacht is a major investment."

I wasn't in the mood for that so I got up and left. It was around midnight. I walked to the news stand on Las Palmas, then to the one on Cahuenga. I thought about the transcript of the trial and everything that had happened and how I could make a book out of it. The more I thought about it the more excited I got. The book was already written. The book was the transcript itself. All I had to do was edit the transcript and tell my side of the story from a personal perspective. I thought about how good it would be to have something to work on every day that was real.

This afternoon I was wakened by Marlow who was in the shower singing "Days of Wine and Roses" in a strained tenor voice. Clouds of steam blew out through the open bathroom door. The plastic curtains that hang over the window and the glassed door to the alley were flapping in the breeze. I could smell the sacks of garbage piled up in the alcove where the hot plate is. Worthington refuses on principle to take out a sack of garbage until Marlow takes one out. I sat up on the mattress and as I looked around I felt a sudden desire to go to Mexico.

Marlow came out of the shower with water pouring off his body and paced around the room, wetting books and clothes and rubbish alike. He pushed his fingers through his hair and flicked the water around.

"Jesus, Marlow," I said. "Use the towel."

"It's too dirty," he said. "I don't even want to touch it. I'll just walk around a while.

Mike Katz came down from his room upstairs. He's small and dark and homely, just the opposite from Marlow.

"Marlow," Katz said, "what the hell are you doing?"

"I'm drying my body. What's the matter, Mr. Katz? Does it make you uncomfortable to see what a god looks like?"

"God, hell. Put you goddamn clothes on, Marlow. Act like an adult for once in your life."

"The gods are ageless," Marlow said seriously.

Katz turned to me. "Did I ever tell you where I found Marlow? At the YMCA. He was sleeping on a couch there because he didn't have any place to go."

"That isn't the whole truth, Mr. Katz," Marlow said.

"When I saw him, curled up there like a big baby, I said to myself, 'There's six and a half feet of child, child, child.'"

"What you saw," Marlow said, "was a Roman god in repose."

"What I saw was a big blond dago. I could tell by the way you were curled up like a fetus that you couldn't take care of yourself. And I was right. I felt sorry for you. That's why I found you a place to live."

"A Jew feeling sorry for a Roman? You must be losing your senses. You did what was right. You saw a Roman in distress and went to his aid. You fulfilled your proper role."

"You blond babies are all the same," Katz said. "You're all either anti-Semites or you bend over for strangers."

"Oh, too much. Too much. In the old days, when the Romans ruled the world, you'd have held your tongue, Mr. Katz."

"You're no Roman, Marlow. You're a dago. Why don't you stop talking that crap? You talk like a dago and you think like a dago. Why don't you get serious about your life?"

I feel like I understand Marlow but I don't understand Katz. There's something real to his anger. He says everything went to hell for him during the war. He was in the navy and spent two years in the South Pacific without seeing a woman.

"That's where I lost my way," Katz says, "in the South Pacific. I read too many books, and that isn't good for you. When you're young like that, inexperienced, too many books can ruin your life. You start thinking it's good to be alive, that there's something to it.

You see everything through rose colored glasses. You get so you believe in God, all that crap. When I think back on it I want to cut the balls off the man who brought all those books aboard ship. It was the captain. He thought he was a gentleman. What he really was, he was the devil."

Today is Saturday and here at Worthington's Saturday night is steak night. During the week we cook noodles and boil potatoes on the hot plate but on Saturday night Katz and Marlow walk over to Hughes Market and steal four or five pounds of steak.

"Come on, Smith," Katz says to me. "Want to go for a walk?"

"Not me. This might be the night you guys get nailed."

"Courage, Mr. Smith," Marlow says. "The little Jew is willing to steal for you. The least you can do is observe his technique."

"I've told you before, Marlow," Katz says, "don't call me that."

"What's the matter, Mr. Katz? Are you ashamed of your people?"

"Come on," Katz said. "Let's go before I lose my temper."

Marlow went to the mirror and combed his hair for the third or fourth time. "The Prince wants to look his best when he goes out on Saturday night."

Katz said they ought to walk to Hollywood Ranch Market and steal some steaks there. "We've been stealing at Hughes two months now. It's not fair to the market."

"I prefer to do business with my local merchant, Mr. Katz," Marlow says. "Don't you have any sense of loyalty? Besides, I'm used to stealing at Hughes. I don't feel guilty about it anymore."

"That night manager's got his eye on you," Katz said. "I think he's suspicious."

"I've done everything I can to get him to arrest me but he won't do it. I put things inside my shirt when he's watching. I stuff my pockets with bananas and jars of olives. Before I go out the door I get rid of everything on the QT. He pretends he doesn't see me. If he'd follow me outside one time and accuse me of stealing I'd sue him for everything the market's got. I'd get my yacht then, and there would always be a place on it for little Mike Katz to sleep."

"I don't need a place to sleep," Katz says. "You're the one who needs help. I have my own room that I pay for with my own money. I have a job, Marlow."

"I'm beginning to hate that night manager," Marlow says. "I wish he would either accuse me of something or stop watching me. The tension's getting to be too much. It's making me itch. How does he know I'm not walking out with something every time I go in there? I think he's being irresponsible. Maybe I ought to report him to the stockholders."

At the last minute I decided to go along and look through the magazines. We walked down Highland in the dark. The street was full of traffic going in the opposite direction to the Hollywood Bowl. Marlow started reminiscing about his father again, the one who went to Germany during World War II and became a Nazi and joined the SS.

"Marlow," Katz said, "get your mind on what we're doing, will you? Try not to ball up this caper tonight."

"My father was one of the ones who got away," Marlow says. "He's been in Argentina since 1946. Working on the Nazi revival, you know."

"Oh, horseshit," Katz says.

"My father doesn't hate Jews," Marlow says sincerely. He puts his hand inside his shirt and scratches. "He just wants to do what's right."

"Oh, horseshit, Marlow," Katz says. "You talk like a man with a paper asshole."

As we approach the market Katz reminds Marlow to act natural, to not do anything to get the night manager's attention.

"Easy for you to say," Marlow says, "but you forget, when I step through the doors of the market it's like the entrance of a God. Every eye turns toward me. Nobody notices you, Mr. Katz. You have to take that into consideration."

Inside the market the night manager is standing at the liquor counter. Marlow walks up to him and puts his face into the manager's face and demands threateningly: "Do you have any matches?"

"Sure," the manager says. He hands Marlow a book of matches and turns back to what he was doing.

Katz says: "What the hell did you do that for?"

"I don't know," Marlow says.

"What the hell are you using for a brain?"

"My cock," Marlow says.

The magazines are full of news about Negroes and civil rights. I think about how the strategy for gaining civil rights is usually fine and how the tactics are almost always wrong. I think about how people from New York like to go down South to work for civil rights but can't find their way into Harlem. Thinking about it makes me angry.

When Marlow and Katz go through the cashier's line I follow them outside and we walk up the hill toward Worthington's room. Katz has a two-pound New York cut under his jacket, along with some gravy cubes and two cans of mushroom caps. Marlow looks disconcerted and intense. Katz asks him what he has stolen.

"I made a mistake," Marlow says.

"What the hell do you mean?"

"At the last minute, I got confused." Marlow is scratching the top of his head. As it turns out, he's stolen a package of cow brains.

Katz throws up his hands. "You disgust me," he yells. "You got no sense. Nobody but a goddamned goy would steal a package of brains. This is the last time I pull this caper with you, Marlow. Do you know we could get arrested for this? Do you want to go to jail for stealing a cow's brain? Now that you stole it, you eat the goddamn thing. It takes a dumb goddamn wop to steal an item like that."

"Don't call me a wop," Marlow says. "I'm the last of the Romans. I don't have any connection with the wops."

"The Morning The Sun Was a Knockout"

(1959)

It wasn't easy for Pamela because her family and friends were everywhere in New York and New Jersey, all of them well-situated, taking life seriously and pointing out to her, in the sensitive way they had, that she'd married beneath her station and that her life was moving in a precarious direction. Secretly I agreed with her family, but my thoughts where busy with something else. Something Pamela didn't know about.

I had discovered that I was being followed. That I was being spied on. The man wasn't someone who I'd been introduced to, not even fleetingly at a party or an East Side bar. A complete stranger. On the dark side. He appeared everywhere, following along in the crowd when I walked the streets. I'd seen him waiting for me on the library steps. One time he was in the lobby of our apartment building but ducked out of sight before I could get a square look at him.

One night after dinner, after the card table was folded up and put away and the dishes washed and the doors closed across the kitchen counter, Pamela and I settled down for a little reading. She had a book on gardening in Eighteenth Century England. I was reading something on Sumerian archeology. I thought we were all right.

After a while Pamela said: "Is something wrong with you?"

"Why do you ask?"

"The way you've been lying on the floor when you read. Is something wrong with your back, Bradley?"

"Nah. I'm happy down here."

"Bradley?"

"Yes?"

"What's wrong with your eye?"

"What do you mean?"

"You've been holding your hand over your right eye when you read. You've been doing it several nights now."

"Oh. I hadn't noticed." I took the hand away from the eye.

"You haven't noticed you've been covering one of your eyes when you read?"

"No, I haven't."

"Brad?"

"Yes?"

"What the hell's going on with you?"

"Nothing's going on with me, Pamela." I tried to not laugh.

"Don't start laughing, Bradley."

"I won't."

"I'm worried about you, Bradley," she said caringly. "I feel something may be wrong with you."

I went on trying not to laugh.

"What does that look on your face mean, Bradley?"

I couldn't stop the laugh. I rolled over on my belly and laughed into my hands.

Pamela said: "You can just go to hell."

That night I dreamed I was in darkest Africa. It was night, there was the jungle, the moon, a wide river. The river was deep and swift and dark. It flowed from right to left. It was my job to cross over it, or through it. Just as I screwed up my courage to begin the crossing I saw something move. A company of naked, black Africans was in the river marching in military formation with spears held upright. They were marching downstream. I woke up.

A couple nights later, lying beside Pamela in the pull-down bed, I realized I wanted out of our marriage. I couldn't think of any good reason. The next morning I walked Pamela to the bus stop on First Avenue as I usually did. 42nd Street was cold and dirty at the same time. I saw the face powder of elegant ladies blowing across corpses. It made me think about Korea. I didn't say anything to Pamela about leaving. I felt rotten and excited at the same time.

When Pamela's bus came I went back to the apartment and packed and within the hour I was off to Mexico. It had always been good for me in Mexico. I caught a bus to Washington, a city bus to Arlington, and started hitchhiking. It was very cold. I couldn't get a ride. While I stood there I kept an eye out for the guy who had been trailing me, but it looked like I'd lost him. When it started to get dark and I still hadn't got even one ride I decided it wasn't absolutely necessary to go to Mexico to get away from the marriage, so I caught the city bus back to Washington and caught a train for New York.

I took a room in a cheap hotel on Ninth Avenue. I went straight up and undressed and got into bed. I would stay there a week, maybe two weeks. Right there in bed. I got out the old Obelisk editions of Henry Miller's *Tropics* I'd been carrying around. Sam Loveman had given them to me when I'd shipped books for him out of The Bodley Gallery on East 60th Street. I opened *Cancer*. It had a red cover, while *Capricorn* was a dark green. What a surprise I got. If you want to know what Henry Miller is all about but don't know where to start, read the first seventeen pages of *Tropic of Cancer*.

I stayed in bed four days and nights reading the *Tropics*, sleeping, and drinking water. I became so intensely happy I felt I was capable of anything. I felt elevated. And all the while, inside, the heart sizzled, sizzled. When I went down on the street again things looked better. It was still very cold, but not so dirty. At first

I was worried about the dark-complected man, but he was gone. I'd lost him on that sudden trip down to Arlington and back. I went from library to library inspecting their books. It amazed me to be reminded how many writers actually finish books. Anyone can start a book. I'd started a lot of them, but it was amazing to see how many others had forged ahead to a conclusion.

Two weeks after I left Pamela I telephoned her at her father's studio on 50th Street. She was there. It was the lunch hour. She was always there at the lunch hour. We met trembling and crying at a Chinese café on Second Avenue. I needed to get laid in the worst way and hadn't known who else to turn to. I didn't really want to turn to anyone else. Pamela was concerned about our relationship and how it would be in the future. I felt moved by her pain, but I needed to get laid. Pamela needed to talk. We talked all afternoon. Neither of us was able to stop the crying. My cock was swollen up terribly. The Chinese waiters didn't do anything to embarrass us. When we left the café the bastard was there again, standing in the entrance to a dry cleaning ship, his black overcoat hanging down to his ankles.

Back at the apartment on the sixtieth floor it was warm and cozy. We fucked and fucked. After a while Pamela lost interest. I decided to give her a little breathing room. Not too much because I had a big problem with the cock swelling up. We lay apart in the darkness, silently. Then she started up again. First, she lit the cigarette.

"I don't know how I should feel," she said slowly and thoughtfully. "It makes me so insecure to know you don't want to take care of me."

"It has nothing to do with my not wanting to take care of you."

"You did the same thing two years ago. One week you asked me to marry you, and the next you quit your position at the gallery and holed up in that awful hotel room in the Village. I don't have to tell you what everybody thought."

"You mean what your father thought?"

"Everybody had something to say about it."

"You know what I like best about your father? How he gets drunk at fancy parties and eats insects."

"I didn't care what anybody thought. I loved you so much."

I didn't say anything.

"I was so sure you were going to be successful."

I remained silent.

Pamela said: "Some men become writers when they're young. Others need a long time to mature. It's one of those things no one should feel uncomfortable about. But in the meantime there are other things to be considered."

I didn't say anything.

"Maybe this time it will be different." She reached over and put her hand on my forearm. "You haven't told me what you've been writing."

I didn't say anything.

"I don't know that you really want to talk to me about it either."

"There isn't much to talk about."

"Oh." She was silent in the dark for along moment, then she said: "Do you think it's something we'll get some money for?"

"I've been writing down my dreams. Keeping track of them."

"Oh."

"I've been dreaming a lot. I mean a lot."

"I see." She lit another cigarette and dropped the match very precisely into the center of the ashtray where it lay on the sheet between us in the dark.

"I can't write stories any longer. I can't keep my mind on them."

"I see."

"No, you don't. I don't see either. It's just the way it is."

"It makes me so ashamed to have to go to work every day and to know you're at the library or just sitting around the apartment and then to know that everyone else knows it too."

"Your father can go hang himself."

"Oh, Bradley," she said, starting to cry. "What are we going to do?"

"I don't know."

"We just have to do something."

"I have this feeling that there's one thing I should do before I do anything else, but I don't know what it is. I can't find out." I was full of remorse. I moved the ashtray and took her in my arms and she cried openly. I cried silently.

Pamela said: "I'm so afraid you'll leave me again. Please don't leave me, Bradley. I won't be able to stand it. I'm so afraid you won't ever be a good writer and we'll live like this the rest of our lives. I'm afraid we won't have children and that my father will never like you. I'm afraid of everything now. It all seems so impossible. I never thought it was going to be like this. And then you picking up and leaving me whenever you want. I'm just terrified."

I didn't know what to say.

"Ohhhhh," she cried out. "It's so unfair."

The next morning I walked Pamela to the bus stop like in the old days. Walking toward First Avenue we could see under the bridge through the fog to the big soft vermilion sun rising up into the winter sky.

"Look at that sun," I said. "Isn't it a knockout?"

"Will you be around when I get home from work?"

"Sure I will."

She looked at me questioningly.

"I promise you. I'll be there when you get back."

She looked at the sun. "It is attractive," she said.

The prick with the black overcoat was everywhere. In the main reading room at the Central Library I sat with my back to the wall so I didn't get any surprises. I'd never forgotten how Bill Hickcock had gotten his. I started thinking about horses, then cats. I didn't get the connection.

I was too restless to read seriously, to read to a point. I walked to the library on 56th Street, then to some others. I decided to walk to every library in Manhattan and read five pages of important text on any subject at each library. My feelings were excessive. Some of the prose I read made tears run down my face. Even newspaper articles. The heart was buzzing, buzzing inside, where it was. I thought I might be getting ready to have a heart attack but it didn't get worse. It didn't get better either. Buzz buzz buzz. Sizzle sizzle.

When it was time for Pamela to get off work I bought some Brussels sprouts and beat it back to the apartment. Pamela loved Brussels sprouts. "They're just so attractive," she told me once. "Like tiny little green cabbages."

I cooked them up for her, along with a curry sauce. I knew it was going to make me fart like crazy. Later that night I couldn't sleep. The heart was buzzing and simmering. I got up in the dark and dressed and went down to the street. I felt charged with energy. I started walking. I farted all over the sidewalks. In no time I was down to the Battery. I kept walking. I walked all night. I couldn't stop. At dawn I returned to the apartment. Pamela was still sleeping. I sat on the couch and waited. When the alarm went off I grabbed a book and pretended to read it. I didn't want to get into it with her.

Pamela said: "What are you grinning at?"

"I'm not grinning."

"Bradley, what have you done?"

I started laughing. "I'm just trying to catch up on my studies."

"What are you laughing about?"

"I'm not laughing."

"Well, you are laughing, and you don't want to tell me why. You can just go to hell."

Pamela went in the bathroom to dress for work. I stopped laughing. The heart was simmering. I felt grateful that we hadn't had an argument. I felt like I didn't have anything to do. Then I noticed a large dark place on the wall that hadn't been there before. While I idly wondered how it had gotten there, it appeared to grow larger. I shifted my gaze slightly to get a clearer look and found that the splotch of darkness was vibrating, or pulsating. I watched it carefully. The splotch formed itself into an hour glass several feet tall. It pulsated in and out, like a black bellows. At the same time it vibrated from side to side. The vibrations moved faster than the pulses, but weren't so pronounced.

The heart began pounding and I heard a laughing sound. I realized it was me laughing. The laugh sounded intimate, but far away. Then the upper half of the hour glass moved in a new way. It was still pulsating and vibrating but now it was nodding as well, as if to get my attention. It had my attention, but it wanted something more. Suddenly I understood that the hour glass was an image of God and that He was trying to communicate with me. I felt myself lifted up. The body lost its sense of corporeality, the brain became weightless inside the skull, and I felt tremendously aware, as if nothing on the planet could get by me.

"Pamela," I called out. "You've got to come out here. I'm having a vision."

I heard her muffled voice through the bathroom door. "Don't start anything this morning, Bradley. I've just snagged another stocking and I feel like screaming."

OH MY GOD, PAMELA. YOU'VE GOT TO COME OUT HERE!"

I paced around the room like a crazy man. I kept saying: "Oh my God. Oh my God," without meaning anything. I was too excited to keep my eye on the hour glass. When Pamela came out I told her about it. I pointed to the wall.

She looked. It was gone.

"I know it's not there now," I said. I was laughing. I understood how ridiculous it must seem to her.

"Are you going crazy, Bradley? What's the matter with you?"

"Isn't that something though?"

I meant about having seen what I'd seen.

Pamela looked at me warily. She still had some last minute things to do before she could leave for work. She went back in the bathroom. I wanted to see the hourglass again but I couldn't find it. I'd lost sight of it by getting so excited. I felt too elevated to feel disappointed. I stood there looking around the room like a happy, plastered drunk. When I glanced down the hallway toward the bathroom the hourglass was protruding from behind the top of the closet door, which was standing open a few inches.

"THERE IT IS AGAIN," I blurted out. "LOOK. OVER THE CLOSET DOOR!"

Pamela stuck her head out of the bathroom. "Goddammit, Bradley, now you just stop that."

I felt a little set back hearing Pamela swear like that. It wasn't like her. The hourglass was gone again. I still felt elated. I felt like I had been chosen, but I was confused.

Pamela said: "Are you going to walk me to the bus stop or not?"

"Sure I am."

"I don't want any more trouble from you either."

I thought it would be a good idea to make some small talk. I said: "I wonder how the sun's doing this morning?"

"Just don't say anything, Bradley. Just keep it buttoned up until I get on the bus."

"Don't I have a pair of gloves around here somewhere?"

"You're wearing your gloves, Bradley."

"Oh, yeah," I said happily. "You're right."

"Don't say anything more, Bradley."

We took the elevator down to the lobby. I didn't say anything.

Out on 52nd Street, when we turned toward First Avenue, the vermilion sun was still there, underneath the bridge. It was a knockout. A real knockout!

"Saved by the Animals"

(1963)

I've decided to sell the typewriter. I've gotten rid of everything else but I'm hedging about the typewriter. It's too heavy to lug around, I need the money, but I'm hedging. Selling the typewriter would make a clean sweep of everything I own except the change of clothes and the stuff in my pockets. The typewriter is from the old life, the one I had until a couple months ago. I want to get rid of everything that was in that life. It was a good life, but the wrong one for me.

I like to say that one place to live is as good as another but I don't want to live in Worthington's room any longer. I can't work here. Marlow and Worthington can't stop talking. Mike Katz comes down from upstairs and hangs around talking for hours on end. I like talking, I like listening to them talk, but I can't talk and laugh and write all at the same time. I have to do them serially.

If I called Pamela she wouldn't let on but I know she'd be glad to hear from me. At night when I'm out walking the thinking turns to Pamela again and again, to her white thighs and her rosy cunt. Thought reminds me that if I'd called Pamela earlier I could be in bed with her right now, instead of walking alone in the dark. I could be turning the pages of a magazine with one hand and diddling Pamela with the other. If she wasn't in bed yet but was at the sink cleaning up the dishes I could stand behind her and hold her breasts in my hands. Usually she'd let me. Or if I found her stroking the cat I could go over to Pamela and begin stroking her, using the same rhythm she was using with the cat. Sunday afternoon we could go driving and I could put my right hand between her legs while I steered with my left.

"Take it out," Pamela might say, scanning the road ahead. "You know what a careless driver you are." Nevertheless.

In my reveries I see myself walking through the rain forests in Guatemala and Yucatan, poking through the temples at Bonampak and Tikal. I see myself walking down through Central America and on to Columbia, Ecuador and Peru. Walking over the Andes and down into the valley of the Amazon. From there I could get a ship to Africa, tramp through the jungles to the headwaters of the Nile and follow it on up to Cairo. Sometimes when I'm daydreaming about next week or next month, thought comes in and says, with just a little more effort you can be free.

I want Marlow to go to Mexico with me but he says he doesn't believe we can live there on twenty dollars a month, which is what my army pension is. He says he wants to work a couple months first, get a bankroll. He says when he has two hundred dollars in his pocket he'll feel secure. In the meantime he's already lost his job with the cab company.

"I pulled into the garage this morning and the supervisor called me over to his office. He said I'm too tall to drive a cab. How do you like that one?"

"It's your own fault," I told him.

"I've already worked three nights. I feel at home there."

"I certainly didn't get so tall," I said. "Worthington's tall but not as tall as you are. Katz got only half as tall as you did. You can't blame the supervisor."

"I know."

"It was your responsibility."

"I know."

"Now you can go to Mexico with me."

"I'm too depressed to go to Mexico," Marlow said. "I've lost my job."

Mike Katz was down here all evening. He was even more unhappy than he usually is. He was brooding about the woman he loves, the one he left behind in New Jersey.

"I was doing all right until I met Dorothea," Katz said. "I was living with my parents and seeing a psychiatrist. I wanted to kill my little brother, shit like that, but I didn't feel worried. Know what I mean? Then I met Dorothea. She had five kids and hustled on the side, but I didn't care about that." He made a gesture with his hands that fisherman make to describe a big catch. "The first time I saw her coming through the doorway, her shoulders out like that (like the big fish), it made me crazy. All I could think about was that I had to have her."

Worthington and me and Marlow were laughing and enjoying ourselves.

Marlow said: "How wide were those shoulders, Katzy?"

"Laugh, you assholes," Katz said.

"The Prince isn't laughing at you, Katzy," Marlow said. "The Prince loves you."

"Fuck you Marlow."

Worthington apologized to Katz for laughing. You can always count on Worthington to do the right thing.

Katz said: "I didn't mind her messing around in the neighborhood. She's a passionate woman. But one day I'm going back to Jersey and murder that husband of hers. I'm going to cut off his balls and send them back to him in the mail."

"Oh, come on, Mike," Worthington said, "I don't believe you mean that."

"I'm telling you," Katz said. "He was against me from the start because I didn't pay her when we did it. Do you think he paid her? Your ass he paid her. His nuts, that's what I want."

Katz paused, brooding introspectively. "I can see it now. The postman rings their doorbell, her asshole husband opens it, and the postman says: 'Here are your nuts, Sir.'"

All I can think about is going to Mexico. I pace back and forth in the room, seeing myself on the highway. At night I toss and turn in the armchair, imagining myself in this village or that one, in my own room working on the book. In my imagination I have no debts and I don't know anyone. Nobody knocks on the door, and when I go walking no one greets me or tries to talk to me. Mostly I see myself in a fishing village lying in a hammock, the afternoon breeze blowing against the bottoms of my bare feet. I can hear the surf on the sand. A gull cries. Day and night those are the images I like to watch.

Worthington doesn't warm to the subject of Mexico but Marlow has some interest in it. He's willing to talk it over with me. He's willing to listen to how it is in Mexico. This afternoon I told him: "Marlow, use your head. Beer is six cents a bottle in Mexico. Women are fifty cents a throw. The weather's wonderful, the air's clean." I gestured around the room at the trash and disorder. "Why live like this when we can live in Mexico?"

"It does sound good," he said. "Maybe when I finish paying off the car."

Somehow Marlow was able to get his hands on a used Pontiac convertible with no down and only a few bucks a month.

"I don't want to lose my investment," he says.

"I can understand that." I could feel the eagerness welling up in my heart. I felt like maybe we'd be off to Mexico after all.

"How many payments have you made so far?"

"One."

"Oh for Christ's sake. One. What the hell kind of investment is that?"

"My car's the only thing I have. I have a suit but it's in the pawnshop."

"Fuck it," I said.

"I'm willing to go," Marlow said. "I just have to get my financial affairs in order."

"Fuck it."

I walked over to Maurice's and started talking to him about Mexico. He was at the typewriter when I got there but he got up and sat on the couch clicking his teeth while I talked. He was sitting on some of his scripts, which kind of bothered me.

"Don't be an asshole," Maurice said. "Take some advice from an older man, from someone who's a lot smarter than you are. From a Jew. You've had your life in Mexico. You lived there three years. What more do you expect from it? My advice is this. Are you listening? Find some broad to live with and get on with your writing. Be professional about it. Any asshole can go to Mexico. Are you trying to tell me you can write better in Mexico than you can here? Are you trying to kid me? Don't try to kid somebody who knows you as well as I do."

"Why are you sitting on your scripts?"

"This is what successful TV writers do. They wipe their asses with their work. If you ever decide to be a successful writer, and from the way you're talking I don't have much expectation that you will, you'll be able to wipe your ass with your work like the professionals do."

That last year in Mexico I knocked around the mountains in Jalisco and Guerrero with a novillero named Emilo Tagores and a couple other guys. We were trying to scare up some business killing bulls at village fiestas. We were hardly making a living. Sometimes we stayed over in Guadalajara with Guillermo Sanchez. A couple years earlier, up in Aguas Calientes, a bull had removed the ligaments from Sanchez's left elbow, which left the arm permanently crooked, so Sanchez had to retire from bullfighting. He had to make a new career decision. He decided to become a tailor. His crooked left arm worked just right to hold the material when he sewed with his right hand.

Sanchez lived and worked in a room on a dirt street out at

the edge of Guadalajara where he slept on a cot and did his cutting and sewing on a solid wood table. I slept on the table. One night Sanchez offered to share his cot with me. I didn't think it was a good idea, but in the end I joined him. The blankets were full of bed bugs. From that night on I slept on the floor on my capote. We were all the same age then, Tagores, Sanchez and me. Twenty-five. I would watch Sanchez measure a man for a pair of pants with his crooked arm and think about how his career with the bulls was finished and how mine was just starting and how I had all the luck.

In the mornings in Guadalajara I'd catch a bus to downtown and walk a few blocks in the sunshine to the old Plaza and train with the capes and the sword. Before noon I'd fold my capes and walk to a café on a torn up street outside the big covered market place and eat a bowl of fish soup, then I'd catch another bus out Jaime Bravo to the dirt street where we were living. There was a courtyard behind the room surrounded by other rooms where entire families lived with all their kids and in the center of the courtyard there was a well with a bucket tied to a rope. I'd take a sauce pan to use for a dipper and a towel and wash up at the well, then set up the typewriter on the cot and try to work on the Korea book. The afternoons were hot and full of flies and if I'd nod off in the chair Sanchez would prick me with a needle or a pair of scissors because it was bad for business to have people sleeping in his commercial establishment. A couple times I got pissed about the needle but I didn't say anything because, after all, I was his guest.

That summer was the last time I tried seriously to do the Korea book. I was also working on a story about Elizabeth, who worked at the soda fountain in her father's drugstore at Gage and Main in South Los Angeles the summer I got out of the army. Elizabeth was a Catholic with a religious turn who made me eat chocolate sundaes six times a week for four months before she'd let me hold her breasts. I got impatient sometimes but in the end it was worth it. Then one evening Elizabeth told me that she had seen a vision. She wouldn't tell me what she'd seen but whatever it was changed our relationship considerably because she entered the convent. I hadn't thought girls really did that anymore. Her convent was the kind that when you get there you have to crawl in through a window and you never come out again. It wasn't a tragedy for me, I wasn't heartbroken, but my hands felt like something was missing.

Some months later I ran into Elizabeth's father at the gas station across the street from his drugstore and he told me encouragingly that Elizabeth was home again. I telephoned her that afternoon and we got together at her house, which was her parents' house. She looked about the same as she had before except her hair was short.

She laughed. "You should have seen me after they cut it all off."

"All of it? Did you like that?"

"I liked everything," she said. "I liked scrubbing the floors. I liked praying and fasting. Everything. After a while they resented me. They voted me out."

"Is that how it works? They vote you in, they vote you out?"

"They resented me because I wanted to do things that were hard."

"I thought convents were for life."

"I was there eight months."

I asked her what she was going to do next.

"I'm going back to work at the soda fountain. Then I'm going to find another convent."

"I've had it with those ice cream sundaes," I said. "I want you to know that." Elizabeth thought that was very funny, but when I tried to hold her breasts again like the old days, she wouldn't let me.

"I'd have too much to make up for," she said.

"You mean in heaven?"

She closed her eyes and laughed.

"Couldn't you spend some time in limbo," I said? "They say it's not that bad in limbo. Whatever we do now you could make up for there."

"Not after you've had a vision," she said soberly. "Visions change your life."

I worked on that story for weeks but I couldn't get it right. I gave up and tried a couple stories about killing bulls which I also could not get right and a couple about childhood and some others I invented. I couldn't get any of them right. Occasionally I wondered about Elizabeth, where she was, what she was doing and so on. Not often.

Last night I took a *Christian Science Monitor* from a sidewalk news rack, drank a few coffees at Biff's on Franklin and Cahuenga, then wandered back toward Worthington's room. For some reason I felt excited, happy, full of energy. I don't know why. I thought about the way the writing was going, all the different projects that were open to me. I thought about how sometimes I'm alert and excited for reasons I can't identify, and how other times I feel depressed and exhausted and how I can't explain that either.

In the room Worthington and Marlow were both sleeping. The air smelled like garbage and stale cigarette smoke mixed. I sat in the armchair and drew my jacket over me but I couldn't sleep. The mind was extremely alert. It was racing. I couldn't keep up with it. I went outside and stood at the corner of the building. An occasional car passed on Highland, its headlights sweeping up the black pavement. After a while the sky grew light along the crests of the hills up above Universal Studios. At first the hills were black silhouettes against the dark sky, but as the gray light came up behind them I could make out the first shapes of the trees and houses. I thought about how wonderful it was to be standing there watching the day come into being.

I must have lost track of time, as if I'd fallen into a trance or something. I was aware of a rosy light appearing over the hills, then suddenly the sun was over the top of a ridgeline and I heard a strain of music I couldn't identify. I felt the face turn slowly, mechanically, upward toward the sun. I felt the warmth pressing against the closed eyelids, the brow, the lips, the naked throat, and then I heard a voice inside me say: "This is God's passion," and at that moment I saw myself soar off the sidewalk into the sky. It happened so quickly there wasn't time to be afraid. I saw myself soar over the San Gabriel Mountains, then over other mountains I hadn't seen before. The entire flight took only an instant. Then I saw myself sitting on a boulder at the edge of a dark lake surrounded by forests. The water in the lake was moving in a foreboding way. That's when the fear started. I understood somehow that huge volumes of water were welling up into the bottom of the lake from underground sources. Then the lake began to throb like a great black heart. The lake was being engorged with water and needed to burst over its banks. I wanted it to happen, but the moment I thought it was going to happen the body turned cold. I was afraid that once the flooding began, I would be swept away. I realized that it was up to me, that in my heart I had to say either yes or no and that the lake would do what I wanted. I wanted to say yes, I wanted to be swept away. I longed to say it but I couldn't. The lake went on engorging itself and the great black watery heart pounded until I thought I would lose consciousness and then at the moment it all started to get out of control I saw animals leap out of the forest and race to the lake and suck furiously at the edge of the lapping water. There were foxes and lions and deer and squirrels. I understood then that the animals were going to save me from having to decide whether to go under or not.

I felt the body relax. I knew then that I was still standing on the sidewalk at the corner of our apartment building on Highland Avenue. I saw the cars passing back and forth on the street, and across the street I saw the parking lot and beyond that the hills and the houses and trees on the hills. I remembered seeing the lake, I still felt the anxiety, but I wasn't actually seeing it any longer.

And then for a moment I saw it again. The sky above the lake was thick and dark and a rain was falling. In the lake fish had come up and I saw their muzzles sticking up through the surface of the black water while the rain fell on their wide-eyed faces. I watched white ducks lift off the water and fly off into the dark distance.

After a while, I'm not certain how long, it was over. I walked down Highland toward Hollywood Boulevard. Bugs were coming out onto the sidewalk to sun themselves. They gleamed brilliantly in the morning sunlight. They were jewel-like. I looked away. I didn't want to see anymore. The heat was still there, inside my chest. I turned east on the Boulevard and walked fast. I didn't know what to do. When I started sweating I stepped inside the shaded entrance of an old office building and sat on the concrete step.

Thought was different somehow. There wasn't so much of it and I had the sense that it was suffused with whiteness. A cockroach walked around the corner of the entrance onto the little green and white octagonal tiles. I watched the roach walk up to the shoe on my left foot and feel the leather with its antennae. With a still, empty heart, I observed the movement and rhythm of each of its legs, the differences in texture among its different body parts, its shadings of black and brown. Thought suggested that with living mechanisms, mechanization may have preceded beauty. For a moment, the idea intrigued me. Then, rather placidly, I began seeing trees. I was getting mixed messages.

"Barney's Beanery"

(1964)

This afternoon I sat on the steps to the back porch in the pale sunlight. The old garden is dead. On the dry grass a blue jay was tearing up a grasshopper. I watched the insect make desperate, crippled little jumps. Inside the house Mother began to sing in her clear pretty voice. She was in the kitchen baking a chocolate cake because today is my birthday. I'm thirty-five years old.

When I heard the newspaper slam against the screened door I walked around the side of the house to the front porch and picked it up. The headline told how another Negro civil rights worker had been murdered. I went in the house where Father was sitting in his rocker in the living room looking at the carpet. I held up the paper so he could read the headline. He raised his head and gazed at it.

"Well," he said, "there's one."

Yesterday I whiled away the afternoon in the library. Today I decided to walk over to Sears and watch the fish tank. I'm very good at fitting my amusements to my circumstances. At Sears I decided to call Morgan. Would she like to meet me someplace? Pass a few hours discussing her neurosis?

Morgan couldn't make it. She was watching a documentary on

television about our boys in France and she was a little weepy. I asked her the name of what she was watching.

"Morgan," I said, "that film is about World War One. All that stuff happened fifty years ago."

"I know," she sniffed. "But it just makes me cry to know how our boys suffered over there." She began relating the history of World War I to me, from the beginning. She was pretty good at it too. I think she was using a reference book. But how much of that do you want to listen to standing in the parking lot at Sears? Morgan is only 18 but her sympathies are all-embracing. They span continents. It's a real bother. Nevertheless, I'm going to wait it out with her.

Back at the house Father was snoozing in the rocker, snoring and gasping for breath. Mother was sitting on the sofa watching the television.

"Just listen to him," she said, looking over at her husband. "One day one of those snores is going to kill him. It's going to just tear everything out of his head."

She leaned across the card table.

"HENRY," she yelled. "WAKE UP. DO YOU HEAR ME? NOW YOU JUST WAKE UP."

Father lifted his chin from his chest and said: "Oh, all right."

He gestured vaguely with one hand.

"Pass me those worms and lights, will you?"

Mother gasped. "Henry," she said, "what the hell have you been dreaming now?"

"Goddammit," Father said, getting a hold on himself. "Just hand me the goddamn newspaper, will you?"

I sat on the couch beside Mother and we watched the black and white television together. A French couple were doing a comic apache dance on a bare stage. The woman was beautiful, her body incredibly packed and ripe, her little costume bursting with glowing flesh. She was full of milk and hot spices. Her luscious odor was so strong it was wafting out of the back of our TV. The scent made my heart pound. I felt shaken, saliva filled my mouth and then suddenly I had her. In my mind's eye I saw myself dive right into the TV screen and fuck her so powerfully her brains popped out her ears. It was over in a flash.

"Isn't she cute?" Mother said, sitting up on the edge of the couch. "Most of those French girls who come over here look like street cleaners, but she's real cute."

Father looked up from the newspaper. "What's that you say?"

Morgan's driving me nuts. Six feet tall, a strong magnificent face. Meticulously groomed, her complexion is a tawny, velvet mirror. A couple abortions last winter set her back a little but now she's picked up the weight she lost and she's beautiful, just beautiful. So long as I remained aloof with Morgan she was aggressively affectionate, but the moment I turned, as it were, and faced her, she withdrew inwardly. She approaches me now wrapped around in fine sheets of clear plastic.

At Barney's Beanery Morgan is a terror. She stares guys down, insults them, spews up on them in erratic fits of scathing anger. One moment she'll keep me at arm's length, the next she'll grab me around the neck like a stevedore and hold on to me passionately. That's her bar image. At home with her mother she's still the teenage daughter, obedient, petulant, eager to please. At the same time, she wants a shoulder to cry on.

Because of Morgan I remember how it is to have the attention of a good-looking woman. Where the hell are they now when I need them most? They can't all have died or gotten married. Where's Freida, I wonder? I want to feel her heavy freckled breasts weighing on me again. And Mary Jane? She's out of the convent now so maybe she's thinking things over. Is Jessie still teaching fifth grade and tricking on the side? I really admire women who can follow two career paths at once. Jo was the best of the lot, and I cared for Jo most. That last night we were together in bed we fell apart sweating like horses and she heaved a sigh and with a note of wonder in her voice said: "My God, but I've had a lot of men."

That night I didn't understand why we laughed so hard at that, but maybe I do now.

In two years a lot of water can go under the bridge.

Lying on the bed in the little room where I grew up, I become restless, then agitated in a way that went beyond restlessness. I started thinking again how I feel stymied, how there's something I need to do, that I'm ready to do it, but that whatever it is it's hidden from me. I went through the house to the back yard to the old shack where I have the typewriter set up on a card table, just like in the old days when Pamela was here with me. There was something terribly sad about being in the old shack again. About the old stains on the walls, the old plywood floor that used to be covered with carpet. About how old Mrs. Carney lived out her life here with her canary and her garden trowel and her breakfasts of mashed avocado on wheat toast.

Standing in the shack, my hands in my pockets, I didn't know what to do. I picked up a manuscript but I was too agitated and too lethargic at the same time to work on it. I had a sense that it was going to start up again. I was exhausted. I sat in the old rocker and put a hand over my eyes. Immediately I saw the image of a white skull. It was the skull of an infant but its jaws were lank and billowing smoke. I hadn't expected it to happen so quickly.

I looked methodically around the shack at the cardboard cartons stacked against one wall, at the manuscript file, the paper bags full of trash, at the crooked-neck lamp arching over the typewriter. Everything was in order. I felt reassured. I happened to glance out the window then and I saw the white skull hovering beneath the little orange tree, observing me. Its long jaws were smoking and there was movement in the recesses of the empty eye sockets.

I understood with perfect clarity that I was seeing a production of my own mind. I couldn't be fooled about that any longer. The hovering smoking skull was in some sense my own creation. Nevertheless, I was seeing it. The fear was building up very quickly. I began breathing in a deep regular way. I shifted my gaze from the skull to the trunk of the little orange tree, at the rotted place that's filled with cement. I noted carefully the grainy texture of the cement, then how the smooth bark of the trunk was enveloping the wound. I made orderly mental notes about what I was observing. My experience is that if I can go on seeing the ordinary things, I won't go off. Then I saw the skull again. It was a lot bigger than before and before I could stop seeing it it moved through the window into the shack and confronted me.

Though I was seeing the skull I was still aware of how I was standing in the shack among my things. I was afraid but I wasn't panicked yet. Inwardly I made a decision to look into the skull's left eye socket. I don't know why. Through the socket I saw an incredible panorama of destroyed and burning cities. Mountains of rubble were smoldering and spewing out poisonous gases. Dead and mutilated bodies were piled up in heaps while vermin the size of horses crawled over them. It was a magnificent view of catastrophic destruction. Seeing it exalted me. I saw myself thrust my arm through the open jaws of the skull. Murderous sensations whirled through my head. I wanted to go down into the madness I saw and finish the job. I wanted to smash everything that was left, pulverize it, smear it into nothing. But suddenly the hand that was inside the jaws caught fire. Then the whole arm ignited and burned with a roar like a turpentine bush. I saw myself leap back, crazy with fear.

The fear was so intense I knew I had to stop seeing or I'd go off for certain. I was able to look out the window and see the orange tree again, but its leafy aspect was terrifying. The skull grew even larger. I sat at the card table, put a sheet of paper in the typewriter and began typing "now is the time for all good men to come to the aid of their country." It wasn't easy. I typed it two or three times. I was conscious of misspelling some words but I couldn't figure out which ones. The skull was swelling and growing. I stood up with my back to the wall and looked at it hard. I would face it down. Sometimes I could do that. Its eyes became long fiery tunnels. I knew I was on very dangerous ground but I kept looking and then I forced myself to leap through the left eye socket into the interior. It was crazy for me to do that and it was at that moment that I went off. Terror wrapped me around and I was no longer aware of being in two places at once. I only knew that I was in the fiery tunnel, that the body was scorching and burning and that the flames were enveloping my face. I saw fat fire demons appear in the tunnel in front and behind me. The demons had bushy coats of fire, flaming faces and black gorilla eyes. They roared down on me, threw me to the ground and held me there while searing blisters erupted on my flesh and marched in military formations up and down the body like troops on a parade ground. I saw everything turn white and then, somehow, I was in a different place.

It was a cave inside the earth. I was still lying on my back, trapped, but the air was cool and dank and a black ape was straddling my chest. I understood I was going to be murdered. I thought the fear would make me lose consciousness, that's what I wanted, but it didn't. From the corner of one eye I caught the image of a pair of pliers. I felt the ape shift its weight, I saw the pliers again, and then with a single backhand motion the animal ripped my throat open. Blood flowed out of the throat and seeped into the cold dirt. I felt the fear relieving itself, as if a tide were going out. I seemed to understand that all of it now was out of my hands, that events had carried me to that place where fear has no significance. The head of a little green snake emerged from the rip in my throat. The head looked around, smiling, red blood dripping off its face. A second snake head appeared from the wound, looked around like the first one had, then the two of them fell out onto the cool powdery dirt and wriggled off. Then I was alone in the cave.

I lay there placidly on the soft cool dirt on my back. I felt empty. Serene. No hurry, no worry. The moment I realized how much at peace I was I saw a bony green hand come slowly out of the gash in my throat. The hand put its fingers inside my mouth, its thumb beneath my jaw and held me in a lock grip while snakes slithered out of the rip in my throat one after another after another. As the snakes left me the body began collapsing inward like a balloon deflating. The toes collapsed into the feet, the feet into the legs. My fingers collapsed into my hands, the genitals into my stomach. When all that was left of me was the head and throat a second hand came out with the first and the two hands grasped my head and smashed it against a rock until the back of the skull split open in two sections. A long simian hand with spidery fingers reached down out of the darkness and scooped up a handful of the exposed brain. I realized that I myself was the ape, sitting on a rock beside the place where I'd been murdered. I understood I was seeing myself as I was forty million years ago, sitting on my haunches scooping handfuls of brain from a smashed skull and cramming them in my mouth. My movements were tremendously energetic. They were wild. I ate some of the brains and rubbed some in my hair. I smeared some on my chest and rubbed it in like a lotion. In my ape eyes there was a stare of stupid concentration. I began masturbating a rectangular ape-prick ferociously while overhead the top of the cave parted to reveal fiery meteors streaking through a black universe in brilliant crisscross designs.

After a while I noticed that I was standing in the shack with my back to the wall. I saw the meteors shooting back and forth through the blackness and I saw the inside of the shack and my different things. For a while it went back and forth. There was the window and outside it the old orange tree. Then I started recalling what I'd been seeing. I recalled the terror, but now the terror was gone. I recalled how I'd had trouble getting my breath. Now I was breathing freely, easily. I used the sleeves of my shirt to dry my face. I felt light, free, winged. The blood was coursing through my heart, foaming. The body was full of energy and happiness. I had seen it through one more time and here I was. One time more. I had accomplished it.

I stepped out into the back yard. The brown grass, the cactus, the old fences were luminous and vibrant in the pale sunlight. The yard pulsated with energy and unused power. It was profound, and I was aware that neither the power nor the profundity was an idea or associated with one. The body was flooded with clarity. My feeling of joy was so intense I wanted to stop having it. I wanted to stop seeing how things really are. I was afraid it would become more than I could bear. Then suddenly I was at loose ends. I was half-overcome with joy but I was restless too. I felt driven but lost. The only thing I could think to do was to go in the house to the kitchen and drink milk.

I started up the concrete steps to open the screened door when I heard a man laugh in an easy, seductive way. I paused, my hand touching the door handle. There was the sound of a flute being played. It was a pretty, piping sound. I turned and toward the rear of the shack near the stunted orange tree I saw myself dancing in a circle and playing an old pipe. I was naked, while at my feet the brown grass swarmed with snakes. My flesh was a white marble tinted with rose, my face a sculptured mask of serene happiness. The snakes too, in their snaky way, were dancing to the sound of my piping. They wound up my legs and around my body. They slithered through my hair. They whirled ecstatically around my legs. They formed themselves into whirling necklaces around my throat and all the while they laughed soundlessly as if celebrating with a joyous abandon their new found freedom.

Standing on the back steps watching myself, I didn't have the fear that I was going to go off. I understood where I was, that my hand was still holding the handle of the screened door as if I were about to go inside, and I was clear too about seeing myself down in the yard piping the snakes and dancing. During that moment I may have understood for the first time the distinction between observing reality on the one hand and forming an opinion about it on the other.

I'd started inside the house for a glass of milk but now I felt so exhilarated that I needed something to calm me down. It wasn't going to be milk. I remembered I had a fifth of Donleavy's Straight Corn Liquor stashed behind Grandmother's rocker in the shack. I tore into the shack and made a dive for Mr. Donleavy. It's the cheapest whisky you can buy down at the corner at Morries. I drank two inches from the bottle as quick as I could. It was a race against time. Within seconds I could feel the warmth and good cheer coming up in me, replacing the terrible burden of joy, level by level.

Calming, I thought about how joy doesn't allow for comfort, on how it stands aside from language and laughter. Then I started thinking on how much pleasure there is in drunkenness and on how the intoxicants have been a boon to mankind everywhere in every age. It made me wonder why I don't drink more myself since I like being drunk so much. Some of my friends think I drink too much but there are times when I drink nothing for days on end. I don't know why. As casually as I could, I borrowed the family car from Mother and beat it over to Braum's place. Braum lives in a storefront on Pico Boulevard and paints pictures of hard-edged creatures that don't exist in daylight but creep out at night from the joints in his fingers. Good old Braum. He believes the North American continent is doomed because it has a wicked shape. He's a geographer of immense proportions, Braum is.

"Full of evil," he told me one night at Barney's, tracing America's outline on the bar top with a wet finger. "Africa now, Africa has soft, female shapes. Gentle. Rounded. The shape of the future."

Tonight he'd finished a self-portrait in greens, bright reds and yellows. We put it in the car and drove to the back entrance to the Parker Gallery on La Cienega. We hung around in the alley sucking on Mr. Donleavy. It was a balmy, tropical night. A warm breeze blew softly through the alleyway and over the buildings. The hair on my head crackled in the electric air. Behind my eyes the eyes were flashing like semaphores.

Inside the gallery, voices hummed. Parker himself was standing with his back to us. I hadn't seen him in two years but I'd have known that dome of his anywhere, bald and shining, creased like a dry desert river bed. Parker likes dirty jokes and young girls, which are two different things. Everybody likes dirty jokes. When I hear of a man who doesn't, I feel a kind of respect for his sensibility and sophistication.

Across the street I said hello to Mrs. Esperanza, who has her own gallery. She's telling several ladies how she has found an endless source of happiness and beauty in the continuum. Then she's telling me something too. Explaining still one more dark corner of the human soul while I stand there grinning oafishly, everything in her special-education monologue going over my head. Maybe what I most needed to know about life had floated past in the middle of my happy grin. Maybe, at that very moment, it was hovering up there against the ceiling, a fat little sausage filled with understanding. Meanwhile, there were all the paintings to look at. Gallery after gallery filled with hundreds, thousands of paintings and plenty more where those came from. No shortage of paintings this year and next year there'll be even more. Ten years from now whole cities will be constructed just to display the paintings being turned out now by the emancipated citizens of democratic nations. I ought to know. I've done a few paintings myself. I'm no stranger to the pleasures to be gotten from dabbing paint onto canvass.

Re-crossing La Cienega who do we run into but Wetzstein, the bankruptcy lawyer. Another figure from my past. I acted as if I didn't see him put his hands in his pockets. I grinned like a bear and thrust out my paw. Reluctantly, he shook it, but he didn't introduce me to his pretty, gray-haired wife. Two years since I'd seen the sour bastard and I hadn't missed him.

On to new picture palaces. Two chic, middle-aged ladies were eyeing a sculpture of a writhing, horizontal nude. Even in metal the body was changed with passion and a dangerous vitality. "I don't know what she's supposed to be doing," one of the ladies said to the other, "but whatever it is I'd love to try it." My heart leaped. My God, I thought, it's time to act. I caught the lady's eye and grinned. I started toward her. She was within arm's reach. I saw her face flush, then she grabbed her girlfriend by the arm and disappeared into the crowd giggling.

There were still plenty of galleries and paintings. Braum is an admirer of Leger, who I don't like at all. A man with a polished steel heart. Some stupid paintings by the head of the art department at UCLA, weeds glued over the surface like rabbit warrens. He's in a fine position to contaminate a lot of students who can pass it on to their friends and their own children. Out in the alley again Braum and I finished off Mr. Donleavy then drove the couple blocks to Barney's. The night was still blowing softly. Automobiles gleamed in the black air, fine looking people called gaily to one another across La Cienega. A lady dressed in white drew the back of her white-gloved hand across her brow, brushing gracefully at a wisp of blond hair. I thought about how Horace had written of such a night. A night for the old, "lightly-living gods."

At Barney's there wasn't much of a crowd yet but the jukebox was blaring. I was ready for a big blowout but I needed more people. Marvin was there on a bar stool, stoop-shouldered and homely as ever, peering licentiously at a couple of girls in a booth, sexual fantasies dribbling from the corners of his mouth. Marvin is an admirer of Proust so it doesn't matter much that he works as a bookkeeper for the city. Morgan wasn't there, but Ross was, the baritone with the mistress who has such a lovely belly. And there was his hawk-faced friend with a big, blond dusty looking woman with a beautifully ingratiating smile.

No thoughts for Morgan now. The dusty blond was the one for me. I backed her against the wall and over the racket of the music I told her about the snows at Lake Tahoe, the hunting habits of owls, the jungles of Yucatan. I delivered a monologue on Hasidic lore, about which I know nothing. My tongue was greased, ball bearings were in my jaw. The blond was impressed. Everyone was impressed except Ross, who was in a drunken stupor.

"You show off very well," the blond said. "Sure, you can call me some evening if you like."

Terrific, I thought. Then I thought, who knows? I wandered off forgetting to get her number. I was at loose ends. Braum had his sketch pad out and was doing a girl sitting at the bar wearing narrow little eyeglasses and a big smock.

"No, I'm not a painter," I heard the girl say. "I'm pregnant."

Braum grinned and stroked the girl's belly.

"I don't have a husband," I heard the girl say. "I'm going to give the baby to a friend in Texas."

Braum gave her belly a couple understanding strokes.

"Oh, you're too much," I heard the girl say. When she hopped off the stool her belly blooped in an interesting, heavy way.

The room was starting to fill up. The music was deafening. I tried to think about why the pregnant girl didn't want to stay with us. I was so drunk I was buying drinks at the bar rather than pulling on a bottle in the men's room. I sensed that someone was looking at me. I turned my head very carefully and saw a female eye with a malevolent cast staring directly into mine. The same thing had happened a couple weeks earlier, the same eye, not twelve inches from mine. I'd never spoken to the lady who owned the eye. I knew she used to sleep with an Armenian painter who'd killed himself. Maybe it was that fucking eye. The first time I saw it staring into mine I was too cowed to ask her what she had in mind. Tonight I was too cowed again. I made my way toward the front door. Joan and Mark walked in just then and Joan began telling me about a new literary magazine being published in Greenwich Village that's called *Up your Ass*, or *Let's Fuck* or some shitty New York title like that. I must not have looked very impressed because she went on to explain that this new magazine is publishing all the newest people, the avant-garde of New York City, nothing less. She said I ought to try it.

"Clearly," I said, steadying myself as well as I could, "what we have here is one more New York literary mag setting out to right the wrongs of the people, of life itself. What do I care for those people? They think the final cure for every ill is to be fucked in the ass by some guy with a dark complexion and no inheritance. They're constructing their literature out of cowardice and perverted sexuality. American letters is being stunk up badly by these literary shit-lovers, these creepy purveyors of black romanticism who sprout like slimy weeds from the gutters and garbage of decaying cities. Even when these guys flower their blooms are black and shiny. Under afternoon suns they exude the malodorous scents, the heavy fumes of steaming assholes." I stopped to take a deep breath because I had a lot more to say on the New York literary scene but Joan said: "I can't take any more of this," and turned and disappeared in the crowd.

Mark was ginning from ear to ear. "Hey," he said, "I like that." Mark's a Jew like almost everybody else I know but Mark's from Milwaukee so he's had a chance to see things from a clearer and cleaner perspective than you do if you're a New Yorker. With Mark's encouragement I began to enlarge on my theme about the growing sordidness of American literature but just then Molly showed up with her boy escort. I followed them to their table and started to tell them about what's really going on in Hamlet, I don't know why, but every time I took a deep breath Molly interrupted me. She was so vicious in her comments that I lost track of what my point of view was. Then I couldn't even remember what I was talking about. She got me so bogged down and confused I couldn't pronounce the words I wanted to say so I just sat there looking at her, wondering how she'd be. That's when Molly signaled her little chum it was time for them to leave. She had a tight little smile on her face. I wasn't sure I still wanted to screw her but I took note of how she had combed and brushed her stringy hair for a change and how that was a point in her favor.

By the time the bar closed I was bushed, sitting alone at a table by the back wall. Braum had disappeared. I didn't care. I needed to sleep. Then Rita came in and I watched her walk the length of the bar to my table. I came wide awake. I couldn't believe my good luck. Rita's a pretty, light-skinned colored girl with freckles.

I've had my eye on her for two years. You never know when you're going to get lucky. It's a question of always being ready. Inwardly I made an effort to organize my thoughts, to work out carefully how I would arrange the night.

She sat down and bumped the knuckles of one fist across her teeth. "Very nervous tonight," she said, her eyes looking in one direction then the other.

"What do you believe it is, Rita?" I said consolingly.

"It's because all my hairs hurt," she said.

"All your hairs?" I considered that in an organized way from several different perspectives but couldn't come to a conclusion about why that would be. I couldn't even form an opinion. Rita didn't say anything more. I was stumped, but I liked looking at her face, which was turning one way then the other like it was looking for something. Then a big Negro from West Covina came and walked directly to our table and Rita left with him. I tried to think why the guy had come all that distance on this particular night at just that moment. There were several possible explanations but no certain one. I went outside to the curbing and vomited on my shoes.

"Secret Spindles"

(1965)

Last night I did my roadwork at a slow steady pace, jogging along in the dark past the old sheds and the brick warehouses. When the rain began to fall I took off my glasses and put them in my back pocket. I felt very intense about something but I didn't know what. As I splashed through the rain I had to convince myself all over again, as I do every night, that the roadwork is really necessary for what I'm planning to do. When I got back to the house Mother and Father were in the front room watching television.

"Thirty-five years old," Mother said, "and he doesn't know enough to come in out of the rain."

"I know enough," I said. "I just don't care anymore."

"Oh pfft," she said.

I felt very intense in an empty kind of way. I more or less understood that something was going to happen. I got a change of clothes and walked through the house to the bathroom. I drew water for a bath and was undressing when it started. I had the sensation that I was in the presence of the Devil again. It was so fleeting I almost didn't catch it.

Instinctively I looked over my shoulder and there He was, like in a hallucination. He was standing inside the closed door, His arms folded across His chest, looking at me with a level gaze. Without taking my eyes from His I put my right hand on the edge of the cool bathtub to make sure I didn't go off. When He spoke it was very matter-of-factly.

"The time is come," He said.

The moment He spoke I felt myself go off. I saw a deep gorge with a tightrope stretched across it. I saw myself walking on the tightrope and I understood I was going to fall. Then I saw the inside of the bathroom door and the medicine cabinet beside the door and the face bowl. Then I saw the gorge again. In the bottom of the gorge there was a square pit. I wanted to cling to the rope with my arms and legs but I knew it wouldn't do any good because I was going to fall no matter what. In the bathroom I sat down on the floor and put my arm over the edge of the tub. I tried to look at all the things in the bathroom and not see the gorge anymore or the pit but I kept seeing them and I understood that no matter how long I tried to hold on I was going down. It was very frightening to be that sure of what was going to happen.

The thought occurred to me that it would be easier to just let go and get it over with. In that instant I felt myself plummeting downward through the darkness. Then I was at the bottom of the pit. I'd landed on my feet. I was standing there looking around. It was gloomy but there was enough light to see by. A ramp led up one side of the pit to a tunnel opening. There was straw scattered over the ramp as if a hay wagon had gone up it not long before. I thought: Others have made the journey before me. I can do it too. I walked up the ramp toward the tunnel but just before I reached it two great medieval doors appeared and swung closed before me. I understood there was something more I could do if I persisted but I didn't want to. I was tired. I began seeing the things in the bathroom then and I felt the fear recede. My legs were cramping and I felt worn out.

I took my bath and afterward went out to the shack where the typewriter is set up. There were the books stacked up against the walls and the piles of old newspapers and magazines. There was the dirt on the floor and the paper bags full of trash. There was the broken radio and the half-finished manuscripts and the files I hadn't opened in months. I didn't know what to do. I picked up a book but I was too restless to read. I thought about going for a walk but I was too weary. I decided to go back in the house and go to bed.

All night I tossed and turned.

~

Every day I watch how little and frail my father is becoming. A wisp of gray hair falls over his brow ever so lightly. In the morning he can't find his trousers and afterward he forgets how to put on his shoes. This morning when Mother got up she found Father in the kitchen standing first on one leg then the other, trying to tie his shoelaces. He kept falling against the drain board.

"Sit down, Henry," Mother said. "Then tie your laces."

Father looked at her steadily for a moment, then sat down.

"It's that goddamn plaster in my bedroom," he said. "It keeps falling off the ceiling and I can't remember a goddamn thing."

This evening while Mother and I watched television Father went slowly from room to room, sometimes pausing as if he'd had a thought. Wandering into the living room he picked up his ashtray and blew the ash out all over the carpet.

Mother put her face to her hands and giggled.

"Old devil-may-care," she said.

Later Mother said to me: "Seriously, Bradley, just look at that old jacket your father's got on. A bandit wouldn't wear it. Now you've got to speak to your father. You tell him you'll go with him when he gets a new suit. I've been trying to get him to buy a suit for ten years. He'll do it if you go with him. And you get one too, and a pair of shoes. I'll give you the money. What's going to happen when your father dies? Neither one of you will have a decent suit. You know all those brothers and sisters of his are going to start dying too and when they do we won't have any clothes while they'll all be dolled up like Aster's pony. You know how those Catholic funerals are. You have to spend a lot of money or you'll go straight to hell."

Mother believes that because Father is absent-minded that he's sick. He'll probably outlive Mother, but in the meantime he keeps her on edge. He throws his cigarette butts in the wastebasket under the kitchen sink and sets the cupboards on fire. Or he turns on the gas in the oven but forgets to touch a match to it. He takes a morning stroll to the corner—"It's such a swell day," he says—then forgets where he lives.

This morning he was standing alone in the dining room, his shoulders hunched up against the cold.

"Father," I said, "do you want me to get your sweater?"

I watched his face light up. "Oh, sure, Son."

My father's hand is the first memory I have of life. Large, solid, hairy, it led me up the street one dark windy afternoon to the top of a hill where we looked down the back slope and watched the trash blowing across the empty lots. When I recall that scene a sense of ineluctable aloneness comes over me.

I remember how Father would hold me on his lap and recite little love poems and how I would cry.

"Henry," Mother would say. "Now don't tease the child."

"I'm just telling him how much I love him," my father would say, and he would laugh softly with his deep voice and my heart would break.

Twenty years passed before I began to forgive him for—for what, precisely? And after that it took ten years more for the forgiving to play itself out. Nowadays, when I'm standing at a window perhaps, or loafing under the apricot tree, Father appears in my arms like a wraith. He's all shriveled and dried out and light as a piece of paper. I hold him very carefully, just as I would a newborn, and my heart warms up.

~

Last night I dreamed I was on the floor of the ocean. There were stony-faced men there encrusted with salt. They performed a ritual dance where they churned up the water dangerously.

After breakfast I drove across town and checked into the Veteran's Hospital to have a hernia repaired. I've looked forward to being here. It would be a relief, I thought, to be among strangers, among people who are of no consequence to me, people I don't have to listen to or talk to. I could say things carelessly here, off the top of my head, and I wouldn't have to be afraid that I'd be thoroughly understood. My every word would not be weighted with a lifetime of intimacy. But how can I relax in a place like this? In the bed next to me a foot is rotting off, television sets and transistor radios are playing one against the other, men are moaning with tubes down their throats and needles in their arms, there's no air and I feel a cold coming on.

This afternoon there was a pleasant diversion. A good looking psychologist took me to her office where I answered some printed questions. The trick was to answer immediately without reflection. Right up my alley. I said that men are hairy and that women are rosy. I said the worst thing a woman can do is forget. I said that's the worst thing a man can do too, which surprised me even as I wrote it down. I said homosexuals are crazy. I said I wanted my father with me.

I asked the psychologist if she had found anything interesting. She looked at my paper smiling. She said: "You seem to be unwilling to commit yourself to either loving or hating."

~

The sniffles have become a real cold and surgery's been postponed a week. I passed the day thumbing through old magazines and reading Jung.

~

Checked out of the hospital this morning with a seven-day pass and went home. On the news this evening they ran some combat film from Vietnam. It made me realize that for several days I hadn't thought about how I'm planning to go there.

It's odd about the roadwork. Once I made the decision to go to Vietnam I began to have recurring daydreams about how when I get there that sooner or later I'll have to run for my life. I imagine myself riding in a jeep that's blown up by a mine. The Viet Cong rush out from the jungle and nothing will save me but my legs. Or I'm living with a lady in Saigon and she deceives me into the hands of the terrorists. There's a tortuous chase through back alleys until I collapse and they kill me. I feel the bayonets being shoved through my back and poking out my chest. They take my breath away. Or I'm run down like an animal and, stupid with exhaustion, I look on calmly while they chop off my head, after which I feel a pleasant sense of weightlessness.

One night recently I dreamed a bullet drilled a hole through my head, entering on the right and coming out the left temple. I sat cross-legged on the ground while my brains came out of my head like sausage from a grinder. A soldier appeared and asked if the wound hurt. "No," I said. "Not much."

Out in the shack reading Jung, I copy out these lines: "It is not so much a question of a 'death instinct' as that 'other' instinct which signifies spiritual life…"

~

Last night I dreamed I was serving with the South Vietnamese army. One morning on patrol we were ambushed and I was taken prisoner by the Viet Cong. I was led to a village in the jungle. There, an unpaved square was bordered by shops and houses with thatched roofs. There was a bandstand in the center of the square overgrown with blooming tropical vines. I believed I was going to be executed. I was willing to tell them anything to keep from being shot. Then I was introduced to the village elder who had white hair and was very kind. He gave me the freedom of his village. Nothing was demanded of me. I couldn't understand it.

I came to know the village tradesmen. There was a printer on the square who had a one-room shop with a thatched roof. He was a big hearty dark-complected man. He printed from square wooden blocks onto thick parchments. He loved his work. I thought about how good it would be to hold those thick pulpy pages in my own hands. One morning I went to him to ask for work. I found him standing in his doorway holding a freshly printed sheaf of manuscript pages. His face was upturned and the sun was beaming down on it. He accepted me as his assistant and my heart swelled with gratitude. I realized I had found a place for myself and that I would never leave the village. I turned then and saw that the village square was flooded with a radiant sunshine.

A dull gray morning. Mooney dropped by. We sat on the back steps and talked about going to Vietnam and getting work there. We talked about how longshoring was going to be slow for a couple months and about how we are going to make enough money to get us by until it picks up again. When Mooney left I walked to the market to read the book reviews in the magazines. I passed three pretty Negro girls and when they looked at me I became conscious of how I haven't shaved for days and how I need a haircut. I was conscious of the sewn places on my jacket and that my pants aren't really clean. It surprises me, the longer I stay in south Los Angeles, how pretty the Negro girls are becoming.

~

A bright pretty morning. Worked comfortably at the typewriter until suppertime, all the while in the back of my mind wondering where I'll be this time next month, wondering what I'll be doing.

I'm setting out to see the world and make my fortune, just like they did in the old days. I know I'm past the age when these things are normally taken care of, but I'm a slow starter.

In the meantime I'm living off my parents' pension checks. I don't feel guilty but I do feel ashamed. I have no money and no job and no automobile. In some peculiar way I'm so weary I don't care about being ashamed. The last three years weigh so heavily on me I hardly have the strength to move my body. My head is clearer than it was a few months ago but it's not right yet. Something very heavy is still pulling me down, weighing on me.

In my daydreams I see myself attached to a South Vietnamese regiment, or traveling with Special Forces teams in South and Central America. I'm writing for a news service and doing a book at the same time. But what's more likely to happen is that after the surgery I'll go to Las Vegas and drive a cab and try my hand at the dice tables again. I'll have so little to lose I might win. With five hundred, a thousand dollars in my pocket life would start humming again. In spite of appearances, in spite of all the trouble I'm having getting myself started again, I feel a gathering process going on inside me. I feel threads of my experience being pulled in from every quarter and wound on secret spindles. Inside me in places that are still dark I sense that forces are building, that expeditions are being provisioned. Before me as far as I can see the life appears clear of obstacles, empty, silent, ready at a moment's notice to receive into itself anything—anything at all.

~

Dreamed I was in the back yard filling in a gopher hole when bugs started swarming out of it. I stomped my foot at the hole. The bugs grew to the size of rats and welled up out of the hole. A filthy duck-billed armadillo scurried out, then fat lizards and insects stuffed with food until they were the size of swollen cats. The thought of squashing one of them disgusted me. A dark woman dressed as a gypsy appeared and looked down into the hole. The insects and animals disappeared. I was very relieved but the woman wouldn't let well enough alone. She shoved the garden hose down the hole and turned on the water full force. The bottom of the hole fell out with a whoosh and became a crater fifteen feet across. In the bottom of the crater was an opening to a tunnel which led off toward the west. The opening was rectangular and shored up with timbers. It was large enough to walk into and I thought about exploring it, but the idea slipped my mind.

A bright morning full of sunshine. Wrote a little, gardened a little, went for a walk, getting through the day as best I could, waiting to return to the hospital.

Mother is growing steadily weaker. She has barely enough strength to go to the market and cook our meals. In the morning she does a little housework but in the afternoon she just lies on the couch in the living room. The stuffing is coming out of the couch so she's put a bedspread over it. She lays her face on a green plastic pillow and covers herself with a blanket I haven't seen since my childhood. She watches television or reads a bit, but mostly she naps. A moment ago when I went in the house and saw her on the couch I thought about how nice it would be to buy her a big soft pillow and a brightly colored lap rug. It's a wondrous thing how deep you can go into a man's psyche and still find the bonds that tie him to his mother. What surprises me is that these ties increase with understanding rather than diminish, which is not how I would have thought it to be—if I had thought about it.

After supper, time dragged. In the shack behind Grandmother's rocking chair I found a half-bottle of Burgundy and that was a help. I loafed and drank the bottle. It wasn't long until I felt something pressing against my stomach. It was a feeling I'd had a number of times before. One day last year I found out what it was. It was one of those days when something comes over me, or happens to me, and I can see myself walking on the bottom of the ocean. That day there was a cave on the ocean floor and I was going to explore it when near the entrance I saw a white rock half-buried in the sand.

I had an inexplicable urge to dig it up. While I held the rock in my hands it transformed itself into a snake's egg with a leathery shell. Inside the egg I could see the form of an unborn child. My flesh crawled, and I was afraid.

I had thought that business was finished some time ago but occasionally the rock reappears, pressing suddenly against my belly while I'm out walking perhaps, or down on the waterfront while I'm working in a ship's hold and I have to go on with the work as if nothing were happening when all the time the egg with the leathery shell is pressing against my belly and the child is waiting to be born and my heart is pounding with fear and expectation.

∽

I was sitting mindlessly on the back steps in the pale sunlight when Joel dropped by smoking his pipe and talking about how well the travel agency is going and saying in so many words that it ought to be very clear after all these years that I don't have much talent for being a writer and that I ought to find a job like everybody else and stick to it and who am I trying to kid anyhow? I always listen quietly when Joel talks about how I am no good as a writer. Afterward he bought the beer and we talked about how it was when we lived together in Mexico City, and about Vietnam, and finally getting around to telling the old stories about Korea that are already fifteen years dead but are still very important and exciting if nothing's going on in your life.

∽

I'm supposed to return to the hospital tomorrow morning but my throat's getting sore again. If I don't get the hernia repaired I won't be able to go to sea and I won't have any way to get to Vietnam. I won't be able to work as a longshoreman any longer either. So I won't have any money and it could be a very long time before I would be able to begin the journey. After the last three years, I'm suspicious of everything. Out walking when I saw by the headlines that "direct contact" has been made between Hanoi and Washington. Disappointment touched my heart. At the library I read something by Kazin: "The age has finally turned all our dreams into books." I had a lot to say about that when I first read it but now I don't understand what it means. Back at the house again I went out to the shack and sat down to the typewriter but my mind was empty. For three years now, in a certain way, I have been helpless, waiting for something to happen to me. I can't act on my own. I am going to have to be thrown back into life by circumstance and events. I haven't got the will to take the first step myself.

When Mother and Father went to bed I turned off the fires and lay on the couch watching an adventure movie on television. In the movie the hero had returned to his ranch in Texas following the Civil War. His family expected him to pick up where he'd left off but he was no longer satisfied with being merely a rancher. He'd developed a craving for riches during the war, and for power and status and for association with other men who had those things. He'd discovered that it was worth his while to lie and steal and murder to gain his end. There was only one way for him, the path of his ambition, and he was willing to risk everything including his life to follow it. Why should he, the hero no doubt said to himself, why should he commit himself to an adventure whose scope was one bit less broad than that of the multi-millionaire business tycoon, or those curious men who became Senators and Presidents? Fate had given him less than his rightful share of the wealth and position of his society and he was going to dare everything he safely had for the chance to beat out his circumstances, to get everything he could picture in his imagination, in his best daydreams as it were.

I pulled my jacket over my shoulders and watched the movie intently. In my ear a voice repeated again and again. "You have lost your daring," it said. "You have lost your daring."

~

When I returned to the hospital this morning I expected surgery to take place at the end of the week. When I was told it would happen tomorrow my heart lunged. In the prep room a little Malay wearing a green smock and cap washed and shaved the "field of operation," that is, from my belly to my thigh. He washed my balls with warm soapy water, and with wonderfully great attention it seemed to me. He told me he'd been doing this work for thirty years. There were two washtubs in the room and every few minutes one nurse or another would pop in to wash her hands. The little Malay, to protect my modesty I suppose, would lay his paw on my parts and pass the time of day with the nurses. He knew every nurse who came in. He had a wonderful way with his hand also and I had to concentrate for all I was worth to not get an erection. When there was no nurse to chat up he talked to me. He couldn't do his work without talking about something else. He didn't stop talking until the moment he stretched up my cock between his thumb and forefinger and began shaving it with a straight-edged razor. His round nut-brown face became set in an expression of such intense and conscious pleasure that it made the sweat run from my armpits.

If something goes wrong tomorrow, I wonder how much of it I'll be able to record? And when I'm old and my life is slipping away from me, how much of that will I be able to get down on paper? I want to be able to feel the necessity for recording my dying just as I do my living but that's the trouble with dying I suppose. You desire less, and then less, until finally you don't want anything at all.

~

A restless night. This morning I started Schaller's book on the mountain gorilla. The nurse gave me an injection she said would quiet my nerves. Pretty soon I felt so good that I tossed the book onto my bedside table and just lay there in a quiet dope-ecstasy.

At ten o'clock I was wheeled out of the ward and left on a gurney in the hallway outside surgery. I looked into the faces that passed to see if anyone was noticing me. My heart was still glowing from the injection. A second patient was rolled up against the wall behind me. He asked what I was going to have. His voice was tense. I wondered if he hadn't gotten his injection. I said mine was a hernia. I asked what his was. He didn't answer. I resented his not answering. He probably was going to have something serious and didn't want to associate closely with someone who was only going to have a hernia. Screw him, I thought. But I wished I was going to have something more important than a hernia. Something better. I heard him speak to a passing doctor. He wanted a glass of water.

"Doc," he said, "I'm afraid my throat's going to close up."

"Nonsense," the doctor said, not even breaking stride.

Faces passed by. When they glanced down at me I tried not to smile. It embarrassed me that I wanted them to notice me. I was wheeled into a room and given a spinal. My hips and legs began to tingle. They grew numb. An arm fell off the gurney and the Negro nurse put it back. My fingers touched something cool and doughy. She said it was my thigh. It was disgusting. The doctors were laughing. They were deciding which stitches to use, they weren't quite sure, and the Chinese or Korean doctor had made a joke. I hoped he wasn't Korean. Who knows what he might have in his heart. I hadn't heard the joke but I wanted to laugh too. My mouth twisted crookedly. The three men appeared and bent over me and the work began.

I'd thought I would be able to feel them working on me and that it wouldn't hurt, but I couldn't feel anything. I'd meant to stay awake while they were doing the work but every once in a while I'd doze off. When I would wake and realize that I'd dozed off I would feel disappointed with myself. The tall Negro nurse stood at my head looking on. She was very attractive. All my parts were spread out under the gaze of a good looking woman but I couldn't feel anything. Then my nose started to itch. I asked the nurse to rub it. She laughed and told me to go to sleep, but she rubbed it. I could think perfectly clearly, more or less, but it took all my strength and concentration to say words. After a while I felt a tugging sensation, a pulling downward from my sternum to my groin. My flesh was being pulled downward and kneaded together. There was a little pain. I was very careful to not move. Even if I had wanted to move I couldn't have moved but inwardly I was very careful anyhow. Then suddenly the pain welled up. It was like a hillside exploding and I could feel the earth lifting up. I tried to shrink away but I couldn't move. I wanted to groan but I couldn't groan.

In the recovery room the pain was more severe than I'd expected. Some of the others were asking for injections but it was my plan to have all the pain I could get. It went on a long while. I tried to not think of anything but the pain. After a while it was too much. I couldn't stand it. It made me feel ashamed but I was going to ask for an injection the next time a nurse came in. But before I could ask for it an orderly grabbed my gurney and wheeled me back to the ward and dragged me onto my bed.

In the ward I couldn't think of anything but the pain. I had wanted to think on other matters when the pain was at its worst and to do certain things but all I could do was think about the pain. At the same time I suspected that I could do what I wanted if only I had more will power, a stronger force of character. I thought about how one day I will suffer much greater pain than I was suffering now and that I'd have to bear it maybe very casually but it was no help because the pain I was having now was enough to deaden my spirit, to make me less than what I wanted to be. I felt degraded, as if I were in the hands of an enemy who was treating me contemptuously.

When the lights were turned off I listened to a radio playing softly in the dark. The pain was very bad but I was ashamed to call the nurse. On the radio then I heard the news coming from Vietnam. I listened to the descriptions of the latest fighting, the newest casualty figures. The war became suddenly very real for me. I could almost hear the sound of the guns. I felt it was possible that the fighting would erupt into the ward itself. I lay motionless, holding my breath. The pain was excruciating. The fighting was drawing closer. I couldn't quite hear it but I could feel it approaching. I could feel the tremors in the building. Then suddenly it exploded into the ward. I felt the shock of the high explosive. I saw soldiers being blown down. It was awful. Tears filled my eyes. War was the same as it had been in Korea, but I had changed. War was no good any longer. No good. I saw the old pictures again— the torn and blasted mountaintops, the scorched forests and men charred black and curled up like burnt bacon. I felt high-explosive blasting through the ward, the mortars blasting, artillery blasting, recoilless rifles blasting, hand grenades blasting. Ferocious blasts of air exploded against my eyeballs, the fiery blasting force of sound blown apart, sound itself blasting through eardrums and heads and blasting bones and splitting rock and the thin little screams of flying fragmentation.

A middle-aged nurse with popped eyes appeared at the side of my bed. "How do you feel?" she asked.

"Fine," I said.

"Do you feel any pain yet?"

"Some."

"Do you want a hypo?" she asked. "It'll help you sleep."

"Whatever's usual," I said.

~

Slept poorly. This morning I read a little Schaller then loafed the rest of the day. At lights-out I got an injection to help me sleep. A warm glow seeped into my breast. I thought about how I had wasted the day. And then I saw a naked woman appear in the dark. She was lying on a white metal table on her back. She was beautiful. I felt confused and didn't know where I was. I turned a little on my side. It was difficult in the darkened ward to see the normal things. Then I saw the woman again. I saw a slice of green melon appear on the white metal table beside her. I saw myself get out of bed and circle the table where the woman was lying. I looked at her appraisingly. I looked like an animal circling its prey. Then the pale green melon merged into the woman and the woman merged into the melon. A spoon appeared in my hand and I watched myself eat the cool delicious flesh of the beautiful woman who was a melon but who was a woman also. It was engrossing and very beautiful seeing it but it was disturbing too. I put my hand on the metal cabinet beside the bed. I rubbed my hands over the blanket and the sheets covering me. I wanted to turn on my side but it was too painful. I picked up Schaller's book on mountain gorillas and handled it. I kept touching all the things around me in the dark that were real until I stopped seeing the melon woman.

~

A very long restless night. After breakfast I caught up on the last two days of the journal then spent the rest of the day watching television and napping. This evening I was disappointed with my lack of discipline. No directed thinking, nothing written, distracted by other patients, made lazy by the effects of the nightly injections.

~

Dreamed I was standing at the edge of the excavation at a huge copper mine. Square shafts appeared in the bottom of the excavation, then deep crevices and suddenly the bottom fell out of everything.

This morning when I first opened my eyes I happened to glance out a window facing east and so help me God into a "rosy fingered dawn."

I was reading comfortably in Schaller when a frocked minister stopped at the foot of the bed and asked if I were not a Protestant? I didn't want to be bothered with that sort of thing, not by someone who works for the Veteran's Administration anyhow, but I didn't want to make the man feel badly either so we had a little chat. By evening I was very restless. I had a headache and a bad stomach. I ate a laxative but it didn't work. When I weighed myself I'd lost six pounds.

~

Dreamed I had a white rat that loved me very much. It nuzzled me with its nose and pressed its face to mine. I loved the rat in return but one day I noticed that its brow line was ragged and unattractive, and that it had the mange. Then I didn't want it anymore.

There's been a lot of dreaming since the surgery but I've been too lazy to record most of it. Still, I've got to stop being so puritanical about the journal. It's perfectly normal to do less work one day and more the next. Why do I feel so guilty about the journal? So obligated? "The courage to be (I'm reading Tillich) for the Stoic is the courage to affirm oneself in spite of fate and death, but it is not the courage to affirm oneself in spite of sin and guilt. It could not have been different: for the courage to face one's own guilt leads to the question of salvation instead of renunciation."

Salvation. When I read that word I was stunned. Salvation—the coming to grips with your entire self in one fell swoop, one terrible plunge into the blackness of your own heart, into the ancient archive where all the lies of your lifetime are stored up on membranous little sheets of film, those stories that will tell the tale that has got to be told when at last I have the will to spit it out. I've known in my heart for a long time that before I'm saved I will have to surrender. But surrender to what? Sometimes it seems I understand. But what does it really mean to surrender? And how can I surrender to something I can't put my finger on? All I know is that until I give in to whatever it is I need to give in to that I won't be able to make my own gestures. I won't be able to think my own thoughts or admit to the beds my desires long to lie down in. When I think of the times I've wanted to surrender to God it makes my head spin. But God is nothing to me, aside from my desire for Him. I would be ashamed to fall to my knees before my own longing. And what does it mean anyhow when a man longs for something he hasn't been able to believe exists? But oh how I long for an easeful going under—not for an end but for a new beginning. I want a new life. I'm ashamed and disgusted with the one I have. I want literally to be reborn. I want to wipe the slate clean with a perfect acceptance. Yet somehow I can't accept-whatever it is, whatever I was. If I could accept—then I would be like the wolf at night when it turns its head to glance at the moon. I would be like the moon going down and the sun coming up. I say I can't put my finger on what it is that I've got to surrender to but that isn't the truth. I know in my heart what it is and where it lies in wait. One day if I'm ever going to save my life I am going to have to give myself up to it. I will have to close my eyes and breathe out and ease into the edge of that blackness that has no end. But what good are images like that? I sit here on my bed offended by what I see, offended by what I smell, by what I overhear, offended by my own body, picking at my toenails like an ape.

Flaubert wrote that the one quality common to all genius is vitality and I believe it. I believe it. It's not good when a man's vitality is insufficient to meet his ambitions.

Jay Cluney dropped by this evening. He's still the same tall narrow boy with the same inhibited narrow walk. The same red curly beard, the same brown eyes flecked with red. Jay's a painter, a writer, a dabbler in cocaine and marriage. It's difficult to believe he's not turned twenty-two yet. He wanted to talk about drugs tonight, about LSD and fantasy. He made me angry. I don't like his habit of belittling consciousness in favor of non-rational experience. I try to impress upon him that it's not necessary. And what's this interest he has now for the psychedelic drugs? Those things are for the triflers, for the faint at heart. A man has got to stand on his own two feet and open his mind like a can of sardines. We don't need anything more once we have found out what our desires really are.

Once I got started tonight it didn't matter what Jay might have wanted to say. I was going to contradict him. Everyone is wrong about everything anyhow. And then Jay's so easy to argue down. He doesn't argue. He frustrated me by allowing me to see my own coarseness, the rigidity of my stance, but I couldn't quit it. I found myself boring in on him as if I were under attack, as if my best defense against him were an offense. I acted as if I were being undermined, as if I had no choice but to beat back the enemy or go under.

"If you go with it," I recall Jay saying, "then there's no danger in LSD. But you have to go with it."

"Yeah."

"It's like life," he said.

When it was time for lights-out I walked him to the elevator. I couldn't stand up straight and I had to walk very slowly.

"What's the matter?" Jay asked. "Got a stitch in your side?"

"Yeah," I said. "A seven gash in my belly and I've got a stitch in my side."

I meant it for a joke but I was too hearty or something and I could see that he was embarrassed for me. The elevator doors opened and Jay stepped inside. We didn't look at each other's eyes again and the doors closed and I walked very slowly back to my bed.

∼

Dreamed last night about huge trench mortars the size of office buildings. The mortars were odd in that when they fired they didn't eject a shell but imploded, blasting out their own insides. After one of the mortars fired I saw a flower seed fall down the massive tube and bounce around on the bottom.

After breakfast I went downstairs to the clothing room and put on my street clothes. I sat on a bench in front of the hospital in the pale sunlight and waited for Mother and Father to drive up. The broad green lawns were still wet from the night. I watched the sparrows and a blackbird hopping in the wet grass among the yellow dandelions. A nurse in a white uniform smiled and said good morning as she walked past.

"Good morning," I said.

I thought about how weak I felt. I thought about how satisfied I was too and about how I had taken a significant step toward getting to Vietnam. I sat there in the cool pale air feeling very weak and very satisfied.

∼

Dreamed all night but made no notes. Sometimes it doesn't seem worthwhile to keep this record. Sometimes it disgusts me to think I have to sit down every day and write out what I did the day before. Sometimes it's so boring it makes me sick, or I fall asleep with my head on the typewriter. Writing down dreams is the worst, but I feel the obligation. At first it's interesting to be able to recall your dreams but after a while it's boring and disgusting. The most fantastic dreams become as boring as any idle conversation or any of the other things that interest other people but that don't interest me any longer and are so boring I can't bear to hear about them.

And yet, as I mull over what I dreamed last night, I recall eating sandwiches stuffed with shit that somebody gave me as a joke. Afterward I was given an assignment to murder someone—I don't know who. Then I raped a woman. Those dreams sound like they should be interesting but they just make me tired.

This afternoon I was in the kitchen looking out the window when Mother came in and tugged at my sleeve. Pulling me into a corner she giggled so that I could hardly understand what she was whispering.

"It's your father," she said, giggling crazily. "He took me in his bedroom a few minutes ago and showed me his trousers all laid out neatly on the bed. I couldn't figure out what he wanted me to look at. Then I saw that he'd pulled one pants leg down inside the other and lined up the cuffs at the bottom so they were perfectly even. We both just stood there looking at his pants like that like we were a couple of idiots."

Mother was giggling so that she could hardly go on.

"And then your father said to me... he said:

'Now you tell me, just how the hell am I going to hang up my pants when they're like that?'"

I thought it was a pretty good story but Mother was completely breaking up over it and holding on to me to keep from falling down.

~

Dreamed I was back in the mountains in Korea. It was night and I was standing on a ridgeline in a broken forest when in front of me a terrible wail came out of a hole in the ground. The sound of it made my flesh crawl. The scene changed and I was here in the living room of my parents' house. Mother and Father were sitting in their favorite chairs staring straight before them with unblinking eyes. They were stiff and there was something weird about them. There was something quite wrong but I couldn't figure out what it was. Something was in the air. I realized then that whatever it was, it was in the kitchen. There was a presence in the kitchen. I understood that it was alive, but was invisible to the human eye. It was a terror.

When I woke from the dream it was still dark. I needed to urinate but I was afraid to get out of bed. I was afraid that what had been in my dream had spilled over into my awake life and that it was dangerous. After a while I got up and walked through the house to the bathroom and when I was in bed again I was still afraid. I wasn't going to be able to escape from it until it was finished. From where I was in bed I couldn't see out to the kitchen. I sat up and with my mind's eye I looked until I could see the kitchen door from where I was. I looked at it very steadily. After a moment the blood began to drain from my head. My arms and legs stiffened. Then I saw myself get out of bed and walk through the house toward the kitchen door. I was afraid. I watched myself open the door. I couldn't see well in the dark but I knew the presence was there. I was facing it. I was very afraid but I thought I'd be alright if I didn't panic and if I stayed alert. I watched for as long as I could but after a while I gave up. I didn't have enough energy to persist against the fear.

After lunch I drove to the hospital to have the stitches removed from my belly. When I lay down on the table the sweat was pouring out of me and my hands were trembling. I didn't understand at first what was going on. Then I remembered the other hospital that other afternoon fifteen years ago. I was sitting up in a wheelchair that time and Doctor Silverman was doing the work. He was removing three dozen stitches from the hand and a couple dozen more from the ankle. I couldn't bear for him to touch the hand. My entire body trembled. My eyes twitched. It didn't hurt, but I couldn't bear it.

"Don't be embarrassed," Doctor Silverman said. "It's only the stupid ones that it doesn't bother. It shows you've got some intelligence."

Today the stitches were out before I knew what was happening. Walking back to the car I had to stop twice to rest.

After supper I was reading Edmund Wilson:

"Lincoln created himself as a poetic figure, and he thus imposed himself on the nation." He created himself. Those three words stuck in my mind. Ideas began lighting up in my brain like matches struck in the night. What's been the matter with me, I wondered? Everyday I sit in this shack stewing and sputtering, daydreaming about going to Vietnam or Vienna, to Africa, Guatemala, Peru or any place at all so long as it's on the other side of the earth but in the meantime of course not going anywhere, not doing anything, telling myself that if only I can get across an ocean I can become a journalist, that if I can get south of the border there will be plenty to write about there, if I can get to the Congo, Tierra del Fuego that fame and fortune will be waiting for me and all the while I sit indolently in South Los Angeles amid the ruins of the most striking and really wonderful riot this nation has experienced in modern times. So what am I doing just sitting here, I thought? I can start my real work right here, right where I am and with what I've already got.

I became intensely excited about the idea of doing something on Watts. My work was cut out for me, no doubt about it. It had been for months but I couldn't see the forest for the trees. I saw it now, I thought, and I half ran to the liquor store on the corner that had been burned down during the riot but is rebuilt bigger and more flashy than ever by its Jewish owner and bought a copy of the *Sentinel*, the Negro weekly. I thumbed through the paper looking for one lead, just one hint, anything at all that would get me started, that would set me running, but there was nothing but the usual stories of businessmen making good and the women's clubs and the shootings. I wasn't half finished with the paper before my eyelids were closing and I was yawning. I dropped the paper in the gutter and walked home.

~

Slept well but no matter, this morning I was tired and downhearted. Drove the folks to the market and thumbed through the magazines. Read several pieces on the tactical situation of the American military in Vietnam. It looks hopeless for the Americans. This afternoon I read a piece on Charles Pierce: "Pierce was a favorite son. He had an eminent father who attended to his early instruction and guided his study; he was subjected to rigorous intellectual discipline and was in early association with famous people who treated him like an adult; his father provided him with a secure position that left plenty of time for philosophy. As a result he began life—as John Stuart Mill put his own case—he began life twenty years before his contemporaries."

I thought about my own father. Then I thought about how I am beginning my own life twenty years behind my contemporaries. What a waste of time there's been. What a sorrowful thing it is to look back and see that I have lived my life the way I have and that now there are disciplines I will never have time to deal with seriously. I don't know if that's true or not, but I'm afraid it's true. I'm afraid that all I am going to be able to do is to be persistent, examine my own experience, my life as if it were a case study of a stranger. Maybe I'll be able to restore to some few others parts of their own lives that they brush aside absentmindedly, like dandruff from their collars. I tell myself that it's not the quality of the data that is significant, but the care with which it's examined.

~

Puttered around the shack all day. The air was bright and chilly. Toward supper time I grew apprehensive. I didn't know why. When it was time to watch the news on television my heart was pounding. I realized that I was afraid to hear that the fighting was going well and that the war would be over before I could get there but I needn't have worried. This war is like a running sore. My chances for getting to it are very good. Still, by the time the news was over my excitement was finished too and I was sitting in the same room breathing the same air I breathe every evening. I went out back to the shack. I read Wilson on Justice Holmes. While I read I felt disgusted. "I think (Holmes wrote) that the sacredness of human life is a purely municipal ideal of no validity outside the jurisdiction…and I understand by human rights what a given crowd will fight for successfully."

I watched a late movie on television. It was a costume melodrama. A man was run through with a foil and I felt myself flinch. Another man was shot down with bullets. I didn't like seeing it. When I was twenty I was able to watch real men being killed without such displays of emotion. What's happening to me?

∼

At daybreak I was still awake. I was thinking about how if I can get to Saigon and get myself attached to a South Vietnam regiment or division command that I can take the part of the Vietnamese against the Americans. I can take the first step toward making a place for myself, as Father used to put it, in high society.

Tonight while Mother and Father were in the living room watching the roller derby I sat in the kitchen with the door shut between us reading Morgan on Nietzsche. Nietzsche encourages me. He charges me with enthusiasm. He makes me want more than any other writer makes me want. "…he who demands and attains great things from himself must feel himself very remote from those who do not do that-this distance is interpreted by these others as opinion about self, but the former knows it only as perpetual work, war, victory, by day and night: of all that, the others know nothing. They talk so stupidly about pride."

~

Dreamed I was a prisoner in a Vietnamese palace. There were other prisoners too and I was in command of them. There was no one in the palace except us prisoners. There were no guards. Yet once before we had tried to escape and had failed. That was before I was in command, however. Now we planned a second escape attempt. We were to make a break for it at twelve noon. I hurried through the palace from room to room urging the men on in their preparations. The work had to be completed by noon or our plans would go to smash. All the responsibility was on my shoulders. I wanted desperately to escape but the others didn't seem to care so much. I couldn't make them understand that if they didn't hurry, the hour would come and go and we would still be prisoners. I couldn't impress upon the others the gravity of the situation. Then it was too late. A crowd of very handsome and fashionable people entered the palace and started up the marble staircase toward where we were pretending to be working. The women were tall and elegantly gowned. Their jewels sparkled brilliantly. As I watched them climb the marble stairs I thought about how much I wanted to be among them rather than among those I did live with and how I too wanted to live in a palace as a free man. Then I realized what I was thinking, what I was admitting to, and I felt apprehensive. I understood that if I gave in to that desire that I would lose more than I would gain. I tried to figure out what it was that I would lose but before I could figure it out, I gave in. I joined with the crowd that was so elegant and rich and gracious. I felt at home with them immediately. I knew I would never again want to escape. Not ever again would I have to suffer the anguish and the desperation of needing to escape and of not being able to.

First thing this morning I went out to the shack and did the journal, as I always do. Tried to review the notes I made yesterday on Nietzsche but my brain wouldn't stand for it. Read in a couple books on guerrilla warfare. I thought about those people I meet who talk so enthusiastically about insurrection and armed revolution. I always want to know who it is, in particular, they want to kill first, and if it happens to be me or someone I know then I'm not very much in favor of it. The radical however always promises you he is going to kill somebody else, somebody neither of you likes.

Browsed in a travel book on the Orient. It excited me. I paced back and forth in the shack. I told myself that I've got to get a ship for Vietnam or someplace else in Southeast Asia. I've got to get in touch with everyone I know who might be able to help me. If I can't get a ship soon, I'll have to do something different. But I have got to do something. I could do a travel book on America like Steinbeck did except that my book would be a sort of frog's eye view of the country because I wouldn't have a car or any money or a reputation or fixed ideas or a nice dog. Or I could do the Indian reservations, walk across them with a sleeping bag from one end of the country to the other. But those are old ideas. I've considered them a hundred times.

Mother expected guests today and cooked a big Sunday dinner but no one came. So we ate in the kitchen just as we do on weekday nights. Father and I sat at the little table and Mother sat at the drain board beside the sink. Father and I ate absentmindedly, without speaking.

"I'm glad you two are so enthusiastic about your dinner," Mother said.

I helped myself to another spoonful of turkey dressing. "Oh, it's really good, Mother," I said. "I always have like cooked bread."

I thought Father was going to kill himself laughing. His head actually turned red. I hadn't thought he would even get it. Mother and I watched him apprehensively, then the crisis passed.

Waited all day to listen to the six o'clock news. There's been a truce in the fighting while the Vietnamese celebrated the Tet holidays. Tet was over today and the fighting should have started up again. There's also been talk of extending the truce. Everything is up in the air. But the news was good. The fighting is picking up where it left off and the worst is now expected. I breathed a sigh of relief and then I was suddenly, senselessly excited. I had to grab the arms of my chair to keep from falling over. My blood simmered. On some high level equal amounts of anxiety and excitement came together. The emotion was very intense. I had no outlet for it. I didn't know what to do. Warning signals flashed behind my eyes. My skin prickled and the blood drained from my head. For a moment I was afraid I was going to lose consciousness or maybe do something that would embarrass me.

I drew water for a hot bath. It was just what the doctor ordered. Immersed in the hot water, my eyes closed, I now felt a sense of perfect well-being. In spite of the circumstances of my birth, I thought, in spite of the bad luck, the shortcomings of my family, my own failings of character, the opportunities I have missed because I haven't been brave enough and because I haven't tried hard enough, I wouldn't trade my life for that of any other man. To have been underprivileged is nothing when you know in your heart that you're fortunate and that you've got the one life that's suited to you. My life, for what it's worth, is in my own two hands. There are times when I understand that even the air I breathe is sweeter than what my neighbor breathes. I feel compassion at moments like these for every man who isn't me simply because he isn't, and I wouldn't trade my future for that of any other man alive.

After dark I was sitting in the kitchen with the door closed wondering what I will write about if I do get to Saigon. The fighting itself isn't important to me any longer. I'm not really interested in the war either. I want to go on examining my own life in new, fresh circumstances. I want to do something for all the others at the same time. I want to tell the tale of one man only but that one returning to society and contending. I need something to put my shoulder against, a partner in life so to speak. That's why I'm hanging on to the idea of Vietnam with so much erratic excitement. If I can get there there's a chance I'll be caught up in something so powerful I won't be able to turn away from it and down into myself again. I may become a part of events that will pull me back once again into ordinary life.

When Mother and Father went to bed I watched an old movie on television about the American air force in World War II. What a tremendous fascination there is in the mind of the public with stories about that war. That's not true about the Korean war. No writer appeared who could create out of that war the necessary romance. It was more difficult with Korea because the issues weren't clear-cut for Americans and because there the problem of what evil is didn't manifest itself forcefully. It was an ordinary, everyday little war. I should have been able to do something with it. I tried but I couldn't. Now I'm getting another chance. Maybe I can make Vietnam my war. Maybe I can create a real war out of whatever is going on over there.

~

It was a lovely morning. Chilled but full of sunshine. Typed busily all day. Toward evening I began to feel the anxiety. I watched the news from Vietnam and thought about how when I get to Saigon my job will be to make the city come alive. I'll give life to the Americans who are there and I might even give some life to the fighting. I know how war is and I know it's not coming across on the television screen or in the newspapers. I watch the newsreels and read the correspondents and listen to the politicians and none of them know how to transmit the sense of how it is when you're there. They don't have a feel for the texture of the thing. I want to be able to tell others what it is that's in the air when a man walks along a street in Saigon. I want to give readers a sense of how the women smell at three in the morning and how it is in the bars and alleys. Why doesn't someone tell me whether the floors in the temples are made of wood or are they stone? How does it feel to be kneeling in an open Buddhist temple with the afternoon breeze moving through it? I want to know how it is to be in the jungle at dawn, to hear it dripping. But more than that I suppose I want to know how it will feel now that I'm no longer a boy to hear the bullets rush and how, precisely, now that I have grown afraid, it feels when the earth blows up underneath me. I want to watch how my dreams change when I put myself into danger and find out, now that I'm growing conscious again, where my necessities are. I believe others will be interested in those things too.

~

Dreamed that Pamela and I were in the yard behind my parents' house digging in the garden. Most of the garden was dead. Here and there a few wilted blooms hung down. Only one plant was flowering. The blooms were disgusting. The flowers were not blooming from the ends of green stems but out of other sickly looking blooms. Pamela dug up a life-sized sculpture of a woman in welded metal. The woman was crippled and doubled over. Then I dug up the roots of a fig tree. It was the tree I had chopped down for Mother when I was a boy. The roots had been in the earth all that time but they weren't dead. They were a rich green and were budding out all over. In the dream a sense of well-being came over me.

When I woke I felt dejected. I heard myself say out loud: "You should not promise a woman like Pamela that you will marry her because if you don't keep your word it will break her heart and she will become old before her time." When I realized what I had said, sitting there wide awake on the bed, I didn't understand what it was all about. I haven't spoken to Pamela in months.

Up at six-fifteen with the idea of going to work. Drove to Redondo Beach for Mooney and we went together to the waterfront in San Pedro. It's too soon for me to start longshoring again but if the marine clerks have any extra work I can do that easily enough. This morning there was nothing. Last month there was still work but from what the men say in the hall it's over now for the winter. On the way back to Mooney's I pulled into a gas station.

"Well, well," Mooney said. "I remember this place. I was going to knock it over last year, but the guy spotted me."

I laughed until I was afraid I was going to rip open the incision. I laugh a lot when I'm with Mooney: a neat, trim guy with thick black hair and pale gray eyes behind black horn-rimmed glasses. His wife is slim and blond and has her feet on the ground, which maybe is not entirely the case with Mooney. Fran keeps house for a woman and the woman's son and the two granddaughters. In exchange, she and Mooney have a cottage on the rear of the woman's property. When we got to their place Fran made us coffee.

"I hate the old bitch I work for," Fran said. "I hated her from the first day. She can't stop talking, and she's a vicious gossip. You know what she was telling me this morning? You won't believe this. 'Little Suzy has the prettiest parts,' she said. Like Suzy is seven years old man, you know?"

"Let's have a look at the kid," Mooney said.

"Shut up," Fran said. "And then the old cunt said, 'But Mary now, Mary's another case.'"

"Kid's got a big hoop, eh?" Mooney said.

"Shut up, will you," Fran said. "You're as bad as she is. Anyhow, then the old bitch told me: 'Mary's got the biggest clitoris you ever saw.' That's what she told me. And we don't even know each other. Then she said she was thinking of having the child circumcised. That's how bad off the old whore is."

"Sounds like it might help the kid," Mooney said.

"Up yours," Fran said. "I mean, you know what I think about all morning when I'm working over there? How to kill her. I was going to push her off the stone steps that go down the embankment to the street but the other night she told me she'd fallen from the top to the bottom just last month and hadn't hurt herself. What can you do with an old whore like that? It just takes the heart out of you."

In the afternoon I drove back to the harbor and picked up a duplicate copy of my seaman's papers from the Coast Guard. I got my papers a long time ago but never used them. Then I lost them one night at a movie on Hollywood Boulevard when Pamela and I were still together. I think that was the night we saw a James Bond movie and Pamela said, "Look at his legs. Just look at them." But now I have the papers again and they're in my wallet and my wallet is in my pocket. So I've taken the second step. Getting the hernia fixed was the first. The new papers the second. I feel satisfied and good.

I've thought more than once about how the Devil appeared to me and how He said the time has come. I don't know what to make of it but something happened to me that night. I lost a kind of enthusiasm for Vietnam that I can't explain. I still feel excited about the idea of going but little enthusiasm, which is not the same thing. There's something to the excitement I feel that I don't want to have to think about.

Sometimes at night when I'm alone here in the shack I become so solid onto myself that I'm like a stone. With a satisfied blue gaze I watch my luck running out. Diamonds hard as fate fill my mouth. Behind my eyes an eye opens up and in the half-light I see my ideas gleaming softly, like silver-shelled eggs. Never before could I have felt so neutral, never before could my hopes have been so high. I have found out something about what it must mean to stand on nothing, to have no foothold and to not want one, to trust precisely in life that which is most ephemeral, most unreliable. For three years now I have had one incredible piece of luck after another. Doors and windows have opened up all over my body and I have been able to wander in and out of myself whenever I wanted. Sometimes I've entered to the side of my kneecap and come out my ear. Other times I went down my throat and opened a window behind my heart. I discovered magic waterfalls, fairy pools that lead to underground seas so vast no man has ever seen their farther shores. I found devil trees that breathe like ordinary persons with wild shocks of white hair and lost species of reptiles that have dog eyes and the bristled jowls of the Great Hog. I saw caves on the bottom of the ocean where tribes of flaming apes battle in constant warfare and the slimy grotto guarded by bushy spiders where the Devil rests on a stone awaiting the chance to fix his eye on you—I know, don't tell me, in this day there's no use going on about the Devil but there's one thing I want to say: He's red, just like they've always said He is. One time I felt the Devil's hand on me and a touch like that I couldn't have thought existed. I saw the dead rising from stony grottoes on clouds of brittle blue vapor, saw them watching me with scythes waving out of lopsided eye sockets. I saw the clothes of the dead come to life and move their flaps of cold flesh dreamily and drift with the tide in my direction. I saw mercury moons shine in cold white heat into the encrusted men, those poor souls who were turned into granite and salt in the days when God still walked the earth blowing His hot breath into the hearts of the chosen, the lucky and the unlucky alike. Hammers and scythes are the tools of God, He who never shows His face, hammers and scythes and leopard's claws. The Lord has come, you can tell it far and wide, to love the leopard. Drawing over me the dripping pelt of a freshly slaughtered leopard I sail up through a perfect blue sky into the breast of the sun. I claw at the flaming flesh. I tear my way inside expecting to see the blazing throne of the Man Himself but fiery spiders attack in waves grinning broadly with torches in their teeth and then the inner arms of the sun reach down with hammer and anvil and with every blow a giant burning spider shoots off sparks and burps up for me alone a tiny figure in green jade of the pharaoh Anknahton, the first little man on earth to see he thought the face of God shining out from the roaring flames of the sacred sky disk and you tell me, you tell me… I don't want to see any more. Not for a while. I don't want to see it. I want to get a job and a woman and some decent clothes. I need my own place to live and a car and enough pocket money to get drunk at Barney's and pay for a cab home if I'm too drunk to drive. I've never been too drunk to drive yet.

~

This morning I left the house at dawn to drive to the harbor. The air was cold, the sky streaked with red. There was no work and when I returned to the shack I filled out an application for "afloat employment" with the Military Sea Transport Service. I've had the application for six weeks but haven't filled it out. I don't know why. I even took it with me to the hospital because I knew I'd have plenty of time on my hands but I didn't fill it out there either. Anyhow, today I filled it out and mailed it in.

After supper I went for a walk. Thin misty clouds were blowing across the stars. Rain is predicted. Back in the shack I read some good stories by Nelson Algren. I thought about how if I can get to Saigon I'll find stories like those to write.

~

Last night I dreamed about the fig tree again. A demon was cutting it down. He was cutting off the branches fastidiously, one by one. I advised him to chop it right through the trunk and kill it all at once. The demon nodded and started following my directions. Then I thought, that's not what I want to happen. I want the fig tree to grow and to bear fruit. I want it to be a better tree than it was when I was a child. I couldn't understand why I had given that advice to the demon.

No work again today.

~

A cold dark morning. Walked to the market for Mother and when I returned home my arms and legs were trembling. I'd thought I'd gotten my strength back but I was wrong. It surprises me that such a simple operation could leave me weak for so long. I've been more than two weeks recovering.

~

This was a long day. Had to fight off sleep and apathy. After supper I watched a documentary on television about Ho Chi Minh, who appears to be an affectionate little guy, at least in public. In the shack I read a story by Algren titled "Stickman's Laughter." It's about a woman who's the peer of her husband and who still is good to him and loving and who on top of that retains her own self respect. The woman brought tears to my eyes just by existing. After reading the story I grew very restless. I paced back and forth in the shack. I was walking in tiny little circles. My hands were closed into fists. I needed something to do. Frustration was like a storm in me. I swore suddenly that I was not going to read any more books. I was going to do something. I was going to stop making preparations and do it.

The very next moment I picked up a book and opened it with an intensity that was desperate. *The Autobiography of Malcolm X*. My eyes fell on a single line: "Anything I do now I regard as urgent…" My heart caught. Here was a man living as I mean to live, as though the day were here. I felt ashamed. It's very moving to see a strong man expressing his hatreds forcefully. But it's not so easy to express yourself when you have no hatreds, when the problem is somewhere else entirely. I used to envy black men. They had their work cut out for them. It was right out in the open for them. I've been afraid I won't be able to find the one thing that I should spend my life doing. What a tremendous relief it would be to know what to struggle against, what to put my shoulder to. But mine has been an easy, a favored life. No one has ever harmed me or taken advantage of me. Sometimes, when I'm most desperate, I think about taking up the causes of other men but the idea makes me feel ashamed. As if I would be evading something. I realize my task still lies before me. At times I can see it as if in haze. I catch a glimpse of a form that is so tenuous and fleeting that I can't decide afterward what it was I saw or if I really saw anything.

I was still pacing in circles in the shack. My head was spinning. I didn't know which way to turn. I felt desperate. My thoughts whirled off to China, the great adventures that have been there for the asking since the turn of the century, to Vietnam, to Africa and back again to Vietnam. My body was aching, literally, with the need to start off somewhere, to get on the road—and then suddenly I stopped short. The shack was filling up with jungle foliage. For just an instant I was confused. I looked around to get my bearings. Everything looked normal, the junk, the furniture, the trash. Then I saw the jungle again. It was dark and lush. I could see it growing and moving. Between where I stood in the center of the floor and the wall a couple feet away, dark receding distances appeared. The jungle became absolutely still, but the distances themselves moved in an uncanny way. It was then that the fear started. I thought of going up to the house where the folks were but I didn't want to go out in the dark. I sat down in the chair and looked at the manuscript I had been working on. I could see the typed characters with a perfect clarity but I couldn't read the words. Then I saw a path leading off through the undergrowth. I saw myself set out on it. I came to a flight of stone steps that led down into the earth. I went down the steps warily. At the bottom where the landing should have been there was a square hole. I looked down into it but couldn't see anything. The hole was black, big enough for a man to fall into it. Then a cloud of vapor materialized over my head. I grabbed the vapor with both hands and hurled it down the hole. Steaming smoke billowed up in my face. I realized then that the Devil was waiting for me below. In the shack I started doing deep knee bends. Then I did pushups, then more knee bends. I was very afraid. I tried to stop seeing the jungle and the hole that went down but I kept seeing them. I understood I had another opportunity to face Him but I couldn't make myself make the decision. I told myself desperately that if there were steps leading down, or a ladder or some other regular way where I could hold on that I would do it, but there was nothing to hold on to. I would have to leap down into the darkness, not knowing. I would have to risk everything. I did pushups and deep knee bends until I became dizzy, then I went up into the house and turned on the television. It took about half an hour to stop seeing the jungle and to see the television steadily without the jungle coming out of it.

~

No work at the harbor today. Stopped off at Mooney's for coffee. We were chatting about this and that when I heard myself say that I might not go to Vietnam after all. "Maybe I'll go to Africa," I heard myself say. "Or South America. I think I might just go wherever I hear the sound of the guns."

After supper I watched newsreels of the fighting in the central highlands. I told myself that I've got to do something more concrete about getting there. I have to make contacts. Have to talk it up. I started rushing around excitedly. I shaved and changed clothes and drove to Hollywood Boulevard where I hurried from one bookstore to another. I thumbed through volume after volume as if I were looking for something in particular.

In Pickwick I heard my name called. It was Marlow. I hadn't seen him in months. His face was a mess. From going home drunk, he said, and falling asleep under his sun lamp. I recalled how Marlow is never without his sun lamp. He's endowed it with a mystique. Three years ago when he and I roomed together and we weren't working and were living on potatoes and rice, even then Marlow had his sun lamp. He'd found it in the alley in someone's trash. It had no stand so he'd tied it to a nail in the wall with a shoelace. He'd lie on the bedspring naked except for his tennis shoes and daydream of how it'd be after he was discovered by a rich fag who'd get him into the movies. He didn't expect his first fag to be a producer, but as he put it, "one fag leads to another."

"To tell the truth," he'd say, "I don't understand why it's taking so long. I know guys who came to Hollywood and got themselves a fag the first week. I've been here a year now and I haven't had one yet. I just don't understand it. Not with this body, this profile. I mean, with my looks, I think I deserve a fag. Don't you agree?"

"Marlow," I'd say, "Listen to yourself."

"Listen to this," he'd say, jumping off the bedsprings and kicking back and forth through the trash on the floor, the sacks full of garbage. "One day I'll run into the fag who was meant for me and when he sees this body he'll start trembling like a leaf in a storm. At first I won't let him touch me. I'll just let him feast his eyes on the bod. One night then, just before he cracks, I'll give him a nibble on the golden wand. Once he gets a taste of that he'll never be able to settle for anything less. I'll have him in the palm of my hand. He'll introduce me to his fag friends in Beverly Hills. The story of Marlow's wand will travel like lightning through fag land. Everywhere I pass, fag tongues will hang out. Sooner or later I'll meet a fag producer and he'll make me a star. I'll specialize in gangster films. I'll be an idol. I have it in me. I tell you, I don't know what's the matter with Hollywood these days. Here I am, ignored, a million-dollar baby going to waste."

It was like old times strolling the Boulevard with Marlow. He works in the studios now as a carpenter and drinks up his money in the lowest bars in East Hollywood. "When I drink," he says, "I like to be superior to my surroundings. It's easier that way to pick up some old bag. You know the kind I like. Hey, Buddha, did I tell you about my cunt with the plastic tits? You have to hear this."

He asked me what I was doing with myself and I told him about Vietnam.

"You must be crazy," he said.

"Why don't you come with me?"

"You're crazy."

Passing a movie we run into Larry Lobel who owes me fifteen dollars. He's owed it to me for four years. He says he's the nephew of Bela Lugosi. I started to touch Larry up for the fifteen dollars but before I could open my mouth he'd taken out his childhood stamp collection from inside his natty top coat and was pitching it to me. Tears came to his eyes. "It's cheap," he said. "Believe me. One hundred twenty-five dollars. What do you say?" I suppose guys like Lobel will always be one step ahead of guys like me.

For old times' sake Marlow and I walked over to the YMCA on Selma hoping to run into Demeric. Sure enough, there he was, sitting alone in the lobby in the dark just like we used to find him three years ago. I have a compulsive interest in Demeric. Except that he's Jewish and dark-complected, we're remarkably close look-alikes. I believe there's some significance in that.

Demeric was glad, in his own way, to see us. We asked him how things were going.

"I'm just plodding along at nothing," he said, "making sure I don't leave any tracks. Know what I mean? When I go to that great computer in the sky I want to be told I haven't left any tracks down here."

We were all silent for a moment, Marlow and I standing in the dark before Demeric's chair.

Demeric said: "A man should make it his business, don't you think, to not leave any tracks?"

"Americans at Sea"

(1966)

It was night and we were steaming south through the Bashi Channel into the South China Sea. The black water was absolutely still. There was no moon, no stars. Out the porthole I could hear the quiet rush of the ship's wake but I couldn't see anything. I sat on the edge of my bunk and used a towel to wipe the sweat off my face. I took off my socks and looked at the splotches on my feet. They were larger than they had been in the morning. In the center of each splotch there were little bubbles of pus.

Rumor had it we would off-load at Qhi Nhon, then steam for India. It was a bad time of year to go to India. It didn't make any difference to me. I was jumping off her in Vietnam. The ship owners had their plans, I had my plans. I was going to become a famous war correspondent. Why not? I'd been at the writing business fifteen years and it was time something came of it. Vietnam might turn out to be my cup of tea. I picked up the typewriter and walked down the passageway to the crew mess.

The heat was stifling. I set up the typewriter on the table and got out my notes. The chief cook was at the other table picking at his guitar. The Chief was black but he didn't play like he was black. Maybe he was a beginner. He had a white towel wrapped around his throat and his sweat had filled it up and was running down his chest. There was a fan at either end of the little room pushing the hot air around. While I typed sweat ran down my arms and dripped off the ends of my elbows.

"GODDAMN," the Chief yelled.

I jumped off my stool ready to run or fight for my life, I didn't know which.

"Motherfuckin mosquitoes eatin my ass UP." He grabbed one ankle then the other. I sat back down. The heart was pounding.

"We're too far out to sea for mosquitoes," I said politely.

"SHIT. These motherfuckers is bred for distance. Don't talk too-far-out-to-sea to these cocksuckers. They flies where they wants to fly. Don't bother puttin them steel screens in those portholes either. That jus makes em angry. Once they gets angry, five, six mosquitoes hit that screen at once an jus blast on inside here. They want in, them cocksuckers? They jus muscle on in."

"I wonder why they aren't biting me?" I said politely.

"Shit," the Chief said. He plucked at his guitar uncertainly.

I tried to get on with the typing. Pretty soon Sal came in looking for someone to talk to.

I said: "Hey, wearing your fancy slippers, eh? Look at that gold braid."

"Big Lucy gave me these last time I was down in New Orleans. Did I tell you about her? Big Lucy was a lady wrestler. One night we…"

"You told me."

"Fuck you then," Sal said. He laid his crooked Italian face on one shoulder and grinned sweetly.

De Marion popped his big stubborn sloped-back head through the hatchway. The sweat was running in rivulets down his thick neck. Apropos of nothing he said: "Best piece I ever had was in Sasebo. Or was it Kobe? I can't remember no more."

He took a stool at the table. The size of his body overwhelmed the stool. It overwhelmed the table.

"Anyhow, it was night and the Japs were having a festival. Lanterns, people dancing in the streets, shit like that. A girl grabbed my arm and asked if I wanted to fuck. She looked about twelve years old. How old are you, I said? She said fifteen. I didn't believe her but I went with her anyway. Har, har, har."

The first cook, plucking quietly at his guitar, looked slyly around at De Marion.

De Marion said: "When we got to her room she started laughing like she was crazy. She was so skinny it was like fucking a couple a bones. She couldn't get enough of the fucking but she laughed all night. I tell you, that laughing can get to you. The next morning she tried to get me to promise to come back later. I told her, fuck you kid. You laugh too much."

Sal said: "When I was in the Philippines I had a girl who…"

De Marion said: "One time in the Philippines I was fucking this broad when I felt something sucking on my balls. I thought, Jesus, this girl really has something going for her down there. But when I looked down it was a little pig."

Sal said: "A what?"

"A pig. Oink oink. Don't you know what a pig is?"

"Shit."

De Marion said: "The Philippines is where the kid shits and the mother wipes its ass with her big toe. Har, har."

"Shit," Sal said.

"Shit?" De Marion said. "Is that all you can say? Don't you have no stories? You got a writer here. You can make yourself famous."

"All right," Sal said. "In Paris after the war there was so much fucking you'd get tired of it…"

"You'd get tired of it," De Marion said.

"Shut the fuck up, will ya? After the war over there, when you took a broad to your room instead of laying her you'd just stuff a silk handkerchief up her twat and the next morning when you went down to the café for breakfast you'd take out the handkerchief and give your friends a sniff. You were so tired of fucking that was all you could handle."

De Marion said: "Last month I met this broad in the park in San Pedro. She had red hair and we got to talking. Her old man had left her. One thing led to another and she offered me seventy-five dollars a week if I'd live with her and her two little girls. I tried it for a week but the kids were too much. They'd jump up on my lap and call me daddy, shit like that. I kept gettin a hard-on. What kind of daddy would I be, I thought? Another week and I'd be finger-fucking both of them and by the time they were ten I'd be peddling their ass. Nah, I thought, this isn't the life for me, and I come to sea again."

"You're a pretty sensitive guy," I said.

"Shit," Sal said.

The Chief unplugged his guitar, gathered up his sheet music and walked out.

De Marion said: "There goes a guy with a sense of humor."

"Shit."

"Can't you say nothin but shit?"

Through the porthole we could see great sheets of lightning illuminating the black ocean and the black sky.

"I'll tell you one thing," De Marion said. "I didn't expect to sail on no bucket of rust like this one. If this tub sinks tonight it won't surprise me."

"What surprised me," I said, "was when I saw the holes in the lifeboats."

"All these old Victories have holes in the lifeboats."

"Why doesn't somebody fix them? Plug up the holes?"

"Oh, what the fuck," Sal said. "If she goes down, she goes down. Who gives a shit?"

De Marion said: "I'd rather ship on a tanker any time. There when you go, it's all at once. POOF. A flash of light and instant death. Har, har, har."

Suddenly a rain began to fall. We went out on deck laughing

and yelling and splashing in the falling water. Half a dozen other guys came out and joined us. It rained hard for twenty minutes then stopped. Inside the midship house again the air was sweltering. I took my cot out on deck and set it up alongside number two hatch. The night air was warm and fresh. I listened to the cool easy rush of the ship's wake. The sky had partially cleared. Here and there stars shone brilliantly in the blackness. Wisps of filmy cloud drifted past. Once, in the early morning, I woke with a dark rain falling on my face.

The ship was gliding through the top of the calmest sea I'd ever seen. On the horizon to the east there were piles of black clouds. Rain fell from the clouds in dark slanting columns into the sea. Somewhere beyond the clouds and the rain lay the coast of Vietnam.

The air grew heavier and hotter. By noon the horizon was lost in a colorless haze of heat. In the engine room the temperature under the blowers, the coolest place there, was one hundred eight degrees. The engine radiated heat through the steel bulkheads, up through the steel decks. The deck hands worked with blue or red kerchiefs tied about their foreheads. At noon mess when I went below and opened the door to the refrigerated box the cold air struck my body like a blow.

The new rumor had it that we were steaming for the mouth of the Saigon River. We were all recovered from going ashore in Yokosuka and the rumor excited us. I got out my map and found Vung Tau. That would be the closest town. About sixty miles from Vung Tau straight up the highway was Saigon. A little swamp, I'd heard, some jungle. I thought about how I hadn't done any reporting before. Now that I was there almost, who would I sell it to? There were things I hadn't thought about yet.

The steward called a meeting of the steward's department. We gathered in the mess at 1400. It was stifling and we were all pissed. Everyone showed up on time except the chief cook and the steward. That's the sort of asshole the steward was. Marlow went topside and found him sleeping in his bunk and rousted him out. Illuminado found the chief cook sleeping on the fantail but he didn't roust the Chief. The steward came down and in his vacant way started to open the meeting.

"We aren't going to have a meeting of the steward's department until the chief cook is here." We all said it.

The Steward said: "All right. Where is the Chief?"

"On the fantail."

"What's the Chief doing on the fantail?"

"He's sleeping, you asshole."

The Steward said: "Illuminado, go roust the chief cook and get him in here."

Illuminado said: "You bein foony, Stew? No thees Puerto Riqueno, no sir."

"Marlow," the steward said, "you want to roust the Chief?"

"Roust him yourself, asshole."

"We'll have the meeting without the Chief," the steward said. "The Chief's been working hard this voyage."

We said there wouldn't be a meeting of the steward's department unless the entire department was present.

"Oh, let it go then," the steward said vacantly. "It's not important."

"Asshole."

After evening mess Haskell and I sat on a plank laid across two line pins and watched the sun go down behind the quiet gray sea. Sundown and sunrise are the two best times when you're at sea. Haskell was pulling on a pint of his apricot home brew. It was the first time I'd tasted it. It wasn't bad. The bosun had searched the ship from top to bottom looking for Haskell's cooker but hadn't been able to find it.

Haskell looked like a direct descendant of one of Quantrill's raiders, tubercular and murderous, his mouth full of rotten teeth. When I first saw him I thought he had a crippled arm but it was just his crab-like way of moving around. At mess he spoke so softly I had to bend over to get his order right. He'd been going to sea fifteen years.

"When I was in Ethiopia I had me an old gal with lips so thin there was just a line where her mouth was."

"Is that right?"

"She lived in a hut with cardboard walls. She had two holes out back. She shit in one and kept her chow in the other. It was some kind of rubbery black shit. What she ate, I mean. I used to get drunk, then I'd be worried I'd go out there in the night and shit in the wrong hole."

"That would have been impolite."

"She'd tear off a hunk of that rubbery shit and chew it up just like it was good. Good for me, she used to say, no good for you. I'd tell her you bet your ass no good for me."

About 2100 a wind blew up from the south. Marlow and I went up to the prow to take a look around. We looked at the black ocean, the black sky. The wind beat our lashes into our eyes. There wasn't anything to see.

At daybreak the wind was still blowing and the sea was a mass of whitecaps. During morning mess I discovered that the ventilation system over the sinks wasn't working. I told the chief cook. He told me to tell the union representative so I told Sal and he told the engineer. The engineer came down, looked up inside the air shaft and said the system was plugged up with dirt. The engineer brought the first mate down and the First said he had already spent more money on maintenance this trip than was allotted him. He said he would speak to the Captain about it however.

When they left I said: "Fuck all of you. I'm getting off her anyhow."

At noon we saw land off the starboard bow. Vietnam. It looked like a lot of other places I'd seen. Low sprawling hills, scrub brush, empty, drab. At evening mess we heard six or seven big, deep explosions in the distance. I thought they sounded like ships' artillery. Most of the guys thought they were bombs. They were probably right. We hadn't seen another ship on the water in five days.

It was too hot in the foc'sle to sleep. Marlow and I took our cots forward and set them up alongside number two hatch. I asked Marlow if he was going to jump ship with me.

"Not if you're going to do what I think you're going to do."

"What do you think I'm going to do?"

"You tell me."

"I'm going to look for the war."

"Oh, boy. What a schmuck."

"I don't really expect you to get off with me."

"If you had a little business deal to take care of in Saigon, I might consider stepping off this tub."

"I'm no good at little business deals. All I think about is the writing."

"Why don't you forget the writing? Think about business for a change. You can't write. You don't have any talent. Haven't you figured that out yet? Give it up. It wouldn't even be a sacrifice. Put your mind to business. Business is the way to get ahead in the world. Make some money. Live like a regular person for a change. You want to live like this the rest of your life?"

"It's not that bad."

"Not for you maybe. You have no future. For someone like me, going to sea is just a stop-gap, a way to have time to decide on something else."

We lay on our cots in the moonlight. The warm wind blew across our bodies and rattled the ship's lines. The sea was up a little and the old Victory wallowed, its booms creaking. Occasionally a solitary figure walked past silently. In my imagination I tried to picture how it was going to be.

Marlow said: "After this voyage is out of the way, let's go to Hong Kong. I'll figure out something to do. Smuggle gooks across from the mainland. Smuggle dope. Something."

"I wouldn't mind living in Hong Kong." I was getting drowsy.

"It'd beat getting your cock shot off in Vietnam."

"I'll never become a famous war correspondent in Hong Kong."

"Who cares? We could wear whites in Hong Kong. We could be taken for retired navy officers. I could anyhow. I don't know about you. I'd tell people you were my faithful bat boy. How does that sound?"

"That sounds okay." I closed my eyes.

"If people wonder why I'm out of service at so young an age I'll say my chief mate ran us aground one night and I took the rap for him. I'll wear an old captain's cap. It'll have tarnished decorations and look like it's seen years of service. I'll act world weary and marry a rich countess. If someone presses me about my background I'll mention the Egyptian navy and act as though I don't want to talk about it."

I was almost asleep.

Marlow said: "In Hong Kong we could …

"Sue Ann, Ruby, Jenny and Me"

(1967)

When Sue Ann telephoned this morning she sounded worried about our luncheon date. That was fine with me because I didn't want to see her. It was too complicated.

Sue Anne said: "If Don finds out about us he's going to be jealous."

"So far there isn't much for him to find out."

"I'm nervous. Sometimes he gets just crazy."

"That's the problem with husbands. They all want to keep their wives to themselves."

"Maybe he wouldn't mind. Oh, I don't know."

"Why don't we have lunch next week?" I said. I was thinking if I could put it off for a week I could put it off forever.

"Oh, Brad," she said. "I want to see you today."

"Let's just have coffee then. It will be simpler that way. Don might not mind that."

"Oh, what a good idea, I don't feel so guilty about just coffee."

A few minutes before one I left my room and walked over to Wilshire Boulevard. The bright sunshine, the blue sky, the breeze- it was a wonderful day. When I reached the coffee shop Sue Anne was already there, the blue eyes, the red hair, the body.

"What happened to your nose?" I said.

"I walked into the doorjamb in the hallway. I was so distracted just thinking about you."

We chatted about this and that. She kept leaning toward me over the top of the table. I felt restless. I wanted to get away. I wanted to walk over to Jenny's and play with Marissa. Marissa was only four but I was falling for her just as I had fallen for Jenny. I liked to just hang around their apartment when one of them was there—either one. Sue Anne had three daughters herself but it wasn't the same. I knew it never could be.

"Stop referring to our relationship as one of brother and sister," I said.

"It's corny, isn't it?"

"It's not accurate. Not from my point of view."

I could feel the erection coming on. I tried to not think about it.

"I wanted us to go for a ride. Don put a new stereo in the van. Don't you want to hear it?"

"Not this afternoon. Maybe we can go for a drive next week. This afternoon I have a little typing to do."

"I don't want to interfere with you writing."

"I know you don't." Outside the window the tops of the trees were blowing in the air. When I looked back at Sue Anne her clear blue eyes locked into mine. I couldn't get away from them.

She said: "I'd like to just kidnap you."

"That made me laugh, I didn't want to start laughing with her, having a good time. The erection was beginning to pound."

She said: "When I asked you to be like an older brother for me, you did exactly what I asked. It was really nice of you. I can't tell you how disappointed I was."

"You have to be careful what you ask of people."

"Am I awful?"

"Sure you are."

Somehow I got myself out of it. I walked back to my room, masturbated, then walked over to Jenny's and climbed the stairs.

Unexpectedly, Jenny and I met in the hallway. There was something hesitant in her manner, as if her mind were on something and I had interrupted her train of thought.

I felt like I had come at a wrong time. That she didn't want to see me. I warned myself to be careful and alert. She turned without speaking and walked into her bedroom. I followed and when we were there she turned and embraced me with her arms, with her legs, her entire body. She pressed her face to my face. I felt the warmth of her entire body passing from her into me. I felt the warmth in my own body rise to meet hers. It was as if something were flowing, melting between us, saturating me.

She said: "I want to stay here forever with you."

"Let's start now."

"I have to take the kids to their grandmother's."

"Do we have a few minutes?"

"We really don't."

"Worse luck." I didn't let on, but was annoyed.

"I was at your room just a minute ago. I left you a crazy note."

"What did it say?"

"I'm not going to tell you."

Jenny got the kids together with a minimum of argument and we all went downstairs together. They drove off in their station wagon and I walked back to my room. There in the typewriter was the note, written on a file index card in an erratic hand.

"Missed you all day with a very deep longing just to be near you. If I could just press up against you and then you would hold me. Well then maybe I could go about the rest of the day without this longing pulling on my insides. I don't want anything right now but to be with you. I almost can't get myself to leave."

In the morning I'd felt lethargic and unable to type. Now I was wide awake and eager to work. It had been a nice change to get out to a restaurant during the day. A little company, a little conversation, a little fresh air. Left to my own devices I don't do anything. I type, I read, I take walks. That's what I do. I was working on the diary when Sue Anne telephoned. She wanted to talk about how it would be for us to have an affair, how we could arrange it and so on.

"I think it would be safe enough," she said. "I don't think either of us would be careless, because if word got out by you Jenny would drop you like a hot potato. I think Don would kill me. I think he really would."

"It doesn't sound like it would be worth it," I said. My cock was swelling up again. "Where are you now?"

"I can't come over now. Don will be home and I have to get supper."

I didn't want to have an affair with Sue Anne, I didn't even want to talk to her, but when she talked about it my cock invariably got hard. It was out of my hands. I thought about the weaknesses in my character, how it seldom seemed worth the while to deny myself anything. It never seemed worth the while. I tried to get the mind onto the typing. Jenny telephoned.

"Just called to say hello," she said in her softest voice. She had a wonderful telephone voice. "Now I'm going to say goodbye. Goodbye."

I figured something was wrong. I called her back.

She said: "I've been trying to call you and your line was busy. Then I tried to call Sue Anne and her line was busy."

I didn't say anything.

Then I said: "It was Sue Anne all right. You're a real detective. She's feeling miserable."

"You ought to just give it to her, Brad. Maybe her cunt would relax and she wouldn't be on the telephone to you all day."

I didn't say anything. I felt nervous at the tone in her voice.

Jenny said: "Listen, I shouldn't have called you at all. Scratch this conversation, will you?"

A few minutes later, Sue Anne telephoned.

"I just feel worse and worse," she said. "I need to be with you. Nothing in my life is worthwhile since I met you. What have you done to me? It's the way you talk. I just feel seduced by how intelligent you are."

"I'm not as smart as you think I am. Believe me. But I'm trying to type now. Don't you have to get supper for Don?"

"I think you're the smartest man I've ever met."

"I hate this kind of conversation," I said.

"I'm making a tamale pie while I'm talking. Pretty good, huh?"

"Look, I have to do some typing."

At five-forty-five I got up from the typewriter, got the Bacardi dark off the top of the fridge and poured a water glass half full. I had a drink and turned on the radio to a rock station. I had a drink and showered, had a drink and shaved, another and dressed. I took a couple more drinks. When I was sober I never listened to rock, when I was drinking I liked it. At seven o'clock I knocked on Ruby's door.

It was good to see her. Smallish, rather than big like Jenny, heavy lidded, shapely, pretty. Fifteen years younger than me. Lebanese and Jewish. She said. I suppose if you're an expert you can tell the difference. We drove to Westwood and ate pizza and drank a bottle of Chianti. This year she was flying to Japan. Last year it was Mexico. We had the same little celebration last year. That time it had been understood that we were going to spend the night together but it hadn't worked out. We talked about Japan, then Mexico, then her latest boyfriend.

"I'm really infatuated with this guy," she said. "He's back East on business and I really miss him."

"Uh huh."

"I guess that's why I called you."

"I see."

She grinned beautifully. "Besides, we have a tradition going, don't we?"

"Not yet," I said. "Unless you think pizza's a tradition."

She laughed beautifully.

I told her about the sexual fantasies I'd had about her the year before, how they'd gotten mixed up with visions about St Francis and a great black hog with fifty arms. She liked that.

"I didn't know you thought about me that way," she said.

I said: "Sometimes my sexual fantasies about you were so powerful I could have eaten you alive."

She laughed excitedly.

"Eaten you alive." I said.

She covered her face with her hands and laughed until there were tears on her face.

She tried to be serious: "Brad?"

I was laughing too. The cock was throbbing.

"Brad. Listen to me." She looked around the dark restaurant to see if anyone was listening to us.

"Go right ahead," I said. "Everyone can hear you."

"Brad, I have my period."

"Your period, Madam, is of no great significance to me."

"My period is very heavy. I have to have a towel under me and I can't move around much."

I looked around at the other tables. "Did people hear that?"

Ruby took my hand on the table top and held it and we laughed drunkenly.

I said: "Maybe by Saturday morning the worst will be over."

"I have very heavy periods."

"Will you stop telling me that?"

"Maybe it won't be too bad by Saturday morning,"

Drinking and laughing we figured out the best time for me to arrive at her apartment on Saturday morning, considering the departure time of the airline and the rate of her flow and so on. I drove her home and we kissed in the hallway. My cock was swollen and she pressed her belly against it. She was very affectionate. It felt good to have my arms around her.

At ten o'clock I was at Jenny's. The Ginzbergs were there. They'd come by for dinner and to talk business with Jenny. Jenny was wearing one of her ankle-length skirts, an Indonesian print in oranges, reds, and gold. She was beautiful. I wanted to tell her how much more she was to me than any other woman I'd ever known. I wanted to tell her there were hardly any others on the planet even similar to her. That she was truly rare. I was drunk. I tried to remember why it was she had chosen me.

They were talking about the hopelessness of attempting to deal with black adolescents with ghetto mentalities. There were two psychologists and a sociologist among the three of them. Someone said the Negro was without hope in his own heart. I disagreed heatedly, drunkenly.

"When I was an adolescent," I told them, "I had great dreams for the future. I didn't have the least idea how I was going to realize them. I didn't have any prospects at all. That wasn't even a concern for me. I was at peace because I expected to be discovered. When you're young everyone expects to get discovered, even black people."

I got a big laugh out of that from Jenny. The Ginzbergs smiled knowingly but Jenny really laughed.

I couldn't wait for the Ginzbergs to leave so that Jenny and I could get at it. But when they left Jenny was suddenly distracted.

"I'm going to bed," she said.

She didn't say it in an inviting way. I felt very alert, and cautious, but the cock was swollen and throbbing. This time it couldn't be denied. I followed her in the bedroom, careful not to touch her. We undressed without speaking. She got into bed. I got into bed. I waited.

She said: "You can't guess what's going on with me, eh?" Her face twisted into a crooked grin.

"No."

"You can't guess, huh?"

Then I knew it was Sue Anne.

Jenny said: "I can't take this business with that broad anymore. I know it's stupid, but I've got to the point where I can't control my emotions any longer. It's just tearing me up."

I remained quiet.

"I hate to talk like this. I'm so jealous of her, of all the attention she's getting from you that I'm half out of my mind."

"I won't talk to her anymore," I said. "She doesn't mean anything to me."

"I don't want that. I know I'm wrong. I know we ought to be able to form a relationship that will allow us to see other people once in a while."

"I'm not so sure of that," I lied.

"What I really can't stand is that she's getting all this attention from you by being weak, throwing herself at you, crying for you to hold her up. She does everything I try not to do. Then she does it and gets things from you."

"She doesn't get very much."

"I just hate myself when I think this way."

We were silent. I could see how she was wrestling with herself, how she was trying to wrestle down powerful feelings of jealousy and anxiety and fear. It was as if there were another, smaller body inside her body and it was thrashing around making her suffer. I didn't know what to do. I felt awful. I felt like I couldn't move.

Jenny said: "Sue Anne's daughter came over this afternoon to ask me something. I can't even remember what. It was when both of your lines were busy. I told the kid if her mother would stop yapping on the telephone all afternoon she could have asked me herself."

I laughed. Jenny didn't think it was funny.

"Later when I went over there, Sue Anne was wearing a bathing suit. She came to the door in it. She was modeling it like a show girl. She said she wanted to be sexy for Don when he came home."

"That was thoughtful."

"I could have slapped her face. It's got to the point where I can't handle my emotions around this." Her voice cracked. "Oh, I don't know what to do."

She turned away from me and lit a cigarette. "Oh, I hate this," she said vehemently.

I couldn't make myself say anything.

She said: "I know you're not going to desert me…"

When I heard her say I was not going to desert her, a sob broke out of me. All of the sudden I felt in my heart, in my gut, how tortured she felt. I was aware finally in my own body of the pain she was feeling in hers. I understood that I had brought it to her, that she had looked into the future and I wasn't there.

"Hey, you goof," Jenny said. "I'm the one that's supposed to cry."

The tears kept coming out.

Jenny said: "If I could cry I guess I'd feel better."

I couldn't stop crying.

"What's going on with you, Brad?" she said caringly.

"When I think about having made you feel this way, I can't take it."

"You're kind of a strange guy, don't you think?"

She began to cry a little. Not much. Two or three tears. She put her face on my chest and went to sleep. I was exhausted. I tried to go to sleep with Jenny's face on my chest but my eyes kept opening up. For a few minutes I had forgotten about the cock but now it was throbbing again. I wanted to wake Jenny but I wasn't sure I should. I considered the pros and cons one by one. I couldn't decide.

"Old Manuscripts, Old Lives"

(1968)

Everybody wants to put a little something away for his old age. I'm no exception. I'm not nervous about getting old but when you're fifty-one you think about it sometimes. You see yourself living alone in a room, you can't walk too good because of the extra weight, in fact you need special supports in your shoes or you can't walk at all, and sometimes your back goes out and you have to crawl to the kitchen table or the bathroom. From the outside it doesn't look like much of a life but still you don't want to give up on it. Though you can't explain why, you want to go on.

Alicia says she'll take care of me when I no longer can take care of myself. She'll let me lean on her shoulder when I have to go pee-pee. She'll wipe the mush off my chin when I dribble and don't notice it. But women come and go, like the years, like friends even, and there's no calling them back.

One afternoon fifteen years ago Jenny and I were embracing in her hallway when suddenly her body stiffened and she gasped.

"Oh my God," I said. "What's the matter?" Her eyes were huge and dark.

"I just had the thought that one day we might not be together anymore. Bradley, I just don't think I could stay alive without you."

Her words had brought a sob from me at the time, but where's Jenny now? Just a few blocks from here to tell the truth. She lives with a script writer who's dark and likes to wear nice clothes. She and I had a beer at the bar at Musso Frank's the other day. She gave me the new biography of Walt Whitman. I'd wanted to give her something too but as usual I couldn't think of anything good.

I've never had any money but I've never worried about the future because for years now I've been putting books in the bank. Good as money I've always told myself. I've even told others about them. They're not finished books, but four or five thousand pages of manuscript in metal files, the carbon copies in cardboard boxes in Mother's dining-room closet. Most of the manuscript is diaries. Every once in a while I take out one or another of the diaries and edit a few pages. Getting it into shape, I tell myself, for that day when I'll need it. No need to worry about a thing.

A few days ago I took out the 1966 diaries. They describe how I worked my way to Vietnam on a tramp steamer intending to jump ship there and become a famous war correspondent. They tell about what I did instead, how the visions trailed off, how I met Jenny. Interesting material. It used to be interesting material. For the first time I am willing to admit the diaries bore me and that I think they will bore others as well. Seventeen years of work. What has it come to?

I don't want to describe the old World War II victory ships again. I don't want to go over even one more time my feelings about the Greeks, the Puerto-Ricans, the blacks, the white southerners, the Italians and Polacks who make up the crews on American tramps. The diaries are all anecdote, no scheme. What was I thinking during all those years? What was I in relation with? I was absorbed by the movement of my own feelings, the thinking that was without direction. I had dedicated myself to observing the organism move about, like those splashy carp I watch for hours in Japanese bars. There was no point to the diaries other than observation, just as there was no point to the living itself. No direction, no idea, no polemic, no story. The story was there but it trailed the fact, like the silver slime of a snail. I was bemused for years with the idea that I should restrict myself to the fact, to the moment. I think now I defeated myself as a writer with that idea.

That June I shipped out on the SS Explorer. I was confident I could jump ship in Vietnam and become a famous war correspondent. I don't know what Marlow had in mind. Every morning we'd drive down to Wilmington to the Maritime Hall and throw down our work cards for every ship routed to Southeast Asia. We got beat out every time by seamen who had older work cards than ours.

One morning I couldn't raise Marlow on the telephone so I drove to the Hall alone. When I got there the work board looked so good I called him again. This time I caught him in.

"I'll have to begin my life as a seaman some other time," Marlow said. "I've got my broad with the plastic tits up here. I can't just walk off and leave her. She needs me."

"I'm serious, Marlow. I think we can both get out on the same ship."

"Do you think they'd let me take her with me? I'd keep her out of the way. I could put her in one of those stand-up lockers. If they'd let me take her the rest of the crew could use her too."

In the background I heard a woman's voice say: "Asshole."

"I wouldn't let the niggers get in it, but the captain could use her in exchange for special shore privileges."

"You asshole," the woman's voice said.

Marlow affected a worried tone.

"Do you think the Captain's a nigger? Small chance, eh? That'd be all right though. Nigger officers are usually half-white anyway."

The woman's voice said: "Asshole, asshole, asshole."

"Bring her along," I said. "Just get down here before the first work call."

I hung around the Hall keeping to myself and an hour later Marlow walked in. He agreed the work board looked very good.

The first regular work call would be at one o'clock. We had three hours to kill. We walked to the nearest bar and drank a couple beers. We walked to the Greek delicatessen and ate lunch. There was still an hour to kill. We hopped in Marlow's car and drove to Cabrillo Beach.

At the edge of the sand there were trees and picnic tables. Some little girls were playing on the sand in the sunshine. We sat on one of the tables in the shade of a tree. There was the expanse of clean white sand, the sunshine, the little girls playing happily and beyond them the blue sea and the empty, bright sky.

Marlow eyed the little girls. "I'd like to round up a bunch like that and put them on a farm to ripen. When they got to be about fourteen I could jam it in and listen to them scream."

I didn't say anything.

"I could record the screaming and later I could listen to the recordings."

Marlow made me laugh as much as anybody I've ever known. He had the custom of revealing the anarchic jumble of his real thoughts and feelings. Bernard Shaw noted some place that there is nothing so funny as the truth.

This morning however when I came across the entry in the diaries about the little girls I felt disgusted. There's a trial going on in Los Angeles this very day where a man is charged with torturing, raping, and killing teenage girls. He recorded the cries and screams of the girls on tape and now the court has the tapes. They're terrible. How many of us in our dreams have done something similar?

I caught a ship that afternoon but Marlow was beaten out by men with older cards. I took the physical then drove to Long Beach where the SS Explorer was tied up and signed aboard formally. The Captain was an old Norwegian—Marlow needn't have worried. He told me the cargo was beer and coffins and small-arms ammunition. I thought: "Just the right mix for Vietnam." Then I drove back to the house to pack. I was thirty-six years old but between jobs, between moving from one place to the next. At that time I was staying with the folks in the bedroom where I'd grown up. When I was home I'd work in the garden and do the typing in the shack out back.

That night I telephoned Marlow to get him to drive me to the ship next morning. He decided to come over for the night. "I can't trust myself to show up if I don't sleep there," he said. He sat in the living room with the folks and talked to Mother. Father looked on happily. Marlow enjoyed my mother. He had his own back East but hadn't spoken to her in ten years, not since he'd been thrown out of college for stealing watches.

"It'd be too embarrassing," he told me once. "What would I say to her? Hi, Mom, this is your son, the thief? The one who couldn't get away with it?"

I stayed in the bedroom and listened to them chatting. I thought about how lonely I felt. I thought about how lonely it would be for Mother and Father when I left. I thought about how lonely it would be on the water.

The next morning I got up to the alarm at four o'clock. I went in the living room to wake Marlow. He was sleeping on the couch with his hands clasped behind his head, his legs hanging off the other arm. When I spoke his name his eyes opened and without pause for reflection he said:

"Have you thought about the things you'll be able to smuggle in from over there? Or are you going into this with your head up your ass?

"Smuggle?"

"Have you thought about the hasheesh, the dirty pictures, the diseases?"

"Good ideas," I said. "Why can't I think of things like that?"

"I wish I was going with you. I'd make a fortune in one trip. I'd show you how to make one too."

"Maybe something will happen," I said. "Maybe you'll get on board today."

"Shit."

I went to Mother's door and woke her. She got up slowly and went in the back bedroom to wake Father. She was pretending it was all right that I was leaving again. I went in the kitchen and put water on for coffee. I could hear her trying to wake Father.

"Frank? Frank? Wake up. Bradley's getting ready to leave."

"I'm awake, Mom."

"Don't call me Mom. Don't you know who I am?"

"I'm getting right up, Mom."

"All right now. Don't daydream."

"I won't. Say, Mother? Is your head swelled up?"

"What are you talking about now? My head's all right. Now get up and put your robe on. You don't have to get dressed."

"All right, Mom."

"Dammit, Frank. Call me Gladys."

"Is Bradley still here?"

"Yes, but he won't be if you don't get up."

"All right."

"Now get up. Here, I'll help you."

"All right."

"Here. Put your legs over the side of the bed. Now get a move on, will you?"

"Mother?"

"Yes?"

"Did you catch any fish yet?"

"Goddammit, Frank. I'm going to get dressed and when I come back in here I expect you to be out of bed."

"Sure thing, Gladys."

When Mother came in the kitchen she was laughing, so I laughed too. She was still very pretty when she laughed.

Some of the stuff in the diaries is fine, but I don't want to go over it all over again. Illuminado Garcia with his silver teeth and big cock. Washington the black Chief Cook ("Listen," he shouted, "you know wha this job is, don you? you washes dishes and you waits tables and you scrubs the mutherfuckin deck. you understan? Tha's yo job. You don't like tha work? Then get off the ship now. Don wait till we gets out on the water then change yo mind and say no one tol you nothin."

"Sounds good to me," I said politely. I knew what was going down. It was pure race.

"We goin get over there in tha viet nam and these mutherfuckin bums is goin drink tha booze and come in here and shit all over your mutherfuckin tables and you goin clean it up. That's yo job. Now, you wan the job or not?"

"That's why I'm here," I said evenly.

"Ah'm tell you zactly how ah feel. Ah hates seamens. Ah've hated them bums all my life and ah'm goin hate em till the day ah die. Seamans is bums. That's what they are. They's no good mutherfuckers and they's bums. Now you wan this mutherfuckin job or don you?"

"Sounds like honest work," I said politely.

I don't want to type out the anecdotes again about the fat, drunken Third Cook falling out of his bunk all the way to Vietnam and back. Or about the Carolina brothers setting up their still in the engine room, or the Steward who wanted me to come up to his foc'sle so we could compare typewriters. I don't want to write anymore about the Greek pantryman who only knew three words in English and shouted them out in a high-pitched whine whenever he was spoken to: "WHO ARE YOU?" Or the blond, steely-eyed pistolero just out of the Virginia State Prison, or the electrician who looked like a frog and put one elbow in his food while he ate, usually the left one.

The time is past for all that.

I don't think about myself so much as I used to. I'm more interested than I used to be in the others, what they're doing and why they think they are doing it. I've discovered I can still be shocked by an idea. I can be more accepting too. I can read racist pamphlets now without going into a rage. I can listen to the anti-Semites and understand what they are getting at. I can refuse to pay income taxes, refuse to fund programs for nuclear "retaliation" where it is guaranteed the innocent will be incinerated for the deeds of the guilty, without being contemptuous of those who do pay. I can consider the proposition that it would be best if the Union were to dissolve without feeling insecure or having my patriotism insulted. Does that make me more than I was before? I don't know, but I like it well enough this way.

The other day I had a plumber in to Mother's house to clean out the plumbing in the bathroom. There was no garbage or trash clogging the pipes, they were full of rust and corrosion. I thought about replacing the old steel and cast iron plumbing with new plastic lines. Some say that water passing through plastic carries cancer with it. What the hell, I thought, it takes twenty years for a cancer to develop. Mother sure won't last that long, and I'll be seventy years old by then. Seventy-one. What difference will it make? Then I thought: Who knows? Twenty years from now the brain might still be functioning. There might still be someone pleasant to talk with. I might still be able to see the day break out of the darkness and the way the worms come out on the concrete walks to sun themselves. I may still be able to feel things and know more or less what it is I am feeling.

We were still in port in Long Beach taking on stores and cargo. I'd finished my day's work and was sitting alone in the crew mess drinking coffee when Marlow put his head through the hatchway.

"Fellow Mariner," he said.

I felt touched that he'd driven all the way to Long Beach to pass the time with me. Then he stepped through the hatchway and I saw he had a suitcase in one hand.

"Are you kidding me?"

"The bedroom utility got sacked," Marlow said. "I was hanging around the Hall when the job was called out." "What a stroke of luck," I said happily.

"It was five-thirty this afternoon. There wasn't anybody in the

Hall except a few niggers and me. Every one of those spades threw down for the job. You should have seen the expression on their faces when I walked over and took it."

"I can't believe you're going," I said.

"I can't either."

"Why were you even in the Hall so late? Hardly anything gets called out that time of day."

"I don't know," Marlow said. "You know how I am. I don't know why I do anything."

Waiting for Saigon to Fall

(1968)

Last night I was smashing cockroaches with a shower slipper when it came to me all in a flash that I find a smashed cockroach, its insides all mashed out on the yellow-tiled floor, as repugnant as I do a dead and torn up human body. What occurred to me then was to wonder if I don't suffer—how shall I put it—some form of ethical maladjustment? But that's just beating around the bush here. What I really want is to write down the one image I can't get out of my mind, the one where the Viet Cong soldier is lying on his back in the rubble and slop of a blasted-out café, his open eyes swimming in blue milk. That's what I can't forget, how his eye-sockets were full of blue milk. It was an absolutely startling, aesthetic experience. It's the most powerful single image I have of Vietnam. Maybe it's the artist in me.

That was last month over in the Chinese quarter of the city. About nine in the morning the firemen came with their aluminum helmets and the hooks with the long handles. They were all grins and as they trotted by some of them threw me a snappy salute. Three of them trotted right into the café to do their work. A moment later they came out again and put on their gas masks. Some of the happiness had gone out of their faces. The man did stink. He had turned dark and had swollen up. His mouth was open like the mouth of a dead fish and filled to the brim with a black liquid. That was the most difficult part to look at, even his teeth were submerged in that mouthful of black blood and who knows what else. When they dragged him out in the street the tips of his fingers trailed lines of black ooze across the sidewalk.

The Saigon firemen keep up a regular line of patter among themselves and little private jokes as they go about their work. They drag the bodies onto stretchers and throw them in the back of pickup trucks. It isn't difficult to watch the collection but when the bodies are thrown into the trucks, I don't like hearing the thuds. Once I saw the firemen miss the bed of the truck entirely. It was with a Viet Cong who had been killed by tank artillery. He'd been cut nearly in half and the bottom part of him was all chewed up. He was such a mess that even the Saigon firemen didn't like handling him. They'd get a hook in one armpit, say, and give a pull and the bottom half of the body would start to tear off or some other rotten thing. They finally got the fellow onto the stretcher all right but they were in such a hurry that they fumbled the throw and he splattered on one of the fenders. The firemen got very angry about that and started arguing with each other there in the street while the Viet Cong hung over the fender like two hunks of meat tied together with a piece of fleshy string.

I've got to hand it to the Saigon firemen, though. What impresses me most about them is their almost constant good cheer in the face of their work.

This morning when I woke I saw my first infant lizard. There are a lot of lizards in the garage where I sleep, they like it up around the tops of the walls and in the rafters, but I'd never seen an infant one before. It was hardly an inch long, squiggling across the tiled floor along the top edge of my sleeping mat. Its features were so tiny that when it stopped I had to put on my glasses to see that its mouth was open. It seemed to be gulping, as if it were trying to catch its breath. I wanted to hold it in the palm of my hand but I was afraid I might rub something off its skin and it would die or get sick. That's how much I know about lizards when I wake up.

The next time I woke, heavy things were falling on the roof, giving me a start. It was children laughing and throwing rocks. I glanced around for the infant lizard and saw that out in the court a swarm of black ants had lifted him up and were transporting him back the way he had just passed. He ate a couple of them while I watched, but what good did it do? There were plenty more where those two came from. And in response the others twisted two of his legs up over his back then bent him sideways into a circle, which pretty well took the fight out of him. Even more annoying, it would have been to me, anyhow, was how in front they were hauling him along by his lower lip.

Rorkman and I are just hanging around, waiting for the attack to come. The papers say there are fifty-one Viet Cong and North Vietnamese Army battalions positioning themselves within a two-day march of the city. Yesterday an American soldier was murdered on the street by two girls riding a motor scooter. The rumors are that the city will be harassed with that sort of thing the rest of the month, and the attack will come during the first week following. Rorkman wants to wait it out because he has bought a new fixed focal-point lens for his camera and wants to get some good photographs before he goes home. He specializes in street kids and refugees and hospitals, subjects like that. For myself—I don't take pictures—what I want is some additional material on the fighting itself, stuff I can use for my book.

That would seem to raise the ethical question again, and while I don't intend to lash myself severely for my failings, I have come to that point in my life where I find such questions interesting. I've always known them to be important, which isn't the same thing at all. The point here is that I know I came to Vietnam for the wrong reasons and have passed my time in the wrong way. If I wanted to right myself in my own eyes I'd have to take up a position against the American military in Vietnam and fight it out to an ending. I won't do that, however; I've waited too long and now it's too late. I am going to have to postpone my ethical life. As a matter of fact, I have postponed it.

Rorkman and I both want to go home to America but that isn't at all the case with Houghton. Houghton loves it in Vietnam. There are so many things to do. For one thing, he's arranging sleeping quarters for a couple dozen street kids (in my garage) and is in with some people who are founding their own news agency. Houghton came here intending to work as a volunteer in Vietnamese hospitals out of a sense of guilt for American war crimes. He couldn't leave it at that, however, so he got a press accreditation and went up to I Corps where he was, unfortunately I suspect, terribly impressed with the behavior of the United States Marines in the fighting at Dong Ha.

After that, his attitude toward the war became complicated. He decided he could do more good for the Vietnamese by founding their first Western theater group (Houghton is an actor now, but he was an Eagle Scout through his nineteenth year). He's written a letter to the editor of the *New York Times* drama department requesting play manuscripts and books on theater, including what I believe is a position paper explaining his new theater and its aims. It's written on such a lofty level I'm not sure I understand it, so it may be about something else. He says it looks good for the news agency to make a profit, but if that doesn't work out something may come from the theater project. If the theater idea falls through he's got a couple monks teaching him guitar and Vietnamese folk songs, which he sings in a clear true voice. Houghton is certain he'll work something out for himself in Vietnam, and so am I. In the meantime he's a good sort who'll go far out of his way for you, who'll laugh at your jokes and overlook your bad behavior. He really is a decent sort.

The trouble with Houghton, and Rorkman and I both agree on this, is that he is a go-getter.

Yesterday afternoon I was drinking beer on the terrace of the Continental Palace when there was a sudden series of sharp cracking explosions. It was the cocktail hour and the terrace was crowded. It took only a moment to realize that the explosions were thunder. Black clouds were rolling in from the north through a milky blue sky. I watched how people turned quickly to each other and laughed. My own intestines and heart were still contracting. The fear, together with the almost instant release from it, made me smile. It was a fine pick-me-up. The very air in the streets became a little brighter.

It isn't easy, just hanging around like this. It might be more interesting if I had some money. I'd lay a few whores then, or go to the movies maybe. I'd get drunk once in a while. The trouble with that is I've done those things for twenty years and I have no more enthusiasm for them. The other evening three women were hanging out the second story window of an old French dance hall, waving me up. They looked like good juicy broads, but it was too much trouble to climb the stairs. Maybe if they'd been on the ground floor.

Periodically I lecture myself about how I am wasting my time. You came here to write a book on the war, I'll say, and now what are you doing about it? It's your job to get out in the field and take notes. Even if you don't use them while you're here, a year from now they'll be invaluable. Tell myself what I will, it doesn't do any good. There's nothing more I want to see here, nothing more I want to do here. If I were on the other side maybe, if I were with the Viet Cong, I might have more enthusiasm for my work.

There was a terrorist bombing at the Vo Tanh movie house this evening. I heard the sirens go by but I was lying on my mat. I didn't want to get up. A while later, when I went out to eat, I ran into a couple young newsmen who work with Houghton at Dispatch. They were on their way to the theater so I walked along with them. The street lights were out and it was beginning to rain. We couldn't get a taxi, which is often the case when there's trouble in the city. No one wants to be associated with the Americans, just in case.

The explosion had been in an arcade of shops along one side of the theater. Houghton and Mike were already there when we arrived on foot. The others went inside to take photographs while I waited out in front. I was thinking about the second bomb, the one with the timed fuse that's left behind after one of these incidents. A policeman told me five people had been killed and fifty-five injured in the blast. The police and the firemen had pretty well cleaned up the mess, but they'd overlooked a man's foot. The truth is, these people don't do very many things quite right.

Houghton came out of the arcade looking distracted.

"It must have been terrible," he said softly.

'Yeah."

"Did you see that foot sitting over there on the pavement?"

"You mean lying on the pavement, don't you? Or standing perhaps?"

"What's that?" he said.

I enjoy correcting Houghton's English. I don't believe he's got enough humility. What sticks in my mind about the foot is how muddy it was, and how the severed place was all shredded and popped out.

My razor is gone again. That's the third one in ten days. One of the kids here in the house is carrying out a vendetta against me. They don't steal Rorkman's razor, or Houghton's. Only mine. I don't pay enough attention to them, that's the trouble, and one of them has chosen this way to get back at me. I don't let them blow their noses on the floor and that upsets them too.

Rorkman spent his own childhood in America in orphanages and now he has this thing about homeless boys. He lets them use his shower, and they can sleep over if they want. He's especially drawn toward pickpockets and the ones with sores. They don't have to sleep on the sidewalk any longer, or in the trash on the steps of the movie houses. Rorkman has a place for them. If your house has been hit by a Viet Cong rocket, if the Americans have bombed your mother and father, you can come over here and get a place to sleep. You may even get a handout for something to eat, but for the most part you're expected to learn how to steal well enough or shine enough shoes to make your own way.

We got all the kids into the bedroom and Rorkman told them they had better stop stealing my razor. "You want steal," he told them, "you go down street, steal there. Very bad, you steal this house. You steal this house again, you no sleep here anymore. Vietnamese boy steal razor, he no fucking good."

Then he slapped four or five of the kids along side the head to show them he meant what he said.

That was last night. This morning my new razor is gone. I believe I know the kid who's doing it but I'll never catch him. He's up and out in the morning before I get awake. He shines shoes for American soldiers in front of an enlisted men's billet on Trung Hung Dao. He makes fifteen dollars a day, sometimes more. I asked him how it is that he makes more money than the other shoeshine kids and he told me he'll throw a blowjob in on the side. The kid's a smart aleck, so I don't know if he's telling the truth or not.

Rorkman and I came in late tonight and there on the corner was Peggy, the neighborhood whore. She's a nice lady but she's terribly slack-assed. Her black trousers just hang on her. Everything about Peggy pleads that you fuck her, or do something to her. The question of money is secondary. On the street she approaches you cunt first, in a manner that with some other woman would be exciting, but with Peggy you're afraid the thing might fall off before it gets to you. She waddles over in her indolent, sway-backed way and shakes your hand and at that moment you half expect her genitalia to drop on the walk. What really disturbs me about her though is what I take to be her submissiveness. I believe she would enjoy being beaten. She would like to lie pliantly unprotected on a bed while fists smash down on her.

The kid who was telling me about how American soldiers pay him to blow them has had all his money stolen. He gave it to Houghton to safeguard last night and Houghton, instead of locking it up in the wardrobe, put it in his trousers' pocket and hung the trousers over the bedroom door. It looks now like somebody got up in the dark and snitched the cash. The kid woke me up this morning with his yelling around about the money, and later on he slashed one of the other kids with a razor. That didn't help, so he tried to saw off one of his own fingers. Rorkman put a stop to that. The little cocksucker has a bad temper, you have to give him that much. I watched him go through authentic paroxysms of frustration and rage, his face twisting up like a Kabuki dancer's. He got so angry he was blowing his nose all over the floor and there was nothing I could do about it. After a while he cooled down enough to cry. When the kids left with their shoeshine kits he stood in the doorway frisking them. Considering how he earns his money, I can sympathize with how he feels.

Steve Eckert is back in town. He's been in Hue two years teaching English at the University. Last week he received a letter from the Viet Cong informing him that he was to be liquidated. The letter accused him of sleeping with his girl students and subverting their minds. Eckert didn't receive the letter directly; it was intercepted by the government censors and he was given a copy of it. He isn't sure the police did not invent the letter for their own purposes. It's difficult to believe anything at all the Vietnamese police tell you, but he's not willing to take any further chances so he's come to Saigon.

An incident like that sets me to thinking about how stupidly I am living my life. Other people come over here and start doing their work straight off. Not me. I can't. Every day it's the same with me. I wake up in the garage to the sun coming through the dirty window. I walk to the Chinese place on the corner and drink French coffee—half coffee and half milk. The owner pours the coffee and hot milk from silver pots into the tall glass at the same time and it is all very sophisticated while a couple tables over a guy is blowing his nose on the floor. I can't decide about the book. I'm not having any luck with it at all. I can't put my mind to the war or to anything else over here.

I have plenty of material, it isn't that. My problem is with my approach to the material, with style. If you agree that style is the man, then you'll see how serious this problem really is. My primary weakness is that I have not been able to make a firm decision about which is the best way to write a sentence in English. For years I have been bewitched by the idea that Hemingway knew how to do it. There were other people, Oliver Cromwell, for instance, wrote good sentences at times, and people like Ben Jonson and Walt Whitman. Those are the first who come to mind. But Hemingway was the one who bewitched me. I suspect there is something in his prose that appeals to the worst, weakest aspects of my character.

The longer I'm unable to write, the more lethargic I get. I suppose I'm depressed. I'm so lethargic now that except to eat and to check for my mail at the press center, I don't leave the house for days on end. Only one subject excites my interest: When will Saigon be attacked? There's very little news in the papers. The other side is lying low. Now and then one of their intelligence officers is arrested reconnoitering one district or another inside the city and when that happens a spark of hope lights up in me, but then the next three or four days pass with no fresh incidents and I begin worrying that I'm waiting for an attack that isn't going to come. At night I lie on my mat and listen to the artillery. There have been no rocket attacks in a month. I don't know what to think. Some other guy, if the war wasn't coming to him, would go out in the countryside and look for it. That's a reasonable idea, but I've no heart for it. Besides, I've already been in the countryside.

I never met Hemingway myself, but I've met someone who has. Patrick the Peruvian has met him, and more than once at that. The first time Hemingway's name came up between Patrick and me was one afternoon during the fighting in Cholon. We were with a company of Vietnamese Rangers when we got ourselves into a bad spot and had to make a run for it. Afterward we stood against a shopfront wiping our faces.

I said, "It's silly of me to get in a spot like that. I'm no combat reporter. That's not the sort of thing I write about. Anyone can do that. It's not worth it."

Patrick took exception in his rapid-fire English with the French accent. "Not at all, my dear. Not at all. That experience will flavor everything you write about what you've seen here today. That's what made Hemingway, you know. He always went where the excitement was."

"Did you meet Hemingway?" I asked.

"Of course, my dear. In the Congo. During the war, don't you know? He had a big presence. Very large."

I started to believe then that Patrick had actually known Hemingway. But Patrick and I had only met that afternoon so I didn't know yet what a great liar he is.

My favorite image of Patrick is of him standing on the cab of one of the fire trucks photographing the bodies of the dead as they were thrown up into the bed. He's a fat young man who dresses in baggy blue jeans, a baseball cap turned backwards, and an armored vest. In Peru his family are aristocratic landowners, but in Vietnam Patrick has the common touch. He doesn't use deodorants so you can smell the vest at about twenty paces. But then he has this thing also about snapping his fingers at Vietnamese waiters. The waiters don't know what to make of it, what with the way he dresses and all.

He waves me up on top of the cab with him. "Come along," he calls down to me. "Don't you take pictures?"

"No, I don't, Patrick."

"Well, come on up and have a look. I've never seen them from this vantage point before."

"You go ahead, Patrick."

"No, you must come up. This is smashing. You really must get yourself a camera."

When I first got to Vietnam I had some crazy idea that it was my responsibility to search out the most terrifying and horrible events and describe them as closely as possible. I found after a while that I just didn't have the heart for it. I understood that my motives were not clear. Understanding that much, I was suspicious of the reasons I had for almost everything I made an effort to see.

At dawn one morning over on Dong Khanh Street I came across a dead girl lying on her back on the sidewalk. She was about eighteen and dressed in stretch pants and pink high-heeled slippers and a white blouse. She had done her hair apparently and had tied a kerchief around it. She looked perfectly all right except for the little chunk of bone knocked out of her forehead. As I walked past her it occurred to me that if she were more attractive, I would almost certainly be more affected by the sight of her. There was a cruelty in the observation that I could not have defended, but in the moment it defined my reaction.

A couple hours later, after making notes on two firefights I had got caught up in, I was returning along the same street when I realized I was going to pass by the girl with the bone knocked out of her forehead. I stopped where I was and looked around for another way to go but there was a lot of small arms fire and I didn't want to take the wrong turn. In a certain way, I was very alert. At that moment I saw I was standing precisely on the spot where earlier the girl had been lying. Apparently the Saigon firemen had been along and picked her up and now all there was left was a wet spot on the cement a few inches from my feet. Before I understood what was happening, a single sob broke out of me. Then I went on as quickly as I could.

Part of my difficulty has been that I can't choose sides in the fighting. I've been like a fish out of water. I'm against every side equally. I believe we have all behaved with such stupidity and such contempt for human life and values that no one has a leg to stand on. I think that no further military advantage that might be gained by any side could possibly be worth what it will cost in human flesh and spirit. I don't know what to do with that idea, because I doubt the worth of my observations. I am unable to decide on concrete positions to work from. I doubt the value of what I feel about what I see, what I think about it.

Not knowing what else to do, a few months ago I decided to knock around the countryside doing combat stories. I was pretty embarrassed about doing it, but I didn't know what else to do with myself. I wasn't on top of the war. The war was on top of me. I decided to travel roads that everyone assured me I would not be able to travel, observing and noting down as precisely as I could the different levels of fear I experienced. That sounds just too introverted, everything considered, but there you are. I learned a lot knocking around like that, saw a lot of things, and I was frightened badly a couple times, but it wasn't until I got back in Saigon that I was able to get into a controlled situation and really find out what it means to me, at this time in my life, to be in a dangerous situation.

I've got such a bad head cold I can't think to write, and last night I couldn't sleep again. First the bat came inside beeping and darting around. If it'd just come in and hang somewhere, I'd ignore it, but it comes flapping around my bare legs and I don't like that. One of these nights it's going to get knocked in the head with a book.

When I write about such things in this journal I sometimes pause to question the order of importance of the events in my life. But all these commonplace little events, they're what underlie the quality of my day, and I take them seriously. For example, another reason why I couldn't sleep last night (and why this morning I am too tired to think on the great questions of the day) was because a cricket got down in a crack in the brick floor near where I lay my head and rubbed its legs together with so much abandon it made my ears ring. I can't imagine what possessed it to be so intense. I poked around at it with a broom straw, then tried to snuff it out with my footlocker, but it was no use. I was dealing with a cricket gone insane. Vietnamese boys have the right attitude toward crickets. They throw them against the wall to watch them bounce. A few hits like that and a cricket is too bewildered to make its noise. Rorkman says the crickets probably do not rub their legs together, but against their abdomen.

Typically when I've had a cold I've blown my nose in a handkerchief and washed it out in a washing machine. That was in America. Here I have to do my own wash on the floor of the shower so I've taken a lot to snuffing and spitting. The Vietnamese are great spitters themselves, so there's nothing improper about it. They spit most any place you can think of but their favorite of all places is on café floors. That takes a bit of getting used to if you happen to come from one of the imperialist countries. It's also one of the reasons that American soldiers are contemptuous of the Vietnamese cafés and won't often go in them. If the floor looks like that, they reason, how's it going to be with the soup?

American soldiers are contemptuous of Vietnamese for a lot of reasons, some of them in part legitimate, but they've got too little sense about when to display it and when not to. One afternoon I was on the Y-bridge during the fighting in the Eighth District when a taxi pulled up from across the canal. The back of the little Renault was packed with hunks of raw pork meat. The driver had just come through an American artillery barrage and a helicopter gunship strike to get his hog to market. In his excitement and gratitude at having escaped with his life he started chattering away in Vietnamese to an American soldier leaning against an armored personnel carrier smoking a cigarette.

"Get that shit out of here," the soldier said. "It's probably dead GI." The taxi driver was a simple guy maybe, but I could see he understood the contempt in the American's voice. It made me feel ashamed.

One afternoon during the fighting in the Eighth District I ran across the Cholon bridge and walked back underneath it alongside the green grass to the pagoda where a battalion of American infantry had its command post. The houses around the green were all destroyed, the entire Eighth District of Saigon, in fact, was in rubble and burning. The artillery was coming in close, exploding in black cracking air blasts while small arms fire came in sporadically through the walls of the Catholic church where the battalion had its supply and aid station.

The American wounded and dead were brought out of the fighting inside armored personnel carriers. The dead were wrapped in ponchos and laid out on the grass in a row. One of the wounded had been hit with a rocket-propelled grenade and he was rather a sight. His trousers had been removed and his abdomen and thighs were all mixed up. When they lifted him out of the back of the APC my heart caught, for while he was alive, it looked like his genitals had been blown off. Everything. I wanted to turn around and go away, but at the same time I was afraid I might be wrong, or I hoped I was wrong, and I didn't want to be left thinking it had happened when in fact it hadn't. I went up close and looked over the back of the medic and there in the middle of all that mess, riding high and dry, were the two balls and the little prick all bunched up together in a cluster. They looked as if they were holding onto each other for dear life, but they were perfectly all right. I felt a rush of gratitude flood through me.

Everywhere I go I ask if there are any new rumors. I'm growing afraid that the Viet Cong isn't going to attack Saigon again. There hasn't been a truly exciting rumor in more than a month. The attack was supposed to come three weeks ago, then last week. Now it's supposed to happen next week. Who knows what's going to happen or if anything is going to happen? There is a rumor making the rounds that when the attack does come that the government will fall. That's not a rumor exactly; that's in a class by itself. I've heard it before, but what a good ending it would be for the book. I'm not wishing a holocaust on anyone, but if there is going to be an attack, if the city is going to fall, I want it to happen sooner rather than later.

Sometimes I tell myself: You talk too much about wanting the attack. You're bringing bad luck on yourself. Even as a joke you shouldn't talk about it so much. Yesterday afternoon it happened to me again. Rorkman and I walked downtown and ran into Steve Eckert and I asked if he'd heard any new rumors about the attack. No sooner were the words out of my mouth than I felt the superstitious fear that I was bringing down harm on myself. Somewhere in the back of my mind I am half-afraid that words and their thoughts exist in their own right, that they can do things on their own. Normally I don't believe it, of course—only when the pressure is on. Then it's as if sometimes I revert to an older way of thinking. I can recall that when I was a child, when I rode on streetcars for instance, I wasn't sure if the other passengers could read my thoughts or not. I protected myself by changing the course of my thinking onto trivial matters, not letting anyone know where my true interests lay. That was simply neurotic I suppose, but only last month when we were being hit with rockets I found myself doing something very close to it.

We were in the room and I was sitting with my back to the wall listening to the peculiar whirring noise of the rockets as they passed overhead and was picturing in my mind's eye how they were sailing in from the countryside over the rooftops and the streets when suddenly I caught myself. If I were to think on the rockets with too much concentration, they would know where I was and I'd be in serious danger. It sounds too stupid when you put it down in black and white, but I stopped thinking about them and forced myself to think about something else. I don't remember what. The idea was to break the connection, the thought line, between the rockets and myself.

All this has something to do with the question of luck. When I arrived in Vietnam I felt unlucky. I had vivid reveries about losing one of my feet, or having an arm shot off. One day it even occurred to me that I might be killed over here. The point is, I'd never had those kinds of thoughts before. All my life I've considered myself lucky, and then without warning I began to feel that my luck had run out. It's no good to say I was having a crisis of confidence. I've never felt stronger and more secure in myself in my life. I am methodically focusing on the weaknesses of my character—not weaknesses as bad characteristics, but weaknesses as weaknesses. Something else is at work here.

One morning soon after I'd arrived in Saigon I stopped at a rickety little stand on Vo Tanh street to eat a breakfast. I was reading a book about the revolution in China during the late twenties. I read again about how Communist prisoners were stuffed into the boilers of locomotives and used for fuel. It's an image I can't get out of my mind. I thought about how impossible it has been for me to commit myself to anything to the extent that I would be willing to risk having my body thrown inside a roaring locomotive (do they close the door?). I sat there on the rickety wood stool thinking about luck and commitment, and when my breakfast was put down before me there were splotches of blood in the yolks of the eggs. I felt the hair lift up off my scalp. For the merest instant I thought I'd received a sign.

This afternoon I was walking on Nguyen Hue when it started to rain so I ducked inside the USO to wait it out. I was thumbing through the magazines when I came on an article about war protestors and their demonstrations. There was a time with such demonstrations, where the President was insulted and vilified in a manner that was so consciously cruel and so purposefully demeaning, that I didn't really understand how anyone could do it. I thought it so out of place. So coarse. This afternoon I understood I no longer feel that way. I'm not sure how it came about that I changed my mind. Part of it is that in Vietnam it has been brought home to me, once again, how men are willing to behave toward one another. It's rather more serious than bad manners.

One evening on the Vinh Long airfield I was drinking beer with some officers from a helicopter assault squadron. They had been on fire missions that day and two of their ships had taken hits. The only man who had not flown that day was a lieutenant who was still recovering from wounds he'd received the month before. They were telling each other about the people they had killed during the day, including one woman. They'd killed most of them with machine guns. They'd been operating in a free-fire zone so they could kill anyone they wanted. Some of the stories were very funny. The best of them were running jokes that first one officer would return to then another over and over again. They were really terrible stories and I tried not to laugh but they were very funny too and I couldn't help myself and the more I laughed, the more the officers elaborated on the stories.

While they related the stories they imitated in outlandishly grotesque ways how the people died. I don't suppose the gesticulations were really very exaggerated, but there inside the club it was too funny for words. The imitations were complete with sound effects and crazy Charlie Chaplin gestures as the bodies got torn up and always ended with the statement: "The only decent thing about Vietnam is killing VC."

One of the running jokes was about the Cambodian mercenaries the Americans hire to fight for them. The Cambodians go hunting in the most difficult country in the Delta and get paid "head" money for each Viet Cong head they bring in. That's on top of their regular salary. Well it seems the American advisors began to suspect the Cambodians of cheating. It's difficult to tell just by looking, don't you know, if a head truly belongs to a member of the Viet Cong or to somebody else, and if the hair is shaved off it, the Americans can't always be one hundred percent sure if the head belongs to a man or a woman. In short, a lot of problems came up so the Americans made a new rule: The Cambodians had to bring in the body along with the head. That meant a lot of extra weight for the Cambodians to carry around, but they agreed willingly enough because that's the sort of guys they are. The new problem however was that the Cambodians were so slipshod that one day they'd show up with seven bodies and eight heads say, and the next with perhaps five bodies but only three heads.

All the officers that night had a story about the Cambodian mercenaries and it really got to be hilarious. I tried not to laugh but the stories were so practiced and so hilarious I couldn't help myself.

Nowadays when I read about how American politicians are being publicly vilified and insulted, I no longer feel the old sense of discomfort and even shame. The question of manners is no longer important to me. In America, the issue of good manners is academic.

"Lt. Han's Brother's Throat"

(1968)

I follow the stories of the kidnappings of unarmed civilians in Iraq by Muslim fanatics. I follow the stories of those who are beheaded, or shot, as if I know from personal experience something, a little, of what they have gone through. The kidnapping of the truck drivers particularly catch my attention. I have a feeling for how it is with them when they are on the road, when they are stopped, and when they are taken.

When I got to Vietnam in February 1968 I had letters from the editors of *Atlantic Monthly* and the *Los Angeles Free Press* stating they were interested in receiving reports from me from Vietnam for publication. Normally that would have been sufficient for me to get press credentials from the US Army. With US press credentials I would be able to go where I wanted, with whomever I wanted.

I waited in Saigon several weeks, but could not get US press credentials. For a while I was okay with that. There was plenty to do. The Chinese Cholon district and the 8th district were infested with Viet Cong, there were attacks in and around the city, and there were many interesting things to see and people to talk to and many ways for me to get in trouble and write about it.

The problem with my getting US press credentials was that, technically, my passport was not quite right. I had worked my way to Thailand as a seaman on an old Victory. We were supposed to have off-loaded in Saigon, and I expected to jump ship there. But while we were still in the South China Sea, the Viet Cong and North Vietnamese kicked off their "Tet" offensive and Saigon itself was under siege.

So our ship was rerouted to Sattaheeb, Thailand, and I jumped off her there. I had no visa, so once in, I couldn't get out. I then had to find a way to get to Laos, where I understood anyone could get a visa for anywhere. It came about that my understanding was correct, which is a very interesting and comic story, and with a Laotian visa I was able to re-enter Thailand legally, then catch a flight from Bangkok to Saigon.

So I was in Vietnam legally but there was a glitch with the passport. The US military wouldn't challenge it, but they wouldn't accept it. After six very interesting weeks in Saigon I went to the South Vietnamese with my letters from *Atlantic Monthly* and the *Los Angeles Free Press*. In about half an hour I had South Vietnamese press credentials.

I did not go to Vietnam to report on the war, that is, to do journalism, but to work on a literary manuscript. For reasons I do not entirely understand, I had chosen autobiography as my form, a form for which there was, and is, no market. A few guys have used the form successfully, but by and large there is no market for it. Particularly if you are no one in particular, and you have no "revolutionary" agenda. Nevertheless, there I was.

There was also something about Korea that I had not quite gotten out of the way. I wasn't certain what it was, but I was aware that it was there. I had been in the infantry in Korea in 1950 and '51. One February morning, in a rice paddy, a Chinese machine gunner had shot me in the head, a slight, glancing hit to the left temple. While the hit wasn't serious, it caught my attention in a way that remained vivid for a long while. It led directly to my deciding to become a writer.

And then in July, in the trees on a mountainside, I was hit by fragmentation from a Chinese hand grenade. I saw the fellow who almost killed me. He stood up from his foxhole directly in front of me with a smoking "potato masher" in his right hand. It was very unprofessional of him to stand up like that, but at the moment I was doing something very unprofessional myself, so we were both just there. I can still see him. A tall, thin young man with a good face, an aquiline nose. While he almost killed me, I was left with a good impression of his face, which remains with me to this day.

A month later, back in Japan, urinating in a trough in the men's room in a club in Osaka, the man urinating next to me said suddenly: "Jesus Christ. Is your name Smith?"

"Yeah?

"Were you in Fox troop, 7th Cav?"

"Yeah."

"I was there the day you got hit."

"Yeah?"

"Is that your hand?"

"Yeah. I didn't lose it. Whose hand do you think it is?"

"I was there that morning."

"I don't remember you."

"We killed that Chink."

"You killed him?"

"Yeah"

"Why did you do that?"

"Why did we do that? Are you kidding me?"

"Yeah."

"Are you drunk?"

"Nah. Are you?"

"You're goddamned right I'm drunk. Why would I come to a place like this and not get drunk?"

"How did you remember me?"

"Are you kidding? You were almost blown off the mountainside.

I saw you. I had only been there four or five days. You had blood all over you. I thought you were hit bad."

"Just the hand."

"Is that the hand?"

"You mean this one? The one with the bandage on it?"

"Yeah."

"Yeah. That's the one. The one without the bandage is okay."

"One good hand. That lets you piss without help. You're a lucky man."

"But you killed the Chinese guy who got me with the grenade?"

"Not me. Some other guys. I didn't even see him. We were busy. I was told later. They shot him in the hole where he was hiding. You want a beer?"

"They have curfew at the hospital. I have to get back to the ward."

It didn't occur to me at the time to ask my comrade from Fox troop why he had been rotated out of line so quickly. He looked okay. I never saw him again. At the same time, I have never stopped seeing the rather elegant face of the young man who blew me out of Korea and thinking that maybe we did kill him. That's what happens when, in a moment of wakefulness, you see an individual face clearly. You remember it, and sometimes you think about it.

Now it was 1968. I was thirty-eight years old. Seventeen years had passed. But there was something from Korea in there, inside me, that wasn't quite finished. I didn't know what it was, and I didn't know how to take care of it. But now I had press credentials and I could go where I wanted and do what I needed to do.

One morning in May I was hitchhiking on Highway 4 in the Mekong Delta between Long Xuyen and Sadec. I expected to be in Sadec by early afternoon. A couple Vietnamese truck drivers hauling onions had picked me up and I was in the back with my overnight bag and my typewriter. About noon the truck turned off Highway 4 and began to head south. I let out a yell. I was ready to throw my gear over the side and jump for it. But the truckers stopped and I jumped out and thanked them.

I was at the turnoff to Rach Gia. I had understood they were going all the way to Sadec, but I had misunderstood their Vietnamese. At the turnoff there were half a dozen little unpainted wooden cafes, or truck stops, three or four little houses, and a gas station. That's all there was. From the intersection on south toward Rach Gia it was all rice paddies, forest, and Viet Cong. To the north it was the same.

I walked across the two-lane road and set the overnight bag and typewriter in the dirt alongside the pavement and began my wait for a military vehicle. I preferred American, but a South Vietnamese army vehicle would be fine, if they would have me. I was rather in the middle of nowhere. The sky was dark and low. The air felt like rain. I didn't try to flag down any more truckers. A bus stopped at the intersection on its way to Sadec, but I had had a bad experience in a Vietnamese bus a couple weeks earlier. I let it go.

By early afternoon I was getting restless. It was good policy to be off the roads by four o'clock, five at the very latest. There were a lot of truckers on the highway headed for Sadec and back toward Can Tho, but I didn't want to take a chance with another Vietnamese trucker. It was too late.

There weren't any American military vehicles. I tried to flag down a couple Vietnamese military vehicles but they wouldn't stop. The men driving them wouldn't look at me. The truckers who stopped at the gas station on their way toward Rach Gia eyed me openly. A few kilometers south there were already villages where Viet Cong cadre knew about the lone American at the intersection of Highway 4. I had to get moving, or get out of sight.

I picked up the suitcase and the typewriter and walked over to the first café. Inside it was dark and empty. I walked to the next one and it was dark and empty. In the third it was dark, but there was a lone ARVN officer drinking beer. He looked okay. I continued down the line looking in the rest of the truck stops. There were a couple more ARVN military and some truckers. I went back to the third café, set my stuff down at the entrance, went inside, and addressed the ARVN.

"Excuse me. Do you speak English?"

"Yes." He smiled pleasantly. "Do you want speak English to me?"

"Yes, I do. I want to ask you to help me."

"Oh, I will help. Will you drink beer with me?"

"Yes, I will."

He stood up.

"I am Lieutenant Duong. I am South Vietnamese officer. I would like very much help you."

We shook hands. He was tall and slender and had a good, intelligent face. He didn't try to impress me with his grip.

"I am Bradley Smith. I am a writer."

"Ahh," he said. He ordered two beers.

"I am a writer too. I work radio station before army. I love be a writer."

Thunder began to roll and the rain hit suddenly on the corrugated tin roof. Lieutenant Duong ordered something from the kitchen and the woman brought pork liver sliced very thin with fish sauce. We dipped the pork in the sauce and drank the beer and the rain fell heavily on the roof and outside the doorway. We asked the questions it is necessary to ask when a Vietnamese and an American first meet. It is very important for the other to know how old you are. Lieutenant Duong was twenty-eight.

We chatted about how dangerous the roads were. He said, "You very crazy travel that way. Excuse me."

"A little crazy."

"Very crazy. Excuse me. Very dangerous. Very, very crazy."

"Okay. Very crazy." It made me laugh. Lieutenant Duong laughed.

"Oh, yes. Very, very crazy. Please excuse me."

We were laughing. I hadn't eaten anything that morning and the beer was good. A couple wet truckers came into the darkness and ordered beer. They watched how Lieutenant Duong and I were laughing. When the waitress brought the two truckers their beer, they raised their bottles and toasted me, smiling. Lieutenant Duong and I toasted them with our bottles.

I dropped a piece of pork from my chopsticks on the tabletop. Lieutenant Duong thought that was very funny. I tried to pick up the pork with the chopsticks but it kept sliding around the tabletop. The truckers laughed and raised their beers. I laughed. We were all laughing happily. In the back of my mind I was thinking about what time it was.

Lieutenant Duong reached over with his chopsticks, picked up the pork sliver I had dropped, and held it out for me. I opened my mouth and he put it on the top of my tongue. He laughed and ordered a couple more beers. I fumbled another piece of pork with the chopsticks and Duong picked it up. I opened my mouth and he put it on top of my tongue. The truckers laughed and raised their bottles. We were having a good time.

"What time is it?" I motioned toward Lieutenant Duong's watch.

"Oh. It is four. I think we go. Yes. We must."

"Where do we go?"

"You stay with me tonight."

When we left the café Lieutenant Duong tried to carry my typewriter but I said no. Then he tried to carry my overnight bag but I grabbed it and said no. I followed him along the edge of the pavement until we came to a barricaded, wooden watchtower. Lieutenant Duong had a few words with a policeman there, then went out on the pavement and stopped the first truck that came along. Lieutenant Duong had a few words with the driver, then we got up in the front seat with him.

We drove about fifteen minutes through rice paddies with tree lines in the distance. We arrived at Ba Ton hamlet. The two-lane highway ran through the middle of the hamlet. There was a canal, an old concrete bridge, and to the south of the pavement a grassy square with a Catholic church. The one-room church was constructed of wood and set up on poles. It was high enough so that a man could walk around underneath it.

We were in a Regional Forces camp. It was a circle of mud bunkers about fifty yards across, thatched lean-tos with the family wash draped around them, the muddy rifle pits, the rolls of concertina wire. The camp didn't look comfortable, and it didn't look defensible. I looked around to see what I might do if something happened. There was nowhere to go, nothing to do.

We took off our boots, put on our sandals, and took a stroll. The rain had stopped. The grass inside the circle of bunkers was thick and wet. Lieutenant Duong wanted to introduce me to each man in his company. I begged off. Wives and children were everywhere. One kid had poked wire through the ears of a rat and was walking it through the grass on a wire leash.

We met First Lieutenant Han who was the company commander. He stood six feet tall and had a skull-like face, and a winning smile. We went out through the concertina and strolled through small groves of mango trees and wax jumbo trees. We chatted politely, Lieutenant Duong translating for us. The air grew heavy and sticky. Insects swarmed.

Strolling back toward the camp we came across a cage made from wood and barbed wire. It was about four feet square. My first thought was that it was to hold a Viet Cong prisoner.

"Oh, no," Lieutenant Duong said. "Cage is give discipline my own soldiers."

"Your own soldiers? From this camp?"

"Yes, yes."

First Lieutenant Han looked at the cage thoughtfully.

"I have never used it," Lieutenant Duong said. "I love my men too much. I love them each one."

First Lieutenant Han spoke to Lieutenant Duong in Vietnamese.

Lieutenant Duong grinned. "First Lieutenant Han ask if you like try our cage?"

"Try what? No. No thank you."

Lieutenant Duong spoke to First Lieutenant Han. Han looked at me happily, his death's head grinning broadly.

The Regional Forces platoon of Ba Ton hamlet was drawn up in formation on the grass beside the church for their nightly inspection. Some of them had boots, some had thongs. Some had helmets, a couple had straw hats. Lieutenant Duong called them to attention, introduced them to the American writer, then went off into an extended oration on duty and country.

Some in the platoon appeared to be listening to him. Some picked their noses, others looked at the sky or scratched their asses. One of the boys was excessively cross-eyed and two others were so dopey looking I wouldn't have trusted them with rifles. One boy wanted to look professional. He stood at attention with his chest blown out to the bursting point, but his steel helmet was on the grass at his feet, and all through Lieutenant Duong's oration the boy stared at the helmet with grotesquely popped out eyes.

Supper was served on a long table in the shadowed light beneath the church. Seated with me were First Lieutenant Han, Lieutenant Duong, and five enlisted men, all in their twenties. Only Lieutenant Duong spoke English. We ate shrimp, string beans, roast pork, bean shoots with green onions and scrambled eggs, a vegetable I was unacquainted with, rice and summer squash with plenty of black pepper. We washed it down with hot tea. There was a lot of talking and laughing. It was a wonderful supper. It was the best meal I had eaten since I left Los Angeles six months before. It may have been the best meal I have ever eaten.

Then there was the sound of singing. It came from inside the church. Down through the floorboards. Children were singing choral music in high pretty voices while below we ate and talked and laughed. There was something odd about the music. I realized then that the chorus was singing in Latin.

I said: "Duong? Do you think the music is beautiful?"

Duong lowered his eyes and shook his head no. I didn't ask him why. I should have.

After supper we all took soap and towels and walked through the wax jumbo grove to the river. There were stands of coconut palms and thatched-roof houses with men and women loafing on the porches. Young kids were playing with a couple of rats, while half a dozen women were washing clothes at the water's edge.

The river was sixty, seventy yards across. Ropes were tied to poles near the bank and trailed in the current. We stripped down to our undershorts and entered the water. The current was warm and very strong. I grabbed one of the trailing ropes and held it with one hand and while I scrubbed my body with the other. Across the river two teenage girls were looking at us, making jokes, and horsing around. They were looking at me. One of the girls pushed the other into the river fully dressed. They laughed like crazy and the Vietnamese I was with laughed and looked at me. I pretended to not see anything.

At dusk we left the river and dressed. People were lighting oil lamps inside their houses. Lieutenant Duong and I went to his bunker to leave the towels. He told me to get my typewriter. Then he took me across the pavement to a little brick house with a tile roof. Inside there were several people who, when we entered, retired to another room. An old, high-framed mahogany bed took up a good part of the room.

There was a small solid table to put the typewriter on, and a lit kerosene lamp.

Lieutenant Duong said: "Now you write." And he left.

I wanted to sleep. The night before I'd been up all night with artillery, and I was tired. But there I was. I worked on the journal dutifully. I didn't want to fail Lieutenant Duong. Insects were drawn to the lamp. A lizard appeared on the table top and ate some of the insects. He was wonderfully agile. After a while I noticed that underneath the mahogany bed, gleaming in the lamp-light, there was the entrance to a heavily timbered bunker.

After a couple hours Lieutenant Duong reappeared.

"Ten," he said. "We have Chinese supper."

Outside there were flares drifting through the black sky and here and there in the distance I could hear small arms fire. I followed Duong across the paved road, through the concertina, across the grassy clearing and underneath the church. My supper companions were there at the table again, along with three civilians. A ten-watt lightbulb hung from a post but there was trouble with the generator so a lighted candle was placed on each side of the table. There were small dishes of fried vegetables and meats and a bottle of whiskey.

Lieutenant Duong said: "These are our farmers. They very pleased meet with you."

We drank the whiskey and Duong did most of the talking and made everybody laugh. When the whiskey was gone Duong said: "Our farmers want you have coffee with them in morning. They very pleased."

First Lieutenant Han invited Lieutenant Duong, me, and his first sergeant, to drink coffee in another part of the village. I was exhausted and half drunk. I thought of making a joke about how it was easier to be chased by Viet Cong than to be welcomed to Ba Ton hamlet by Lieutenant Duong and First Lieutenant Han. I thought better of it. I resigned myself to sitting under the church in the candlelight drinking coffee with people I could hardly converse with.

Lieutenant Duong said: "No. No here. Other place. No give VC time fix us."

"How close are VC?"

"Eh?"

"VC far away?"

"Oh yes, very far. Half one mile. More. We very safe. We move here, move there. They not fix us. Very safe. We move now."

"I see."

"First Lieutenant Han very good soldier. VC like very much kill him. We move."

"I see."

We walked across the pavement into the hamlet. There was no moon, no stars. I could see a few feet ahead of me. We took a couple turns among the houses and I lost my direction. I felt myself come absolutely wide awake. We came to a tiny café with a kerosene lamp turned low. The proprietress was a good-looking middle-aged woman. The baked dirt floor had long open cracks in it. I heard the trill of an AK-47. Then another.

We drank coffee from tiny cups and ate little sweet breads. I needed the day to end. Lieutenant Duong was being charming to First Lieutenant Han. It was obvious he respected the man. Small arms fire sounded from one direction, then another. I seemed to be the only one who was aware of it. Finally it was time to call it a night.

I followed Duong back to his bunker, and inside to the lean-to. The entrance was so low I could hardly get in. The bunker was just a hole in the ground with a sod roof. The hole had a foot of water in the bottom of it. There were no firing slits. In the little lean-to, there was a cot and hammock side by side. Duong's bodyguard and servant had left a candle burning for us on a piece of wood. A little pile of clean clothes was stacked neatly on the end of the cot.

"My man did that. He with me two years. I love my man very much."

When I lay down on the cot in my clothes and socks, the thatched roof of the lean-to was close against my face. I could barely turn over. The small arms fire was everywhere, but not too close. I was too exhausted to feel anything. The camp was not defensible, but I went to sleep anyhow. Once in the night I woke to find Lieutenant Duong in his hammock writing in a pad by the light of the candle. I heard the rain falling on the thatch above my face.

"I write something for you," he said.

"Do you?"

"I want you have rememberings this time together."

"Thank you."

I watched the candle burn. I listened to the small arms fire. I listened to the rain fall on the thatch. I slept.

In the morning the sky was clear and the sun made the thatched roofs steam and the steam rose off the thick grass and the roof of the church. The whole camp was steaming. Military men and their wives and kids emerged from their bunkers and lean-tos and stretched and ran their hands through their hair. They brushed their teeth in little tin bowls.

I walked to a place I thought was private to urinate. The urine stream steamed in the chill air. I looked over my shoulder to make sure I wasn't being watched. I saw a young militia man elbow his wife and point toward me. His wife giggled and pushed her hands against his chest, looking at me all the while.

I followed Lieutenant Duong across the pavement to the café we'd been to the night before. I was fully dressed, including my boots. Duong was wearing his blue striped pajamas and rubber thongs.

The café was about fifty feet from the highway. We ordered coffee and sweet breads. I felt completely at ease. Lieutenant Duong took out his long ivory cigarette holder, put a cigarette in it, and asked the proprietress to light him up. We grinned at each other. Lieutenant Duong was content. I was content.

There was the sound of an explosion in the near distance, then another.

Lieutenant Duong said: "VC."

"It sounded like a mine. A land mine."

"Oh yes. Mine. Every night VC mine highway."

"So close?"

"Oh yes. Very close. I show you?"

"Oh, yes."

Lieutenant Duong understood that I had made a joke. He laughed. "Oh yes. Very close."

We finished the coffee and the sweet bread. Lieutenant Duong finished his cigarette. I followed him back across the highway. A couple hundred yards to the west I saw a little French bus on its side, half off the road. First Lieutenant Han's platoon was forming up in the grassy place beside the church. Some of them looked like idiots. I followed Lieutenant Duong to his bunker. I supposed he was going to dress. A moment later he came out, still dressed in his blue striped pajamas and thongs, but now with a beautiful, slender, walnut-finished cane.

We followed the Ba Ton Regional Forces Platoon through the concertina and up the highway toward the bus. The platoon ambled along leisurely. Some of the men had put lavender flowers in the barrels of their rifles. Others had put flowers or ferns on their helmets. A hundred yards out we came to the narrow bridge. The river was about fifty yards wide there. Duong paused and we looked upstream. The platoon ambled on toward the bus, still a hundred yards or so down Highway 4.

Lieutenant Duong pointed his cane upriver. "Many VC there."

There was the broad river, then the banks of trees on either side.

"How do you know?"

"Oh many time they shoot us here on bridge."

"Here on this bridge?"

"Oh, yes. Right here." He looked at me and laughed. "We stand here enjoy beauty, they shoot us."

"It is very beautiful here."

"Oh, yes. Very beautiful. Every morning, I look at it."

"The VC shoot you right here on the bridge?"

"Oh, yes."

"That's very interesting. Right on this spot?"

"Yes."

"That's very interesting." I looked across the river to the trees.

"One month past they shoot First Lieutenant Han—his brother, you know?

"Right on this spot?"

"They shoot him in throat. Ugghrr."

"This very spot?" I pointed at the ground between us.

"Oh, yes." Duong laughed a little. "Very sad."

"Oh, yes."

Lieutenant Duong said: "Machinegun. You know?"

"Oh, Yes. I know the machine guns."

"He bled river. You know that song?"

"I think so."

"First Lieutenant Han, his brother die here. Lose his blood."

"I see."

Lieutenant Duong gestured across the river with his elegant walnut walking cane.

"You see big tree? Over there? VC machinegun. Shoot us all time."

"I see."

It was a beautiful sunny morning. The blue sky. The cool fresh air. The paddies, the river, the trees on the far side of the river. It was all very beautiful.

And there was Lieutenant Duong in his blue striped pajamas and rubber thongs. Up the road a bit was the little bus blown over on its side where the men of First Lieutenant Han's platoon were pulling things, and pieces of things, out of it. In the trees along the other side of the river there was the big tree, and maybe or maybe not, the machinegun that had shot First Lieutenant Han's brother through the throat. We were standing on the very spot where First Lieutenant Han's brother had bled his river and died. And there I was.

I had a ride to catch.

"Che Guevara in Saigon"

(1968)

When I saw the first light of day come in through the window I pushed the three paperback books I used for a pillow against the wall and rolled up the reed mat and stood it in the corner of the room. On the bed, Bryant turned onto his side snoring lightly. Bryant's a Quaker, but he still snores.

I was in the little cement bathroom shaving in cold water when I heard the measured chugging of the fifties start up out in Cholon. It was agreeable to me to know they were still there, that the routine of the battle had not altered. An hour, half an hour later the fifties and even the sound of tank artillery would be lost in the noise of traffic as the city began to go about its business.

Down on the street I walked quickly with my hands in my pockets against the chill while young men in white uniform shirts and billed caps bicycled toward the gates of the National Police compound. They carried their identification cards gripped in their teeth so that the guards could check their photographs. I cut over to Tran Hung Dao and began walking toward Cholon. There was no more money for cabs.

I walked fast along Tran Hung Dao for half an hour then walked through a wide wooden doorway into a courtyard where workers straddling bicycles and wearing pith helmets were eating soup and drinking tea around a green wooden stall. I bought a cheese sandwich on a French roll and a bottle of orange soda pop. While the workers watched me carelessly I stuffed the sandwich inside my shirt and the bottle of soda in one pocket and started walking again.

I walked past the police barricade at Dong Khan Street to the corner of Thong Duc Phoung where one company of the 35th Vietnamese Rangers had its aid station. The medic and the two stretcher-bearers were sitting on the curbing in front of their jeeps. The two blood-spattered stretchers were standing upright against a shop front. Ahead, the pavement was covered with rubble and some of the buildings were smoking. A pagoda had collapsed and I walked around the orange tiled roof that had settled down intact onto the street. I could hear the AK-47s and M-16s now. I walked past Rangers standing silently in doorways with their weapons and then I saw Captain Thatcher sitting in his jeep with his American driver ready to advise his Vietnamese counterpart if his counterpart asked for advice, which was not very likely. It was good to see Thatcher there. Every morning it was as if I could count on him.

"Good morning," I said.

"Good morning," Thatcher said.

"How's it look today?"

"It looks like shit. The way it always looks with these people."

"What was the tally yesterday?"

"Three dead, seven wounded. Ours."

"Not bad for all that shooting."

"Light casualties, no progress. These people are satisfied with that."

"They do seem to be."

I was satisfied myself. I didn't want to say so. I wasn't very interested in progress, in victory or in defeat. I still thought I was interested in the process. I believe I still believed that I was convinced that in the process of risking death something significant could be identified.

It was a very nice morning. The sun was bright but the air was still cool and fresh. I had my sandwich and something to drink. I had my notepad and two ballpoint pens with black ink. I was set for the rest of the day. Up at the next corner there was on-again off-again small arms fire. The tension was there. The possibilities. I strolled over to the nearest shop front and looked in through the open doorway. It was a stationery store. The inventory was in a real mess. The next shop sold children's and women's clothes. Everything was in order there except for the Viet Cong corpse in black pajamas lying on its back in the center aisle. The open eyes were full of a sky-blue liquid. I gave the bottom of one of his feet a little kick just to make sure and ripples passed through the blue in his eyes. Out on the street I saw Thatcher watching me.

"What did you think of that one?"

"I don't know what that was. I can't figure it out."

"I can't figure any of this," Thatcher said. "You want to see what these people can do when they're in the mood?"

I followed him into a bicycle repair shop. Small arms fire was rattling in bursts on the streets on either side of our street. As we entered the bicycle shop Thatcher gestured toward some holes that went through the brick wall. Inside to the left there was a row of shattered glass display cases running toward the back about two feet out from the wall.

"Last night Truong set up a fifty on that balcony across the street and waited. He sat there all night and this morning at dawn he shot the shit out of this place."

Four Viet Cong corpses were strung out in a line in the aisle behind the glass cases, each one on its belly with its head toward the rear of the shop where a crawl hole had been knocked through the side wall into the back of the shop next door. When they were still alive the corpses must have moved to the front of the shop to look for targets where Captain Truong had heard or seen or sensed them and started up his fifty. The corpses that weren't corpses yet dove frantically behind the display cases and scrabbled one after the other back toward the hole in the wall they had come through. One by one they had been made into corpses until the one in the lead was halfway through the hole where he had been caught with his ass in the air and his head down on the floor on the other side.

"This one's easy to figure out," I said.

"Pretty, isn't it?" Thatcher said.

"The storyline is straight as an arrow. It's so straight it's eerie."

"It's a story with a happy ending. It's the kind of story we ought to see more of around here. If these people'd show a little imagination we'd see happy stories like this every day."

"Nothing beats a happy story."

"That's what we're trying to do here, create lots of happy stories."

At mid-morning one platoon of Rangers formed up and headed single-file into a maze of alleys and buildings. I went with them. The idea was to get in behind one of the two thirties the VC had trained on the intersection. We left the alleys and walked through passageways covered with tin roofs and chicken wire screens and came to the rear entrance to a large brick building. The lieutenant signaled us to get down and we sat down, some of the men with their back to the building wall, some of us facing it. I sat facing it. The lieutenant cranked up his telephone and was talking into it quietly when there was a terrific cracking explosion inside the building. There was a moment of frozen fear, then the realization that no one was hurt. A couple of the Rangers grinned. We went on sitting quietly against the walls on either side of the passageway. The lieutenant talked quietly into his telephone. I began making notes on my pad.

There was another sharp crashing explosion. It reverberated wildly under the tin roofs. A moment later I heard a soft human sound and a Ranger sitting across from me fell slowly forward until he was lying on his face. His back was opened up like a great bloody flowering plant. Then one explosion followed another and I understood it was our own tank artillery firing into the building ahead of us and that we were getting it too. Another Ranger fell forward, the noise became catastrophic, then part of a head came skidding across the stone alleyway on its hairy side and we all understood at once we had to get out. It was something like terror. There was yelling and running and yet enough courage to use enough time to carry out two wounded and the corpse with part of its head sliced off. No one bothered with the part.

As we came out of the alley, Thatcher was standing at his jeep watching. At that moment thought reminded me that at thirty-eight years I was the oldest man there. I was older than Thatcher. I was holding the ballpoint pen in one hand and the notepad in the other.

"Vietnamese tankers," Thatcher said.

"I figured." Then I saw the blood on the front of my shirt and pants, and I felt ashamed.

After lunch the Saigon firemen showed up with their aluminum helmets and the long poles with the hooks on the end and began dragging the corpses out of the smoking shop fronts. Some of the corpses were still fresh and soft and when the firemen threw them up in the back of their flatbed truck little clouds of ash poofed up from them.

In the late afternoon it was decided the Rangers would force the intersection in a company charge and occupy the four-story hotel further up the street. There was a café on the corner, behind it a couple one-story shops, then the hotel. There were two Sherman tanks with Vietnamese crews to lead the attack, the two that had killed one of us a couple hours earlier.

At sundown the Ranger Company was still formed in a column of twos along the east side of the street. Overhead the sky was growing dark. On the street the air was humid and thick. The battalion colonel had arrived and was arguing furiously with the tank commander, who was standing half out of his turret yelling down at the colonel, and holding up a bloody thumb. I walked over to Thatcher to ask what was going on. Just then the lead tank fired off a round and I jumped about a foot in the air. When I came back down I was pissed.

"What the hell was that for?" I said.

"The tankers are getting frustrated. They don't like the plan, and now their leader has hurt his thumb and wants to go home."

"I don't blame them for not liking the plan. Why doesn't Truong send some people over the roofs there and get down on top of that thirty?"

"There's a lot of things could be done in this situation if these people had any imagination."

"I've never seen an officer refuse an order." I watched the tanker telling his colonel to shove it along. "This is a first for me."

"Be sure to write it up that way," Thatcher said.

"If the Americans are going to train these people, they ought to train them right."

"You can only do so much with these people."

"The people up north do pretty well with them."

Thatcher didn't say anything.

Suddenly both tanks gunned forward firing their artillery. The lead tank blasted the corner café and through the wall behind it while the second fired up into the hotel beyond. Then the Rangers let out a great cry and broke into a run in a column up the sidewalk past the closed shop fronts and there was the noise of a hundred men in full gear, their boots striking the concrete, their equipment thudding and clanking and then they were charging across the street past the café and into the café and there were Rangers crumpled on the pavement in the intersection and there was the patter of the thirty out of sight around the corner.

Then there was a tremendous explosion and flash of light in front of the hotel and the lead tank didn't pause but continued right on up the street as if it had someplace else to go. As the second tank started to pass the front of the hotel firing its artillery I saw a figure in black lean out of a second story window and drop a package that looked like a fat briefcase. There was a terrific explosion and light-flash over the top of the second tank and an instant later the lid of the tank turret opened and a tanker jumped down on the pavement and staggered across the street, the fingers of one hand spurting blood like four or five open faucets.

The charge petered out and Captain Truong yelled and pushed his men up the sidewalk, he pleaded and threatened, but they wouldn't go out anymore into the intersection where they were being machine-gunned. I had never seen soldiers refuse to follow an order and while I watched something inside me turned around painfully. I watched while individual Rangers who tried to rescue their comrades who had fallen in the intersection were machine gunned themselves.

When B-40 rockets began exploding inside the corner café and a Ranger walked out without his helmet or his rifle and sauntered across the street toward us I noted on my pad the peculiar smile on his face and when he reached us the way his friends embraced him laughing and slapping his back and how the Viet Cong machine gunner had refrained from killing him and I jotted down in my notebook, "Why?"

I watched while the Rangers tried to make it back from the café one by one as night fell and how they were machine gunned before they could get even a few steps or how they made it, one shot through the neck but making it, one shot in the hip who made it too, limping and grunting and when he was safe with his comrades how one of them picked him up piggyback and carried him up the street toward the aid station.

I watched one Ranger shot in the stomach very carefully crawling across the pavement toward us whimpering and crying until two of his buddies ran out into the bullet storm and dragged him back over the curbing and how the last Ranger who was quite tall for a Vietnamese made it almost all the way across before he was jerked to a stop in mid-pace with a handful of bullets in his chest and how he staggered, caught himself, took two more steps forward and fell into the arms of his comrades.

Of course there were many things I missed seeing. Then the shooting stopped, and it was dark. Buildings were smoking and burning everywhere, for the fighting had taken place on many streets and intersections, not just where we were. Flames illuminated the tops of buildings in eerie, gorgeous ways. One Ranger had been shot in both arms and wouldn't allow anyone to lift him off the pavement. He moaned in a peculiar way and in the tortured light from the flaming buildings I could see his face turning to stone.

Two Rangers were trying to take a green wooden door off a storefront. I watched them working at the door fastidiously, as if they didn't want to damage someone's property. When I realized they wanted to use the door for a stretcher I went over and tore it off its hinges and threw it in the street. I was in a rage. The three of us stood there looking at each other and I still had the notepad and the pen in one hand. I put them in my shirt pocket and we put the wounded, strangely moaning Ranger on the door and another Ranger came over and the four of us picked up the door carefully and started back toward the aid station. We moved slowly in the dark through the rubble. We carried him past the pagoda roof. The wounded Ranger wasn't moaning, I realized; he was chanting in a low, rhythmic voice. It didn't resemble anything I had ever heard.

At the corner of Tong Duc Phuon it began to rain. We carried the door inside a dark drugstore and set it down. Outside, wounded Rangers lay on the sidewalk in the dark in the heavy rain. Their comrades spread ponchos over them. Rangers who weren't wounded pressed back with their weapons into doorways. Thatcher was standing in the entrance to the drugstore making entries in his little black notebook. I knew he was doing the tally, one column for wounded, a second for dead. Every evening at sundown Captain Thatcher started his tally. On the other streets all across Cholon at that moment American advisers were standing in doorways out of the rain with their notebooks and ballpoint pens recording the tally.

I moved down the street and stood in a doorway crowded with half a dozen Rangers. It was very dark. No one spoke. The rain poured into the street. A few blocks away fires burned out of the tops of the buildings, beautifully illuminating the great cloud billows of smoke. After a while I heard Captain Thatcher's driver start up the jeep and a moment later it pulled up at the curbing in front of the doorway where I was standing among the Rangers.

"Time for beddy-bye," Thatcher said. Every evening at nightfall for ten nights Thatcher had given me a ride toward the room.

"I'm going to hang around for a while."

"Big plans are one thing," Thatcher said enigmatically. "Taking care of business is something else."

"I suppose so," I said. I didn't have the least idea what he meant.

"See you tomorrow then."

"Yeah."

When the jeep taillights were lost in the rain I started walking in the downpour. I walked through the roadblocks toward Trung Hung Dao. It was after curfew and the streets were deserted. Trung Hung Dao is one of the main thoroughfares in Saigon but there were no streetlights and not a single window had light coming from it. I walked as fast as I could in the rain. I hadn't thought that part of the city would be so deserted. I went out in the middle of the street and started running to keep warm. That made me think how I could be shot for the wrong reason and I started walking again but I stayed in the middle of the street.

Memory began going over what I had seen during the day. It recalled what I'd seen the day before and the day before that. It played back the scenes from over in the Eighth District, then the ones from First District. It produced pictures of what I saw around Sedec in the Mekong and on the road to Tay Ninh and outside Mee Tah. There was no particular order of appearance. The pictures just kept coming, one crazy, bloody scene after another, like those dreams that appear pointless but have an insanely driving persistence.

It took about an hour to walk to the room. It rained hard the whole time and the streets were empty and dark. I was defenseless. Then I was climbing the flight of stairs to the room and when I opened the door Bryant was sitting on the bed in his shorts with his back to the wall reading *Time* magazine and listening to his Beatles recording of *Sgt. Pepper's Lonely Hearts Club Band*. He looked up as if he was going to ask me a question, but he didn't say anything.

Then he said: "You look like you've been to hell and back," and he laughed. In the bathroom I looked at myself in the medicine cabinet mirror. I was sopping but I looked normal.

Bryant said: "When you opened the door and I saw you there, it was the expression on your face."

I showered in the cold water and dried off with a clean towel and put on fresh shorts and a clean shirt. I rolled out my mat and lay down and drew the three paperback books beneath the back of my head. Bryant put another Beatles recording on his machine. Outside I could hear the rainwater rushing off the tiled roof and splashing on the street below. The Beatles music was cheerful.

Bryant said: "Well, how'd it go out there today?"

"Just like the other days. Same, same."

"I thought maybe something unusual happened."

"No. It was exactly like the other days."

Books and magazines were scattered around the floor as usual. I picked up the magazine closest to me. It was a recent issue of *Ramparts*, the one with Che Guevara's portrait on the cover painted in flaming reds and he in a beret looking rakish and heroic. It was the issue where *Ramparts* published Guevara's "Letter to the Bolivian People."

The "Letter to the Bolivian People" recounted a feat of arms. Guevara had directed where his guerrilla group had ambushed a

Bolivian army patrol and bushwhacked four of its members. The letter was a sensitive apology to the mothers of the four dead soldiers and an explanation of why it had been necessary that he, Guevara, shoot their sons. It was a touching letter. There was a certain generosity to it.

Guevara empathized with the pain and loss he understood the four mothers were experiencing. He wrote that he had no personal grievance against their sons and had shot them not as individuals but as representatives of the Bolivian State under General Baronets. Guevara then spoke to all the mothers of Bolivia, explaining that he would soon begin shooting their sons too, and it was necessary for all Bolivian mothers to prepare to bear the pain he was going to bring them in order to set them free.

Uncertainly at first, then with the growing understanding of an avalanche, I saw that the revolution Guevara was making in Bolivia belonged to him, not the mothers he was addressing. The mothers hadn't asked him for it. He hadn't asked the mothers if they wanted it. Guevara wanted it himself however and he was going to give it to the Bolivian mothers whether they wanted it or not. He was ready to kill every mother's son in Bolivia who got in his way. That's how dedicated Guevara was to his imagination. That's where his revolution began, in his imagination, and for him that would be the only place where it could end. The people he had already killed and all those he planned to kill when he could make the right arrangements for it would be dedicated to the turnings of his imagination.

Inwardly I began arguing with him. Inwardly I shouted: "Why don't you start at the top you asshole? Why are you starting at the bottom again? Why don't you keep it among your own kind, you shit? Those who have a passion to use others for their own ends? Eh? You don't like the way Bolivia is ruled?" I yelled inwardly. "Kill the ruler, you fucking intellectual. What is it about you people? You always kill the people the tyrant rules, never the tyrant. Kill the generals, not the soldiers. Kill the politicos, not the citizens. When will you ever understand?"

"Bradley?" I heard Bryant say quietly.

"Yeah?"

"Are you okay?"

"Yeah. I'm okay. Why wouldn't I be okay?"

"Are you talking to yourself?"

"I'm okay. Let's let it go."

"All right."

After a moment, Bryant said very quietly, "Maybe tomorrow you'll want to talk about it."

"Bryant," I said. "Let's let it go. Okay?"

"All right."

"And turn off that fucking music. Will you do that?"

"Veil of Maya"

(1973)

Up at six this morning. I listen to the rain falling from the eaves. I dress quietly in the dark, careful not to wake Susan. In the kitchen by the light of the open refrigerator I mix half a glass of grapefruit juice with some mineral water. The rain is splashing on the concrete walk outside the back porch. I picture puppies sleeping in a heap in the dirt underneath the house. Dry and warm. Just like myself. Cozy. When it's raining, any roof is a luxury.

In the study I turn on the lamp and sit down to my table. Here are the notebooks, the manuscripts, the dictionaries, the typewriter, the blank paper. Oftentimes I wonder: why do I still make the effort? What's the purpose? In the beginning there was no wonder. Twenty-five years ago I began passionately to write things down. No training, no direction, no purpose. Only the driven need to record one certain experience on paper. At first it was mindless, but after a while I began to write things down when I did not feel driven. It wasn't mindless then, and I began to write in relationship to ambition. And I thought a lot about the future.

Last night I sat on the couch in this little room filled with the sound of rain and read about the death of Malcolm Lowry, his last years, his final months, the last night when he died of alcohol, barbiturates, and self pity. He was a sot, a contemptible husband, pathetically unable to take care of himself. While I read—and I was unable to put down the story—I was aware of how contemptuous I felt toward him. Where is the good in writing a book and living a life like Lowry's? That isn't what my aim is. His attitude seemed to be that because he had written some work that was praised by literary people he could forego acting like an adult. I was contemptuous of Lowry, but I was uneasy also. This morning I woke thinking about him. I feel aimless, and wonder again what it is all about. Most likely the whole affair, this life, this living, is about absolutely nothing whatsoever. No meaning, no purpose, no consequence. Nothing but happiness, pain and boredom.

The trees outside my window become visible one by one. The evergreens, the palm trees, the round-topped dark green trees whose name I don't know, the pepper tree hanging low over the pavement of the street. How many times have I described the dawn? What for? Still, there's something about doing it I like. For example, the dog is up and I can hear her walking her nails across the old hardwood floors. The cat is awake also. I can picture her in my mind's eye. She is on one of the chairs in the dining room taking her morning stretch, and I hear her scratching at the rush in the seat of the chair. Pretty soon Susan will be up, then Jon and Jen. Rather, Jen will be up, then Jon. Jon is not too good at getting up.

In 1951 I was a rifleman in Korea. I was twenty-one years old. Occasionally, as we climbed around through the mountains, a magazine would make its way from squad to squad. I received packages regularly from my mother and perhaps this was a copy of *Time* that she had enclosed along with her cookies and the canned fruit. There was a review of a new play, or a movie, based on the story "Rain" by Somerset Maugham. There was a profile on Maugham that caught my attention. I can't recall why. Perhaps it was his travels in the orient. "Rain" was described in glowing terms as a work of literature, and Maugham was praised as an important author. I wrote my mother asking her to send me the "book."

I was quite conscious of asking her for a work of literature. I had never before turned to a book because I understood it to have literary quality. Literature was not esteemed in our family, or in our neighborhood, and no literary matter was ever discussed in my presence by anyone. A month or so later I received my copy of "Rain" that Mother had run down for me. It hadn't been easy, she had had to go to Hollywood to get it. I remember that our battalion was in reserve, how I sat in the frozen rice paddy in front of my pup tent and opened the package. When I saw that "Rain" was only a short story I was excruciatingly embarrassed. I had asked Mother to send the novel, *Rain*, and had worded the request in a manner meant to display a considerable sophistication, a sophistication I knew she did not have. I could not tell from her letter, which accompanied the package, whether she had understood that intent, and I could not tell if she understood how little, as it turned out, I really knew about the matter. It was horribly important to me to feel she had not understood, but I was really afraid she had.

Still, I was excited by having the story, and I read it immediately. It didn't take long. It was over very quickly, too quickly. It wasn't much of a story so far as I could tell. I had expected something tremendous, earth-shattering, a story that would move a mountain. I don't know what I expected, but "Rain" did not fulfill that expectation. After all, if it was a work of literature, if it was written about in one of the world's most important magazines, it had to be something. When I finished the story, it occurred to me immediately that I could write a better one. And that moment was the beginning of twenty-five years of effort and use.

I must have not thought about it for long though, not at the time. "Rain" probably got passed around and lost. I don't recall discussing it with anyone. Winter passed, spring, and then it was early summer. One hot noon day we were lying behind the ridge of a hill covered with pine scrub and flies. Across the valley a Chinese soldier was pacing back and forth on another ridge, silhouetted darkly against the sky. Some of the guys were taking pot shots at him to break the boredom. The Chinese did not even break his stride. No one could figure what he was doing, or what he thought he was doing. He was probably showing off for his friends. After a while our 57 mm recoilless rifle team climbed up to the ridgeline and took a bead on the Chinese. They couldn't hit him either. Nothing could kill that Chinese and nothing could faze him. We got to whooping it up and cheering for him and shooting at him at the same time. We got to seeing how marvelous he was and imagining how he was swearing at us, giving us the finger (whatever the Chinese do), making his own comrades laugh, just as we were laughing, and admiring him also for putting his life on the line to make the whole thing go.

I remember lying in the dirt, sweating, the flies swarming over everything. Two of the guys were talking about a new book that had been published—*Forever Amber*. I listened to them talk. I had heard about the book also. I read a review of it that was disparaging, probably again in *Time* magazine. The book was supposed to be sexually titillating and it was that sexual aspect of the story that they were talking about. After a while I broke in on their conversation and remarked that the book had gotten poor reviews. It was implicit in the words I chose and in my tone of voice that I knew more of the matter than they did and that the quality of my understanding was on a higher level. That was how I intended it anyhow. If they had questioned me about my motives I would have denied my real ones. I would not even have believed what my motives really were. I wouldn't have understood. I was not accustomed to examining the motives that lay behind what I said or did, but only judging the correctness of my acts. I felt I was probably correct in what I said about the book. After all, any reviews published in a magazine knew more than two guys in my own squad, and I was conscious of the rewards I got by saying it. I had placed myself above the two others. I had placed myself in a position that was superior (that is critical) to that of the author of *Forever Amber*, and I had created a certain image of myself that I imagined the others would see and which would take the place of the one I believed they did see. I had created an image of myself that I wanted the others to see. It gave me an apparent stature I did not feel I otherwise had. I don't know why I can remember the incident so completely. Perhaps it was that day when I got a whiff for the first time of a role that was open for me to play, one that I could in fact play. I found a technique for appearing significant. The other role I had dreamt of playing was savior of my nation, my people. That role called for too much sacrifice, too much effort, too much blood. I hadn't been able to conceive even how to go about it. But being a writer, being a critic, there was an activity anyone could get into. After all, what was involved in writing a story, or criticizing a story? What was at stake?

By the end of July I was in the hospital at Camp Cook, California. The hospital was close by the ocean, and the mornings were cold and foggy. The wards were single-story barracks connected by covered corridors that creaked beneath our feet. Sand drifted over the linoleum floors in the wards and in the passageways. There was nothing to do. I was very tired. Some mornings I would get the paper and pass the entire day reading short paragraphs from it and dozing. Some days I would sit in the recreation room in the back of the ward and watch the fog drift across the deserted dunes where weeds grew in brown clumps. Sometimes, when I was spoken to, it was difficult to understand what was being said.

One morning without any forethought I walked through the covered corridors to the PX and bought a fifteen cent notepad. I would give anything to know the train of events that morning that prompted me to do it. I returned to the ward and sat at the table in the recreation room. The fog was blowing against the windowpanes. It was cold on my feet and on my back. I wrote a description in the notepad of how it had been that last day with my company—rather, that last moment with the blast of the hand grenade, the rifle torn out of my hands, the shock, the bubbling blood, the whiteness of the bone glistening wetly in the sunshine, the shock, the way I sat cross-legged beneath the tree and searched through the leaves for the finger I thought was gone, the shock, the look of the little emptied artery splayed open like an exploded flange.

I worked at it all day but couldn't get it right. I was wide awake and excited. The way I put the words together did not convey the reality of what happened. I couldn't make it strong enough. I kept leaving things out. What had happened, the movements that had proceeded that last moment, were more complicated than I had known, even if I had previously thought about it. Each separate movement had itself been proceeded by at least two additional movements or possibilities and those proceeded by two others. What had happened to me had been so powerful an experience I did not want to leave out even one single aspect of it. All of it was important. But no matter how I described it, the words I used did not have the power, the sheer reality, of what I had experienced. Compared to what had actually happened, my description of it was weak, like watery soup, and inadequate. The experience itself rode like a mountain over the passages of my notepad, which were frail, and without life. The next day I bought another fifteen cent notepad, and the day following that I bought another one. And the next day.

And I have written about it for years and it has never come out right, and I have never made it as real as it really was. I have become impressed by the superficiality of memory, the uselessness of it. I am struck by how I use memory to fill up the gaps in my life. Oftentimes I am in a state of remembering for longer periods of time than I am aware in the present. I am one of those for whom the selectivity of memory operates in the present fashion. I recall the most moving incidents, the most beautiful landscapes, the loveliest women, the most exciting, most fulfilling times. I recall easily the quality of the sunlight during specific moments ten years ago, the contents of interesting dreams, the visions, the hallucinations, the fantasies. I love to remember the most important incidents of my life during childhood, at school, with friends, by parents. I can dwell for hours on what happened to me when I was a soldier, when I traveled, when I was with the bull in Mexico, living in Greenwich Village, the nights at Barney's in Los Angeles. So much of my time now is spent in ways that are not pleasing or moving, that I prefer to live in memory rather than in my real life. It appears that I would rather pass time recalling pleasant moments out of the past than to live fully in the life that I am truly living now. But then, I believe that this may have always been the case. I don't really believe it is anything new.

It may be that it takes more energy to see, to be aware of, what is happening in the present than what has already happened in the past. Memory can float easily to the top of consciousness, simplified as memory is, while whatever is happening at this moment is varied, multifaceted, complicated. It is easier to deal with the present after it is over, after it has become the past, and sorted out by memory. It occurs to me there is no word comparable to memory that we can use to describe forgetfulness. Clearly there is more forgetfulness in memory than there is remembering. Memory must be made up of two aspects, forgetting, and remembering, the balance between the two depending on what we want from memory, what our desire is. The psychologists must know all about this, yet I don't hear this talked about. And then of course when I am bored with remembering what happened to me in the past, I can always start imagining what I would like to happen to me in the future. Anything but what is going on now. Anything but what is real, what really is existing at this moment.

Why is it that the present moment most often is not so important as the past or the future? Probably, I see this now, it is that we figure out what the present moment is. I want to be able to describe it, and it is indescribable. It is too varied, too complicated, too full to describe, to identify, to delimit, to embrace. For the first time I see what is meant by the idea—of thought itself—as being limiting. Experience happens too quickly for thought to identify it and sort it out and understand the significance of it. By the time that process has even begun, that process of identifying, and then through comparison making a decision on what is important, the moment is gone and I am faced with a new one where I have to begin the thinking, identifying, comparing process all over again and then that moment too is gone.

With memory, on the other hand, I have all the time I need to dwell on the remembered and forgotten experience. I have the time with any certain memory to try to identify it, to explore it, to compare it to other experiences and to what I wanted during the first living out of the experience. I can perhaps find out what was pleasurable in the original experience, why it was pleasurable, and think about how I could get a similar kind of pleasure from it.

In real life, the real present living moment, where the quality of experience changes from moment to moment quicker than the eye can see, what good does thinking do? Thinking cannot keep up with it. The problem, probably, then is to be in relationship, nothing more, nothing less, whatever that means. To be in relationship then means to be completely aware without thinking, completely open, the entire system experiencing the reality of the moment, not merely the mind.

How can thought keep up with the moment? It's impossible. It is demonstrably evident that we cannot think so quickly as we can live. Thought is one part of living. It is produced by living. Life is not produced by thought. We live in spite of everything, then we die. But while we live thought is a segment of living. Memory is a segment of thought. Why do I choose again and again to live with a segment of a segment of my life, rather than with the entire thing?

It is very arduous to live in the present. It is very unpredictable, unsure. I am not often satisfied with living in a way that my reward is not assured. If I were to live this moment without remembering the past, without hoping for something in the future, I don't know what would happen. Rather I do know something about it, but it is so arduous an experience I feel ambivalent about having it. I am actually somewhat afraid of it.

I am so trained by my own habit of remembering and imagining that it is very difficult to live without either diversion for more than a moment at a time. Sometimes it just happens to me, or I let it happen, or there is some coincidence where for the moment I become completely alert to what is going on in my presence while at the same moment thought is absent. Those experiences are profound ones. It is as if I see right through something. Memory shifts to the left, like a sheet withdrawing, my imagination moves to the right, and through the opening in the center I see the world as it really is. The beauty of it is incredible. It brings tears to my eyes. It does not last.

One day after work I walked across the street to the Villa Italia for a beer. This particular evening when I walked outside I felt content and at ease. The sun had set behind the hills but the sky was still quite light. I didn't immediately notice anything unusual, but I hadn't taken more than eight or ten steps when I happened to glance toward the corner and got the feeling that something was different, that something was "in the air," as they say. Then I noticed the traffic light on the corner. It was signaling stop, and the red light was on. I was struck by the quality of the light. There was nothing about it that was different from the hundreds of other times that I had looked at it, but there was something about it. The light changed from red to green. The green light looked perfectly like any other green traffic light I had ever seen, but somehow for the first time, I saw how lovely the green was colored.

When the signal changed again to red I saw how lovely and glowing it was. I realized that I had stopped walking and was standing there watching the traffic light change. The red and then the green were so lovely. Then tears came to my eyes.

I changed the direction of my gaze and looked up Montrose Avenue. I saw the signs on the drug store, I saw the dress shop, the sewing machine store, the appliance store, and farther up on the next corner I saw the post office. The storefronts and the signs looked just as they always had but there was a reality about them, a concreteness, that was totally new. I looked across the street at the lumber yard, then up Honolulu Avenue. Nothing was changed from earlier in the day, everything was in its place, but the sheer reality of what I was seeing was so moving I began to cry. At first the building looked washed and clean, spotless, glistening. Then I saw that they were soiled and worn just as always, but that I was seeing the dirt and the wear and tear perfectly clearly and that the imperfections and the dirt itself were beautiful. I thought at first that my faculty for sight had become somehow charged, powerful. Now I realized that everything was charged, the traffic light, the pavement, the buildings, the store signs, my own eyesight. It was all more real, more incredibly concrete than I could explain. I was wiping the tears off my face with one hand then the other. I didn't understand what was happening.

I walked across the street to my car. I was aware of everything going on around me in the ordinary way, but I was aware in this new way also. My relationship with the street was not different, but I was aware now that the street itself was different from what I had previously thought it to be. It was glistening and beautiful. No one part of it more beautiful than any other part, or less beautiful. I drove up Honolulu through the mall. I wasn't sad but I was so moved I thought my heart would burst. Only a few minutes had passed since I had begun to see things so clearly. It was still quite light. I drove down a residential street of small houses built in the twenties and thirties. I saw a man standing in front of his house watering the lawn. I saw the colored flowers, the green grass, the water spewing from the hose. It was so moving. I could not contain my feelings. I drove slowly up and down the streets. I didn't want to stop because I was afraid someone would see how I was crying. Here and there people were puttering in their gardens, mowing their lawns, sitting on their front steps. It was so lovely. Every single thing was absolutely in place and in perfect relationship to everything else. My tears were so profuse that I had to pull to the curb and park. I decided then that I had had enough.

I wasn't frightened, there was nothing scary about the experience, but I couldn't stand to see things that way any longer. I resolved not to look at anything anymore, to wait for darkness so that I could not see so clearly. I waited a long time, sitting there in the car. Dusk came but it wouldn't get dark. I had to do something. I took a chance. I drove back toward the mall. I kept my eyes on the pavement in front of the car. I forced myself to think about other things. I can't remember what, though that would be interesting, now, to know. I pulled myself together as best I could, wiped off my face, and stopped at Avignon's. I had the idea that if I had a couple drinks I would stop seeing so clearly. The alcohol would interfere so to speak with my sight. I had three quick ones. I was restless in the bar, and out of place. I went outside. It was dark. Now I saw things more in the usual way. I was relieved. I wanted to be relieved of everything that was not ordinary. I wanted to rest. I was not tired. I didn't realize I was not tired until I had had the thought that I wanted to rest. I did not need rest. I needed to be relieved of the burden of seeing so clearly. I drove home and got the kids and we went out to play some pinball at Barney's. I saw everything in the ordinary way again, and we had a pleasant time playing the pinball machine, the pool table.

It is not possible to describe accurately what happened to me that evening. I cannot describe accurately, in the sense of describing fully, what the experience was. It is not that I cannot get into it everything that I saw or that I was aware of, as it was with the incident with the hand grenade, but that the later incident is perfectly simple, uncomplicated. Nothing happened. I saw the faces of buildings and passing automobiles with a purity of sight that changed my understanding of their reality. Reality did not change.

My senses opened up somehow. My capacity for perception functioned with more clarity than is usual for those few moments, and I saw things in a new light—literally. That was not the first time I have had that experience, nor would it be the last. But it was the first time I realized consciously afterward that the reality of that particular experience cannot be described.

This morning when I came to look over what I had been typing, I saw things written down that I had already forgotten. When I was reading how I described moments when memory and imagination draw aside, as the curtains from before a movie screen, my mind made a connection with the concept of the "veil of Maya" that one reads about in Eastern literature. Perhaps what I experienced that evening coming out of the Villa Italia would be described in that literature as the veil of Maya withdrawing from before me, revealing to my gaze a reality so concretely beautiful that comparison between the good and bad, the ugly and the beautiful, would be meaningless. Everything is there. That is all there is to it. And it is wondrous. That must be what all the hoopla is about.

In the hospital after I wrote about the incident with the hand grenade, I wrote about two dreams I was having recurrently. I was able to describe them fully and accurately to my own satisfaction. Dreaming is significantly easier to deal with that wakeful living. Later on I wrote down other things. I wrote the outline for a movie script (based on a movie I had already seen—*Sunset Boulevard*—but with a certain twist in the plot). I wrote parts of a story or two, perhaps some recollections about childhood. I can't really recall what all the scribbling was about. I am certain, however, that the greatest part of it was the effort to get right what had happened at the moment I was wounded with the grenade fragment, and that I was never able successfully to do it.

The season is changing rapidly. Last night there was thunder and lightning followed by a rainfall. This morning the sun is shining on the trees and the flowered vines and on the east facing walls of the residence for elderly priests. The sky is pale blue, and the birds are flitting around in the eucalyptus tree and I can hear their various songs and calls. The very tips of the pepper tree, as they hang down over the street, are moving ever so slightly, and I understand that the cool morning air is beginning to form its currents. A moment ago, trying to distinguish one insistent bird call from all the others, I discovered it was in fact a particular sound this electric typewriter is making.

"The Journal"

(1979)

Last night a wind was up. I lay on my pad in the dark on the living room floor. I felt content. I listened to the wind chime hanging on the front porch. It was so delicate and pretty. When I tired of laying on my back I turned on my side. By dawn the wind was blowing only occasionally. Once, in a little puff of air that came in under the front door, I caught a whiff of skunk. I thought about how the skunks and possums and raccoons had been out in the night among the houses and garages and how the warm wind had blown through their fur.

~

Tonight I took some ice cream home and was dishing it out when Mother wheeled into the kitchen and said: "That's what makes your feet hurt, Boy." I was struck by the complicated compression of her thought—that I'm overweight, that ice cream is fattening, that I eat too much, and that after the jogging my feet hurt.

Reading the Sunday paper I find that Ira Glasser, executive director of the American Civil Liberties Union, wants to force me by law to participate in a program (Medicaid) to pay for abortions on demand by pregnant women. I don't want to. Glasser suggests I don't want to because of my religious beliefs. I don't have any. Not only does Glasser want to direct my acts of conscience by the threat of force, but he wants to justify his initiation of violence by falsely attributing to me beliefs I don't have.

Glasser writes that the beginning of human life in the fetus is essentially a religious question but that there's no religious consensus about when it happens—and no scientific consensus either. His response to lack of consensus by priests and scientists is that I should follow the direction of government when I have to decide what value a fetus has. What could be more vulgar? Just as I don't worship a god, or a godless science, I don't intend to fall on my knees before the idea of an all-knowing government.

Glasser draws an analogy between the anti-abortionists now and the conscientious objectors to war in the past. He points out that while government gave to the conscientious objectors the right to not personally kill living people, that government did not exempt him from paying taxes so that government itself could get on with it. The point being that while the government gives me the freedom of choice to not personally tear the fetus from a living woman, it insists that I fund the program whereby government does it in my name. What kind of (aborted) sense of "freedom of choice" is that? I am not going to comply with it.

I have a different attitude toward freedom of choice than that of Ira Glasser and the ACLU. I don't feel that government has the right to control my acts of conscience through forced taxation and the threat of imprisonment. And I didn't come to feel this way because I'm religious, or scientifically trained, and certainly not because I'm a lawyer. I might as well admit it. I don't know how I came to be the way I am.

∼

This morning I thought I heard Mother calling me. I was lying under my covers on the living room floor. I realized that I'd turned off the alarm at five o'clock but hadn't felt like getting up. Now the room was filled with the gray light of breaking day. When I realized where I was I understood that the voice I'd heard resembled Mother's but wasn't really hers. Something in my own brain had called out my name in such a way as to give the impression it was her. Why? I got up and dressed. I felt good. I felt healthy. I thought about how it might be a good day to begin a fast.

At the newsstand on Cahuenga and Hollywood Boulevard I looked through a copy of *Soldier of Fortune*. There was a long article with photographs of the French Foreign Legion and their drop in Shaba Province in Zaire. The story excited me, the adventure of it, the colorful historical connections with other campaigns, other wars. I never buy *Soldier of Fortune*, but I note that I always look at it. I can't deny the way it appeals to me, or the embarrassment I feel because of that appeal.

Began fasting this morning and by early afternoon my head was aching over the right eye. By late afternoon the eyes felt as if a breeze were blowing into them and they couldn't blink. By tonight the head was worse and I went to bed with it. I hate it when the head aches. I tried to not make so much of it this time, to not take it so personally, as if I am I and the head is the head and the head can hurt if it must but I am someplace else.

∼

Walked to the office this morning, aware that the headache was gone, aware of how good I felt. Typed and napped and typed all day. In the afternoon my eyes felt as if there was too much air against them. By five-thirty I was tired of drinking plain water. Tried some diluted consommé. That made me uncomfortably hungry. I could see I was at the edge of ruining the fast. I am unwilling to experience even a moderate level of hunger without taking it very personally. To get away from the refrigerator, I went out walking. It was cold. I wore my sweater and put my jacket on over it. I went straight as an arrow to El Burrito and ate a soft tostada and a tamale and drank a cup of coffee with sugar and milk. Then I went next door to Me and Me and ate a Bavarian creme with chocolate syrup. Then I beat it across the street to Jumbos for six chocolate covered coconut drops. I staggered upstairs to the office to read. I felt awful.

~

Billy Carter has been partying with some Libyans and now he's being quoted as having said: "There's a hell of a lot more Arabians than there is Jews," and that: "the Jewish media tears up the Arab countries all the time, as you well know." What an uproar. Our own Congressman Waxman waxes absolutely hysterical over it, calls Billy Carter an anti-Semite and demands that President Carter publicly disassociate himself from his brother.

While I'm not sure Billy Carter is an anti-Semite, I do know that there are more Arabians than there are Jews, and that the American press has been pro-Zionist for as long as I've been reading. The truth is that for thirty-five years Jewishness has been a taboo subject in this country. It isn't my experience that Jews are better than other people, but the policy of the press and government in this country has been "hands-off" and it still is.

The Libyan government is a dirty little thing and no one with normal sensibilities would want to associate with its representatives. My guess is that Billy Carter's failing of sensibility is not rooted in anti-Semitism but in a cultural and moral shallowness that is not able, and has no interest, in identifying what government, his own or any other, actually does. While he enjoys partying with the Libyans, that doesn't mean he wouldn't like to party as well with Samoza of Nicaragua, or members of the Supreme Soviet, or perhaps Pol Pot. Billy is interested in partying, not in what the partygoers do next day when they're on the job. If that were not the case, Billy Carter would disassociate himself publicly from the President for reasons of conscience.

Restless, out walking the streets, thinking about how I am publishing myself and all the things I can do with my own periodical, I got myself into a state of high excitement, my mind flying from one subject to another—licensing boards (let's get rid of them), the Confederation of Iranian Students (Marxist-revolutionary), Joe Karbo's book on how lazy men can get rich (send for it, send for it), the California Arts Council (get rid of it), Libertarians (they want liberty), socialists (they want to help the needy), the manufacturing cost of a hydrogen bomb (how many people could be fed for how long at the same expense?). Decided to drive to Cal State to see an exhibition of California literary magazines.

At Hughes Market one of the lenses fell out of my eyeglasses. Just dropped out beside the garbage bin. The frames are beyond repair. I bought some white glue and glued the lens back in. It didn't look too good. At Cal State the exhibition of literary mags was closed down. Drove to downtown Los Angeles and went to the library. I felt at loose ends. Went through a couple back issues of *Libertarian Review*. I was still agitated, couldn't concentrate. Leaving the library I spied a large photograph of Nikola Telsa in the foyer. In a letter dated 1892 he wrote: "Is there anything more fascinating than the study of alternating currents?" I looked at Tesla's photograph. I couldn't stop grinning.

Out on the street the air was chilly. Sat in the pickup in the parking lot and ate some old bran muffins and washed them down with club soda. I felt myself calming down. I took a nap. When I woke it was dusk. Ahead, to the West beyond the Union Bank skyscraper, a few clouds were faintly tinted with red. Above, the sky was already dark. The twin black ARCO towers loomed up to the left, the Bonaventure Hotel to the right. The great buildings with their lights turned on were beautiful against the black sky and against the red and gray light on the horizon. The lights of the Bonaventure were small and warm compared to those of the Arco and Union buildings. The exterior elevators of the hotel, a light at the top and bottom of each, glided up and down between the round, black, mirrored towers like silent carousels.

When the horizon grew dark I started the pickup and drove out onto Fifth Street. I turned on the radio. A Tchaikovsky waltz was playing. It was lovely sitting in the warm cab listening to the music. I drove up the Fifth Street entrance onto the Harbor Freeway. Ahead, the traffic was backed up solidly. The lines of red taillights stretched out before me beautifully in the clear black air. Columns of white lights swirled down off the interchange and swept past in the opposite direction. The warmth inside the truck cab, the music, the red and white lights in the blackness, the great expanse of view toward the northeast, the tremendous buildings—all of it together created in me a sense of elevation. I felt moved by the wonderful accomplishments of people everywhere.

~

A photographic display of scenes of the Holocaust has opened in the Martyrs Memorial at the Jewish Community Building on Wilshire Boulevard. Students from three Catholic high schools were the first official non-Jewish visitors. "We would like to see this program expanded throughout Los Angeles," said a spokesman for the American Jewish Committee. The purpose of that program would be to spread the "Holocaust lesson" to all faiths.

What exactly is the "Holocaust lesson" that the American Jewish Committee wants to spread? That it's not right to incinerate living persons? That it's not right to starve people to death, and gas them to death, and shoot them to death. All the kids I know already know that. I think something else is going on. I think that the memory of the Holocaust is used as a technique to unify and bind together the "Jewish people," and as a way of creating for Jews a special place in the consciousness of all of us. It creates "Jewishness" on the one hand, and on the other it creates a "space" for them to be.

The drive Jews feel to "share" the Holocaust with others also performs other functions, among them the tendency to be absorbed with a repression that exists only in memory at the expense of repressions that are living realities today. The difficulty in talking about these matters is that those who lived through the Holocaust are still so seared by the experience that they don't believe others have earned the right to comment on how they feel or what they do with how they feel.

But the Holocaust was then, and here we are now. Why not get on with it? I've never met a fifteen-year-old kid who would think it proper to incinerate his neighbors. But I know plenty who were willing to grow up and incinerate foreigners under the direction of the United States Government, and I know one boy today who's looking forward to joining the Air Force where he will sign a contract with the American government agreeing to incinerate or otherwise destroy any living person that the government chooses in exchange for learning how to fly airplanes.

I maintain a studied indifference to the Holocaust.

I was at my table this morning typing my daily entry into the Journal when I saw a black snake glide across my crumpled sweater onto the table top. I felt something like an electric shock pierce my heart. In the next instant I saw that the snake in reality was my black-bound copy of Jaynes' *The Origin of Consciousness in the Breakdown of the Bicameral Mind*.

~

On the television tonight the newsmen were talking about what a difficult strategic position China is placed in by the fall of Cambodia to the Vietnamese, what with the Russians on her northern border and so on. My suggestion is that the Chinese government try something unique—that it just go about its business. People in government love a crisis just like people in news love one. It's their key to having others thinking they are needed.

A newsman interviewed our Senator Cranston who talked

about the problems of getting the state budget under control in light of Proposition 13. The interview was followed by a commercial for the California State Colleges urging people to register for instruction on how to become a photographer's model. What a wonderful coincidence, I thought. Here's the State claiming the right to extract money from my wages in order to instruct people I don't know on how to pose themselves for photographers. I don't want to bother paying for something like that. It's ridiculous. No wonder there are so many people unwilling to contribute to the state educational system.

~

Worked in Topanga Canyon today. At noon it was raining heavily. I sat in the truck cab eating a sandwich and reading a paper while the rain poured down on the metal roof. A photograph of a feminist named Adrienne Rich showed her to be in her forties with short-cut hair, square hands, a comfortable face. Some way into the interview it was revealed that Rich had been married and had mothered three children.

At that moment I realized that I had adopted the attitude toward Rich that she was a lesbian. There was nothing in the interview itself that suggested that was the case. I'd formed the opinion, somewhat below full consciousness, on the basis of her haircut, her (feminist) point of view, the shape of her hands, the fact that she wore no wedding ring. On the grounds of her being lesbian I had discounted something off everything she had to say. I was taken to observe how abruptly my attitude toward her softened and grew more accepting the moment I discovered she had been married and had borne children.

Then I realized that while she might well have married and borne children, that is no assurance she is not lesbian. I saw what a swamp of confusion I had gotten myself into by attempting to imagine what her motives might be for saying what she was saying rather than simply listening to her carefully. I had been unwilling to be in a simple, straightforward relationship with Rich as she was being interviewed, but had chosen rather to complicate the matter by shoving into it a (prejudiced) projection of my own imagination. I might have been correct in what I was assuming, but even if I had been, how would that help me understand clearly what she was saying? In the end, she said what she said, that's what she gave to me, and she gave it freely, and the least I could have done was to treat her as simply and clearly as she had treated me.

I oftentimes have feelings of hostility toward the opening gambit of feminists. I resent the implication, the repeated observation, that I am somehow responsible for the plight a feminist finds herself in. Men and women are in this thing together and have been from the beginning. That's what I insist on. We have all been in it from the beginning—together. To say that we live in sexist societies is one thing, to say that these societies have been created by men is to suggest an almost unimaginable lack of responsibility on the part of women, an abysmal failure of courage in the face of history, a profound weakness of character, lack of imagination, self-serving repression, and the pathetic cowardice of an entire gender.

My own experience with women doesn't suggest that that's how it is. If men are responsible for what men do, and men are responsible for what women do, what are women responsible for?

Drove the five miles up the mountain to check on the construction site where I still have a little work. The rain fell steadily. I became mesmerized by its movement and by the sound it made. When I drove back down Topanga Canyon toward the sea the rain was falling so heavily and the sky was so dark it seemed like night was falling. Turned north on Pacific Coast Highway toward Malibu to pick up some blueprints. When I got there it was five o'clock. I realized it really would be dark in just a few minutes. I felt confused. It was at least three hours later than I'd thought it was. I tried to recall what I had done between the time I had finished my lunch and the time I'd driven up the mountain to the construction site. I must have lost my awareness that time was passing. I must have sat there under the falling water and its sounds for three, maybe four hours. I thought I had taken only enough time to eat and read the paper. I can remember, very sketchily, observing prehistoric scenes of humans living in dark forests.

~

Drove up the coast this morning to Malibu, the rain falling heavily. Rocks and small boulders fell off the cliff sides and bounded across the highway. Traffic drove around mudslides. An unrecognizable little pile of guts and bones and flesh was near one of the slides. I wouldn't have known it was, or had been, a living thing, except that in one place on the mangled pile was a tuft of red hair that moved softly in the breeze from the car ahead of me. Farther along a coyote lay in the middle lane, seemingly unhurt except for the blood running out of its nostrils and eyes.

Did some business with the county engineer, then tried to get through Malibu Canyon but it was closed by slides up at the tunnels. Back down the coast and up Rambla Pacifico Canyon. At six hundred feet I stopped and looked down through the rain to where the creek was pushing its muddy water in a perfect half-circle out into the gray sea. At fifteen hundred feet two new waterfalls were pouring over flat glistening rock faces. At twenty-four hundred feet, up on the crest of the mountain, the rain fell off. I could see out over the San Fernando Valley to the San Gabriel Mountains and beyond them to the San Bernardinos covered with snow and thick white clouds.

Driving down the grade to the site I saw that some more of Gary Harryman's "For Sale" signs had been broken off and thrown down. Environmentalists. The "Save-Our-Topanga" people, with the emphasis on "Our." The "Save-Our-Topanga" people don't want any more development in Topanga Canyon. They want it to remain like it is because it's so beautiful. They're enraged at the real estate people and developers who are willing to go on selling and developing and changing it. They don't own any of the empty land in Topanga Canyon; they just want to control it and manage it. They're willing to use violence and coercion to do it. They're particularly eager to use the government to control and confiscate the property of others to enforce their own desires. It's never occurred to the Save-Our-Canyon people in the past to put their money where their hearts are and buy into the land, and from what I hear it doesn't occur to them now. They're not willing to organize, collect money, be responsible to get something done on their own. Always the turning to government, the exploitation of the force of the state apparatus to see one's own will enforced.

Worked on the site a couple hours sealing windows, everything wet and cold. The storm broke up, patches of blue appeared among the clouds. I felt disappointed. I love it when it storms in the mountains. Driving down the grade I caught myself looking for signs that the storm was coming back in, wishing for it to build up again, wishing for the thunder to roll, the rain to fall, the clouds to close in on me. I saw how I was trying to hold on to something that was finished, how I wanted to manipulate, direct the future. And how at the very moment I was trying to do both those things that I was out of relationship to what actually was. That I was full of disappointment on the one hand, and longing on the other, and that the possibility of the moment was escaping me. Driving around a turn in the road then I saw the whole basin laid out before me in the pure rain-washed air and the great city spread out between the sea and the mountains all creamy and white and perfect.

~

Bella Abzug was quoting Eleanor Smeal, president of the National Organization of Women: "…we will never trade the rights of one group of women for the rights of any other group…" I think that concept is so admirable I should like to have it applied universally to all persons. That the rights of one man or woman never be forcibly traded—and especially by the courts of this country—to someone else.

~

Samuel Beckett says that "the problem is to find a form that accommodates the mess..." Met Jim Hubler on the street. He's been to Ireland, sports a new beard and moustache, and complains about the degradation of Irish beer by the arrival of American breweries. The conversation turned onto libertarian thought. "I agree with what they're saying," Hubler said. "But will it work?"

"I think it's mostly educational," I said.

"Just talk, eh?" Hubler said. "Just like the socialists. All talk." I felt annoyed. As if my people were being disparaged. But I'm not a libertarian, and I don't intend on becoming one. I've got good reasons. It's the attachment to party that's so destructive in human affairs. Every day's a new day, every issue a new issue. Attachment to party causes thinking to become "historical-minded." That's what obscures every issue. It isn't now what it was then.

I think if one libertarian and one Marxist could join themselves together that between them one decent person might be created, free and compassionate.

Driving down Hollywood Boulevard I see a man on crutches crossing the street. He has a cheesecloth sack over his head and face and tied closed at his throat. He moves confidently through oncoming pedestrians so apparently he can see where he's going. A sign on his chest hangs from a string tied round his neck. There's one word on it. "Corrupt." There's smaller printing beneath that one word that I can't make out. Other pedestrians cannot help but notice the masked man. I try to guess what he is protesting. There are no clues. I think about how I probably could never do what he's doing. That I would never take the chance he is willing to take to appear foolish in public. I think about how the desire to not appear foolish to others is one of my particular weaknesses.

~

Reading Timothy Crouse in *Rolling Stone* on Black Harlem. The mindless, stupid violence. The mindless, stupid way of living. I find myself raging inwardly against the law, against the prohibitions on dope, sex and gambling, against the impotence and servility of the courts. I find myself asking why the local residents don't form vigilante committees, take the law into their own hands. People in Harlem are being murdered because of their supine respect for aimless, incompetent, corrupt city government.

Government is absorbed with law. Government is law. Without law, no Government. Law is always good for government, that's why government has so much of it. Government swills law like a hog gobbles truffles, and it waxes fat on its hog diet. Men who work for Hog Government ought to look carefully at what they force down the gullets of the citizenry, trading off the rights of these for the rights of those. In Harlem, where the going gets tough, government gets out. If the law isn't working somewhere, why not do something else? Law is the government's game. The game for a living person is right relationship.

~

Ali Hassan Salameh, Arafat's top security officer and the man thought responsible for organizing what turned into the Munich massacre of Israeli athletes, has been reported assassinated, blown up in a car filled with high explosives, detonated by remote control. It's not known who killed him, but it's thought the Israelis did it. I hope so. I think that up to this point the Israelis have been altogether too discreet with respect to the PFL. They should have knocked off Arafat years ago. They've killed enough other people, tens of thousands of them, so why they don't get rid of that creep is beyond me, especially when they're perfectly willing to murder Lebanese and Palestinian children with bombs and artillery shrapnel.

I was rather set back at seeing the photograph of Hassan Salameh in the paper. Young, trim, handsome, modishly turned out, an appearance that would have fit him in well at the discos in West Los Angeles. Knowing the sort of acts he's been responsible for I'd expected to see the photograph of a snake. Someone who looks like Arafat perhaps? I'm fascinated by Hassan Salameh's photograph. Perhaps by the thought of what attachment to party can cause a good face to do. Perhaps by my confusion over what significance a good face can possibly have and what it means to have a good face. It shouldn't seem to mean anything, yet we put so much store by it. All of us. The fear and hatred of "monsters" is universal. If one's eye is even slightly out of place, if one's head is rather too small—the size of a grapefruit say—if one should discover a second tongue sprouting from an armpit ever, these little irregularities would cause disgust and even horror.

This evening Irene was helping me transfer some manuscripts from one place to another. "Be careful with that file," I said in Spanish. "It's got two years of my life in it."

"Doesn't weigh much," she said, grinning at me.

˜

Dreamed I was in a bare-fisted boxing match with a man much bigger and stronger than myself. I kept in close, hit him repeatedly in the face. My tactics were good, correct, but my blows were weak. While I fought for all I was worth I sensed that my aggressiveness was going to make my opponent grow angry with me personally, that I was going to get myself into bad trouble, but I couldn't stop attacking.

At daybreak this morning I parked the truck on Las Palmas and was walking toward the side entrance to the building where my office is when I stepped on something crunchy that squirted up inside my pants and all over the calf of my leg. From the crunchy sound I'd heard I supposed I'd stepped on a snail. I started to feel disgusted. Then I saw I'd stepped on a container of strawberry jam, one of those little individual servings packaged in a plastic tub that I get in a café when I order toast. I rolled up my pants leg and wiped off the jam with my handkerchief. I felt relieved that it hadn't been a snail.

When I returned to the house for brunch, Mother had just gotten off the phone with one of her elderly friends who has been stricken with cancer. Mother was giggling. It seems the other night her friend had gone to bed with a heating bag on her stomach and had fallen asleep without turning off the pad. The next morning while she was dressing she noticed three burn marks on her belly and got scared. She telephoned her daughter at work and said: "Oh, honey, please come home as fast as you can. That cancer has eaten right through my stomach."

Mother thought the incident was just too funny. I thought it was funny too, but it made me feel uneasy.

"I think you could understand the ethical muddle of the Western world today, perhaps better than any other way…by making the distinction between the idea of men being equal and that of men being brothers…" (Malcolm Muggeridge discussing Solzhenitsyn in *The Human Life Review*.)

~

Sitting at the kitchen table this evening reading the Jaynes book, *The Origin of Consciousness in the Breakdown of the Bicameral Mind*. He describes how in Ur the rulers were sometimes buried alive along with their retainers. What caught my attention, what made my hair stand on end, was that some of the people were buried crouched over. It seems so horrible to be buried alive, but to have your body manipulated and held in certain positions while being buried in dirt was just too rich for me. I felt the horror at first, then the anger that one person would do that to another, and then I had the curious, repugnant sense that that is what any animal would be willing to do to another animal, that it's only animals that use each other, and that when men do it they are mere animals and that the use of the other is what makes animals of us all and what connects us most strongly to the animal kingdom.

It's all really unclear, but it was something like that. I only got a glimpse of it, the hint of a revelation.

~

Stopped at Topanga Center for brunch. A tanker from Gene's Pumping Service was in the parking lot pumping out a cesspool. The odor sickened me. At the entrance to the café I stopped, considering whether to go some other place. I asked myself why I was at the point of nausea, whether it wasn't merely culturally induced. I suspected it was. I asked myself why I should habitually fall for something like that. I went on inside and ate—lightly. The smell of shit was everywhere.

Afterward drove up the mountain to the Saddlepeak site and marked out the distances on the driveway to be built up with a berm. Driving back down toward the canyon there were icicles a foot long hanging from the sage along the tops of the embankments.

~

On the television tonight a man named Friedman talked about flying saucers and was at the point of convincing me they exist when a commercial break came on. Suddenly I had to void my bladder. I made a run for the bathroom—I didn't want to miss anything the flying saucer man had to say. But in the bathroom I decided I should change into my caftan. Then I thought: No, I don't have time. I'll miss the next segment of the flying saucer program. Then I decided to go ahead with it anyway. If I got organized, if I focused, I could do it. But I wasn't quite sure. I probably could do it, but I was not absolutely completely sure. All this back and forth took only one fleeting moment, but I was aware that time was passing. I made my decision. I would do both at once. I could do it, urinate and change my clothes at the same. Trying it, I pissed all over everything.

~

The rain fell and the wind blew all night. It was very nice. This morning when I woke on the living room floor, I didn't get up right away. After a while I became aware that I was watching a hypnogogic dream. I watched myself enter the reception room of my superior, which was richly furnished, where I was greeted coldly by a tall, dark, middle-aged secretary. Over her left shoulder a vertical, rectangular light flashed on and off. That startled me. I sat up and looked out the front window. Sunshine was flooding the little yard. The asphalt street sparkled with points of light. The needles of the south side of the Japanese pine were tipped with points of light.

By the time I was down on the Boulevard a storm was blowing across the city. Telephoned Jonathan to ask him to breakfast but he said he was going skiing. I felt a trace of envy. When I was sixteen I wasn't in the habit of going off skiing with a bunch of chums. No one in our neighborhood skied. I recalled how my own father had pointed out to me how his boyhood had been so much more strenuous than my own. It was the truth. Mine had been easier than his, and now Jonathan's life is more fortunate than mine had been. I wondered if my father had been envious of me. I supposed he had. I'd never thought about it. I made a mental note to tell Jonathan about what I had thought, how I'd felt, and how it is with the fathers.

End of January 1979

"Libertarians, Aliens, and Malcontents"

(1979)

I'm on the mezzanine of the Bonaventure Hotel in downtown Los Angeles. A Libertarian Party convention is taking place and there are a lot of people milling around. As I walk through the crowd I pause to accept a photocopy of a newspaper article that a man is passing out. The man quickly starts telling me that the stories about six million Jews being killed during World War II are not true.

I'm stunned. It's as if some character from an outer space movie has come down to earth and zapped me with a beam from his ray gun. I've heard about people like the fellow who is confronting me, but I have never actually seen one. He's a small, thin, middle-aged man with a white pointy beard, clear blue eyes, and a ruddy complexion—the picture of health. He speaks fast, in a well-mannered, articulate way, as if he's afraid he might lose me to some other interest.

In the first instant I don't truly grasp what he is saying. Then I understand that he is telling me that the stories about German gas chambers are not true, and that many of the stories I have heard all my life about gas chambers and the Holocaust are meant to gain sympathy for Jews at the expense of Germans. I feel sweat appear on the palms of my hands.

The first thing I want to do is to get away from the man. I'm excruciatingly aware of the many other people around us, that they can hear what he is saying. He has almost certainly proselytized those others before I arrived. The others, then, have already heard what I'm hearing now, and in my imagination each of them has one eye on me, waiting to see what my first move will be, waiting to judge me.

I feel ashamed listening to the man talk about Jews. I feel ashamed holding the photocopied article in my hand. I'm listening, but after the first few words I don't understand anything he's saying. My brain has closed itself down in self-defense. And yet, at the same time, I'm aware that the man sounds knowledgeable, and even sincere.

I feel trapped between what I take to be the man's sincerity and my own embarrassment. I want to get away from him, to hand back his flyer and turn away so that those who are watching can see that I reject, out of hand, everything he is saying. At the same time, because of his honest and open manner, I don't want to cause him to feel ashamed by rejecting him publicly. I have never looked into the history of the Holocaust. I'm ignorant of the whole business. What right do I have to do something that will embarrass another simply because he's saying that he does not believe what I believe? And then the man makes my decision for me. He turns to a new arrival and begins his spiel all over again.

Thankful, and at the same time feeling defiled by the fact that I am still holding the flyer in my hand, I walk toward a large trash can. Even at that moment I know that the problem for me is not so much that I am holding the flyer as that I am being observed by others to be holding it and that they know what it says. I had accepted the flyer innocently, in deference to another's sincerity. The shame I feel, the defilement even, does not come from inside me but from the others, from what I understand to be the standards of my peers.

As I approach the trash can I glance down at the flyer's headline. It's titled "The Problem of the Gas Chambers, or The Rumor of Auschwitz." What rumor, I wonder? What problem? There isn't anything there that rings a bell for me. The author of the article is a certain Professor Robert Faurisson. I've never heard of him. Then I notice that the article had originally appeared in *Le Monde*, the Paris daily. It's confusing. I have no idea at all what the "problem" of the gas chambers might be, or what the "rumor" of Auschwitz refers to. It sounds crazy. And I have never heard of Faurisson. But I am familiar with *Le Monde*. *Le Monde* is one of a handful of world-class newspapers.

What, then, is *Le Monde* doing printing an article critical of the gas chambers, the Holocaust, or whatever? I had intended to drop the flyer into the trashcan on principle. In my circle you just do not read materials that might make Jews feel uncomfortable. It's a principle. At the last moment, the mind caught by the mystery suggested by the association with *Le Monde*, I fold up the flyer and put it in my back pocket.

All day I go about my business at the convention, the flyer in my back pocket. Tonight, alone in my room, like a thief, I take it out and read it, all the while conscious of the fearfulness in my behavior, the lack of self-respect. I am aware that I am reading something that everyone I know, and all the people I like best, will think is bigoted and dirty, and that I am doing it at a time and in a place where they cannot find me out. I have spent years learning to accept the weaknesses in my character and to stand aside from them, yet here I am, forty-nine years old, hiding in my room with a photocopy of a translation of a newspaper article, fearful and ashamed.

Several weeks pass. How can I possibly explain what has happened to me? I have read a newspaper article written by a professor I have never heard of, which has been translated from the French by who knows who, given to me on a hotel mezzanine by a stranger who is probably a crank, forwarding a thesis that is outrageous—and dangerous.

Outrageous because it makes claims that I have never dreamed I would hear made. Dangerous because —why? I don't know. But a sense of tension and danger envelops the thing. I sense immediately into the reading that if I do not reject everything that this Professor Faurisson has written, I will be in danger of suffering great losses, though I cannot say exactly what.

At the same time, I was willing to read the Faurisson article with something of an open mind. Very carefully. Why?

I'll probably never know the why of it. But the source of original publication is given, along with the date, so theoretically it is possible to check the accuracy of the translation. Key statements in the text are sourced. Anyone willing to spend an hour or so in a good library could discover for himself if Faurisson is being honest in those instances. I am impressed by the simplicity of his claims, the objectivity of his tone, dealing as he does with a matter of tremendous significance, from a point of view that is absolutely radical.

My being willing to read the article with an open mind, if I can use that term, might be due simply to my ignorance. I have never read a scholarly work on the Holocaust, and have not paid much attention to the stories of Holocaust "survivors." Maybe it's because there are no heroes in the stories I have heard. Masses of sheep-like people being herded to the slaughter. Helplessness, passivity, pathos. No heroes to create tragedy from catastrophe. Maybe that's it. Ignorance, a disinterest in suffering unredeemed by heroic action, and finally a kind of primary boredom with a wretched story told and told and retold far too often.

That being so, how is it that I remain so stunned after reading Faurisson's thesis? If the stories had not interested me in the first place, why should I be affected so profoundly by the discovery that there are those who do not believe the stories? Doesn't my lack of interest in the Holocaust annul my right to be shocked by the possibility that Faurisson has his finger on something?

The really surprising fact for me is that despite my ignorance of the Holocaust and my realization, on reflection, that I was bored with hearing about it, I have believed everything I have ever heard about it. Not the shadow of a doubt has ever crossed my mind about even one Holocaust story, and over the years I have heard hundreds of them, some over and over and over again. I have believed every eyewitness account about German monstrosity that I have ever heard. It has never occurred to me to compare what such people say about Germans on the one hand, and what they say about Arabs and Palestinians on the other.

Maybe that's why something broke in me that night in my apartment when I read Faurisson's article. Maybe I had believed too rigidly for too long. There has been no room in my mind for doubt. The Germans committed every monstrous crime against the Jews that they have been accused of committing. I have absolutely believed that. My mindset has been that of an absolutist. There was nothing there that would allow me to give a little. I was absolutely rigid in my believing. Intellectually then, psychologically, something had to break. My mind welcomed it—but in my heart I felt the awful anxiety that only great insecurity can create.

I knew that first night that I would have to do something about the break, the suspicion that had entered my mind. I knew that first night but I have done nothing. Week follows week and I do not lift a finger to check out a single assertion made by Faurisson about Auschwitz or the gas chambers. I keep a daily journal, the purpose of which is to make an honest man of me, but there is not a whisper in it about one of the most stunning moments of my life. I'm aware of the evasion. I can't make myself move on it.

Today, three months after the central event of my recent life, the last day of December, I telephone the Central Library in Los Angeles and ask the history department if it has a copy of Arthur Butz's *The Hoax of the Twentieth Century*. I don't think they will have it, but they do. I ask the lady to hold it for me at the desk. I feel a little apprehension, a little excitement. I try to identify the moment that I decided, at last, to make the telephone call, what was behind it in that exact moment after all the other moments that have passed these last three months, but I can't.

As I climb the library steps I feel the body growing heavy and burdened. It's comical. I feel an exhausting load accumulating on my shoulders. I can see the whole thing operating. It's pathetic. I understand that I am afraid that I am going to find out something that I really do not want to find out. I'm not certain that I will find it out, but I sense that I will. I want to find it out, all right—curiosity killed the writer. What I do not want is to experience what I am afraid I will experience if the German gas chamber stories do begin to unravel before my eyes.

A middle-aged woman is at the reference desk. As I approach her to ask for Butz's book I feel the shame rise up inside me. When I ask for the book the lady appears to avert her eyes as she hands it to me. It's as if she recognizes the shameful act that I am about to perform but does not want me to see it in her eyes—that she understands that I want to read a book that no person with decent sensibilities would want to read.

At a reading table I discover that Arthur R. Butz is an associate professor of electrical engineering and computer sciences at Northwestern University. Electrical engineering? Computer sciences? Butz tackles this issue straightaway:

> There will be those who will say that I am not qualified to undertake such a work, and there will even be those who will say that I have no right to publish such things. So be it. If a scholar, regardless of his specialty, perceives that scholarship is acquiescing, from whatever motivation, in a monstrous lie, then it is his duty to expose the lie, whatever his qualifications. It does not matter that he collides with all "established" scholarship in the field, although that is not the case here, for a critical examination of the "holocaust" has been avoided by academic historians in all respects and not merely in the respect it is treated in this book.
>
> That is, while virtually all historians pay some sort of lip service to the lie, when it comes up on books and papers

on other subjects, none has produced an academic study arguing, and presenting the evidence for either the thesis that the exterminations did take place or that they did not take place.

If they did take place then it should be possible to produce a book showing how it started and why, by whom it was organized and the lines of authority in the killing operations, what the technical means were and that those technical means did not have some sort of more mundane interpretation (e.g. crematoria), who were the technicians involved, the numbers of victims from the various lands and the time tables of their executions, presenting the evidence on which these claims are based together with reasons why one should be willing to accept the authenticity of all documents produced at illegal trials. No historians have undertaken anything resembling such a project; only non-historians have undertaken portions.

"With these preliminary remarks," Butz writes, "I invite your study of the hoax of your century." I am struck by the self-confident and dispassionate tone of his voice. Who knows? Maybe he doesn't have a case against Jews. I suppose—I am certain—that that is the question around which so much of my apprehension and evasiveness circles. While I understand, intellectually, that reasonable men can openly question the truth of any historical question, in my heart I have not believed it. In my heart I have believed that only men with an ax to grind against Jews would allow themselves to question the orthodox history of the Holocaust.

I begin looking carefully through *The Hoax*. It takes me less than two hours to decide that something I have believed for 35 years with all my heart and all my mind, that a uniquely monstrous German regime had intentionally murdered six million Jews in an attempt to physically destroy them as a people, has probably not been demonstrated to be true. Less than two hours.

The gigantic, brutal transfers of populations by the Germans and Soviets, the tremendous chaos of the war itself, the fact that the sources of "post-war primary data are private Jewish or Communist sources (exclusively the latter in the all-important cases of Russia and Poland)…"—if that's true, there was no way to know how many Jews were left in Europe in 1945 or to know accurately how they were distributed around the planet.

It is not only that I have believed the "six million" figure with such certainty, but that I have believed so deeply all the implications—including the endless torrent of accusations of unique German monstrosity—that went along with it. I have believed without reservation, but in thirty-five years I have not made the slightest effort to substantiate what my believing has accused others of. I have been willing to live my life believing something that morally condemns an entire people of complicity in horrific criminal behavior without ever bothering to investigate the evidence supporting a single charge made against them. The very least I could have done was to say: "I've heard the stories, I have heard them over and over, but I don't really know if they are true or not."

The only way I can explain such intellectually immature and, finally, contemptible life-long behavior is to admit, simply, that it has been easy to believe what everyone else believes and difficult not to. The believing takes no energy, no courage, no common sense. Trying to find out the truth about such terrible accusations against others would have taken all that and more. Merely standing aside from opinion and not participating in that of others—that would have taken energy, too. In my laziness I had allowed myself to be swamped with belief.

I go to the desk and ask the librarian to help me run down some comment on Butz's *Hoax*. She takes a run at it but can't turn up anything. I return to the text. I peruse the acknowledgements, the final remarks. I go over the appendices, notes, references, the index. *Hoax* is extensively documented, the established history of the Holocaust is confronted openly, and discounted in scores of places. And yet, so far as I can find out by consulting the standard indices and guides, not one periodical, not one newspaper, not one historian, not a single journalist, critic, or scholar has published one word to either confirm or deny one statement, one shred of the evidence presented by Butz to the effect that the poison gas chamber stories are falsehoods and even deliberate lies.

The mind is racing and shooting around like crazy. I walk through the library from one department to another, upstairs and down. Something is wrong with the gas chamber stories. Something is wrong with the story of the six million and what is wrong is being covered up. Something is wrong with the silence that has buried Butz's book. Something is wrong in the academic community, and not only among the historians. Something tremendous is going on, or not going on as it were, and the ramifications could prove to be endless. There is an immense amount of work to do. The air in the library is thick with complication. I feel as if I'm swimming in a sea of suppression, censorship, and evasion.

Out on the street the crisp, late afternoon air is electric. Men, and men and women, speak to one another with an animation that is extraordinary. They stand on street corners laughing and making plans. I remember that this is New Year's Eve. While I have not spoken the words, while I do not know precisely what the words are, I understand that a resolution has formed inside me that will change my life from this moment on.

"Love at the Nirvana Arms"

(1979)

The alarm goes off at four-thirty in the morning and when I get up to turn it off I see it's raining so I mash a couple cockroaches and go back to bed to think things over. The next thing I know it's eight o'clock and too late to kick up the typewriter. So I dress and walk through a light rain over to Pinehurst Road and up the canyon to Mother's little apartment to pick up the truck.

When I get there I decide to go in the house and make some coffee. In the kitchen the glass coffee pot is full of water and ready to go so I boil the water and make a cup of instant. It's awful. It's horrible. I sniff the milk carton, the jar of instant, the saccharine. Everything is okay. I make another cup. This time the milk curdles when I pour it in the hot water. I sniff the milk again. It's fine. I'm standing there at the stove wondering what to do next when Mother wheels her chair in from her bedroom. I tell her about the coffee.

"Did you use the water in the glass coffee pot?"

"Yes, I did."

"That pot was full of vinegar, you idiot. I was cleaning the stains out of it."

I explained how I had carefully inspected each of the ingredients that had gone into the water but hadn't checked the water itself. I had thought I was being thorough. In reality I had gone everywhere but to the heart of the matter. The glass pot looked clean. The water was crystal clear. I saw it with my own eyes. I was an eyewitness for Christ's sake. How could I have been so wrong? In her wheelchair Mother is laughing, her hands to her face.

"Oh, Bradley," she says, "you're so dumb. I just don't understand how you can be so dumb."

I drive over to Jenny's to get the company mail. Jenny is there at the dining room table going through her purse. She looks terrific. It's odd being together in the house with her again yet being a world apart and knowing that's the way it will be the rest of our lives. I talk about how we'll finish the last house in a couple months and how I will be out of a job again. I can feel the anxiety. Jenny says maybe we'll all do something together right here in Hollywood. That's good news.

Now I start telling her about *The Hoax of the Twentieth Century*. It's been in the back of my mind that I have to tell her and a few minutes ago when I first saw her standing there, I think that's what started the anxiety. I speak very carefully. Her family on both sides lost a lot of relatives in the Holocaust. Jenny and Sol both grew up on the Holocaust story. One night in Westwood Sol and Betty and Jenny and I watched a movie called *The Garden of the Finzi-Continis*. It was about a family of cultured Italian Jews, including an elegant daughter about Jenny's age, who were rounded up and sent off to the Germans to who knows what. By the end of the film Jenny was sobbing uncontrollably. Her body was actually convulsing. It was unnerving.

This morning the first thing she says is: "Well, Bradley, where did all those people go?" She's smiling very broadly like she does when she's challenging someone and knows that the other person knows he's being challenged. I say that nobody's really looked for them yet and maybe there aren't nearly so many missing as we've been told. I say: "The Germans said they put them in the Soviet

Union. Who knows? The real issue is the gas chambers. It's an easier approach to the problem. You don't have to run down six million people one by one. The gas chambers were either there or they weren't. I think Butz might be right. He says they weren't there."

She asks if I've been to the Simon Wiesenthal Center to ask the scholars in residence there what they think about Butz's book.

I say no, I haven't. We speak very quietly and carefully, standing across the dining room table from each other and in the end she says: "Well, Bradley, it sounds fascinating. It really does. I don't know how it's going to add up. It's going to make trouble for you, that's for sure. But it's fascinating. I have to say that."

"I was worried about telling you."

"Were you, Bradley?"

"Yes."

"Wait until you tell Sol."

"I guess so."

"Sol won't feel the same way I do." She's smiling very broadly, in her challenging way.

"What worries me is that I'm afraid I'm going to be reviled."

"You will be, Bradley. You're going to be associated in everybody's mind with all the worst kind of people. It's all set up. It's all set up. It's right there waiting for you."

"I really look forward to this."

"It makes me think you've found a new way to be on the outside looking in."

I drive over to Sawtell Boulevard to pick up a laborer. The rain falls steadily. People are driving with their headlights on. The lights are brilliant in the rain-washed air. The traffic lights, especially the greens, are beautiful against the dark gray sky. At the Nu-Way Chile Dog on the corner of Pico I buy a couple papers and a coffee to go. Outside, raindrops pop into the uncovered coffee. The designs they make in the top of the jumping coffee are attractive and interesting. Out past Malibu at the job site in

Las Virgenes Canyon the rain is very heavy. The slopes of the hills facing west are green while the those facing east are still brown and barren. At one place a lone red and white heifer grazes on a green hillside. At noon it's still raining so I drive the laborer back into town and drop him off.

This morning at the typewriter I watch a cockroach climb up the side of my cup and fall over into the coffee. It floats there quietly, thinking things over. The roaches were here when I moved in and no matter how many I mash I can't get rid of them. One time they just got up and left. It was like they had gotten marching orders from Central Command. Weeks passed and I didn't see a cockroach. I started thinking about them, wondering where they were, what they were doing. Why had they left in the first place? I stopped changing the traps and putting the poison around, then one night in July I saw something black floating in half a glass of milk on my nightstand. Even in the dark I knew what it was—they never learn—and the next morning there they were in the kitchen sink and on the drain board.

At the Nirvana Arms the most orderly and circumspect tenants are the middle-aged men. I guess I'm a middle-aged man and that may have something to do with my judgment. The worst tenants are the young whites who dress like punks and pretend they're living dangerously. They dope, they drink, and if they forget their keys they bust through the front door of the building. But the building is aswarm with Mexicans. They live five or six to a room and lie about it to the manager. They don't take out their garbage, they have beer busts on the fire escape and throw their bottles and cans on the lawns below. They sit at the curbing with their car radios blaring at midnight. Sometimes a dozen Mexicans will sit in the hallway outside my door drinking beer and horsing around. I don't like it when I'm typing so I put on my pants and go out and tell them to knock it off. They're very cooperative. The first time I did it I thought it might be the last my mother saw of her son, but when I explained the situation to them in Spanish they apologized and went somewhere else. I was kind of touched.

There used to be a few elderly white men living in the building but now they're gone. One died in his sleep, and the story is one put his head in his kitchen oven. A third used to have an apartment near the front entrance. One afternoon when I walked by his door it was open. The old man was sitting on the edge of his wall bed in his shorts looking around vacantly. His gray hair was uncombed and the room was a mess. As the story came out, the shower in the apartment above him had overflowed and the water had come through the old man's ceiling. And while I didn't know it that afternoon, his wife had died the day before. She'd been in a nursing home for years and every day after lunch the old man would dress in coat and tie and walk over to pass the afternoon with her. That day, when I saw him sitting there on the edge of his bed in his shorts, I thought he was being patient, waiting for the plumber. But what he was really doing was thinking about life. That night he walked over to Hollywood Boulevard, rented a room on the twelfth floor of the Roosevelt Hotel, and jumped out the window.

Saturday morning James calls to say it's time for Rose and him to take me out for our annual breakfast. They always take me to a natural foods restaurant, so I feel safe with them. This time we go to the Old World on Sunset Boulevard. James parks his Roto-Rooter plumber's truck around back near Old World's garbage bins. The place smells like a Calcutta sewer. James tells me that he and Rose are moving to Medford, Oregon. Medford is considered by survivalists as one of the better places to be when the catastrophes begin. Prevailing winds will keep it clear of fallout after the nuclear exchange. The population density is low and there's a lot of farmland so when plague and starvation break out in the great urban centers, Medford will have plenty of food and water. The people are mostly white so the coming race wars won't affect the community.

"It sounds ideal," I say. "It's beautiful up there too. Jenny and I were in Medford one time. We were all through that country a few years ago."

"Well, Bright-Eyes," James says, "why don't you come up with us. You can be a starving writer in Medford easier than you can in that tenement you live in here."

"If Mother would do the right thing, I could go with you."

"What do you mean, if she'd do the right thing?"

Rose looks at me in a peculiar way. "I like your mother," she says.

"I like the sensible way I live now," I say. "I live in a nice old brick building that's going to collapse in the next real earthquake. I eat processed food and food that's packaged in cancer producing containers. The city is surrounded by oil fields, petroleum processing plants, aircraft factories and nuclear and rocketry research centers so that when the commies make their move me and my neighbors will be incinerated. The air I breathe is filthy, the streets are filled with foreigners who resent the original population, the blacks strong-arm you and shoot you and likely as not I'll step in a clump of dog shit before the day is out. You want me to move to Medford where everything is clean and people are white and treat one another decently? I don't know, James. I'll have to think about it. I may be too depressed to live in a place like Medford."

This morning I'm driving up the coast toward Malibu with two laborers. I'm thinking about how I'm going to have to write something about the Holocaust. I feel kind of disgusted with myself and at the same time I see how rare and beautiful the morning is. Palm trees are outlined darkly against a Hiroshige sea, soft mists hide the horizon, a wonderful fresh air washes in through the open windows over my arms and face. Then thought recalls the summer morning when I was a child watching my father and two other men cut down the two great old palm trees in our front yard. A rope is tied high up on the trunk of one palm and Father is out on the street pulling on it while the two other men chop away. A pain touches my heart as I watch my father pulling and directing everything. I wonder about it. It's not a lot of pain but what purpose does it serve?

In that instant thought recalls an image I had seen on television showing Mother Teresa comforting some old bag of bones in her death hostel in Calcutta. The man has a wonderfully sweet smile on his face as he gazes up at the wizened little nun. She'd picked him up off the pavement someplace where he was about to give it up to starvation and age. He has no family, no friends, no money, no food, and no history. No history! No one he knows even knows where he is. At any moment he'll disappear forever. As I drive up the coast toward Malibu I watch how the gazes of the two old strangers pour into each other's eyes and I understand that in that one moment of the dying man's attentive and beatific smile there is no thought and no imagination so there is no desire and no loss and it's all quite all right.

North of the Rambla Pacifica turn-off a young man stands at the side of the highway thumbing a ride. Bare-chested, his shirt in one hand and a can of soda pop in the other. He's saying hello to a woman walking past. The boy has big pimples on his chest and a scraggly beard. He's a homely kid but he's laughing and being easy on the lady too and going somewhere in the cool morning air and during the instant of my glance he looks like he doesn't have a care in the world.

And thought, never stopping, asks: Why are you so distraught over having to write about the Holocaust? What do you care what people say about you? What does it matter that you are not a historian? You're a man. A citizen. Why do you go over and over it? All the accusations that are going to be made, the misunderstandings that you will never be able to clear up. The way you are going to be humiliated. Why?

And thought says: If you can't do it with a light heart, stay out of it.

This evening on the television I watch *Meetings with Remarkable Men*, after the book by Gurdjieff. An empty film.

Sometimes I wonder why I go on living in the Nirvana Arms. I suppose I kind of like it here. It's a nice old building that's suffering socioeconomic problems like the rest of Hollywood. The room is large and has ten-foot ceilings. There used to be a wall bed but that's gone. The kitchen and breakfast nook have their own hall entrance. There are chutes in the hallway to shoot your garbage down to the basement but they're sealed up now. In 1929 this was a classy building just off Hollywood Boulevard behind the Grauman's Chinese Theatre. The Nirvana Arms was designed in the Grauman's architectural style, a school that began there and ended here.

If I didn't live here where would I live? I have no desire to live in any particular place. I don't want to improve my lot in life. I want to have enough time to do the typing and enough money to pay the rent and that seems to be about it. I still need friends and an excuse to get drunk once in a while and plenty of talk and I need a woman around. If I didn't have to work to pay the rent, that would be nice. The desire to make money and buy things is something that's missing from my character. My inclination about money is to make do. That's my inclination about almost everything. No matter how low my luck sinks, there's always a way to make do. If I came into a fortune today my life would remain largely the same. I would still have to struggle with the issue of right relationship. There would still be the problem of when to cooperate with the State and when not to. I would still feel devastated by what I found out about the Holocaust and I still wouldn't understand why. How would the money be able to change any of that? I would still want to get up at three or four in the morning and go to the typewriter and commit myself to my life's work.

After living half a century I understand that if I'm going to get to the bottom of my life with others, and to the bottom of the authoritarian ideal, I'm going to have to depend on myself. I can't count on the books taking me there. I can't count on the professors or the other intellectuals or their libraries either, no matter how much information they're choked up with. I started reading books forty years ago and here I am anyway, alone in the Nirvana Arms and feeling pretty much at home.

The variousness of the book of daily life is wondrous beyond everything we can imagine. I remember Huxley pointing out that the productions of earth are far more various and intricate than what human imagination can produce, no matter how we stimulate it, because mind is a fragment of the whole and can only be fractionally productive compared to the whole. Huxley probably explained it some other way.

When Nietzsche writes that the surface of life is more significant than what lies beneath it he's saying something similar. Maybe he and Huxley got their ideas from books, but maybe they didn't. Readers make up only a tiny percentage of those who reside on the planet. Am I supposed to write off the couple billion of us who can't read or don't want to? I haven't forgotten that Stalin could read, along with all the rest of that bunch. How are the poor and illiterate to judge what's true and false, right, wrong and good and bad? I spend sixty or seventy hours a week working in the mountains behind Malibu and in Topanga Canyon and getting there and back, and still have the same obligation as the philosopher to support the truth and dismiss what's false, according to my own best light. At the end, working men have the same responsibilities as the professors and the intellectuals. We live in a real world, not an academic one. I'm obligated to develop a sense of what's right and good and what isn't. I'm not going to leave the responsibility for understanding those things to men who have the leisure to read books.

Men who read believe it's impossible that men who can't or don't are able to lead responsible and honorable lives in a modern world. In one of Castaneda's books he and Don Juan are in a café someplace in Mexico and a couple of street kids are eating the garbage from the plates of customers who have left. Castaneda wonders how the two scavengers will be able to make a life for themselves. Don Juan comments that all those he has ever known who became true warriors were once like those two boys, hopeless and abandoned. Maybe that's the best place to start.

Tyrants today use books and intellectuals as weapons against the poor just like tyrants before them used priests and their voices from heaven. Every horror committed by the State against the people has been done in the name of books by book-reading despots or despots who claim to have privileged information given to them by their book-reading experts and advisors. *The Communist Manifesto*, *Mein Kampf*, the Constitution of the United States, the New Testament, the Old Testament, the Koran, Mao's *Little Red Book*—those are only a few of the writings beloved by the book-reading tyrants of our age and by the professors who look down their noses at the illiterate and uninformed.

Uninformed about what?

Thousands of books are published every week in a hundred languages I can't read. Maybe the answer to my life was published recently in a book written in Swahili. A real misfortune for me, or don't you think so? On the other hand, if the answer is in books published in English only then maybe we should strike off the rest of the race. Life is full of small misfortunes. I don't see how the answer can be put in a book. You get pleasure and power from books. That's why the West is such a miracle in history. But understanding depends on something else. Something to one side of intellect and power.

In one of his books on Zen, Blythe writes that all questioning is a way to avoid the answer, which we already know. That we already understand the answer but wish we didn't. "Every man knows he must love his enemies, and sell all he has and give to the poor, but he doesn't wish to know it so he asks questions." Blythe is talking about the spiritual life but what am I talking about? When the old Calcutta man and Mother Teresa lose themselves in each other's gaze at the moment of death they don't have much use for their library cards. They see the situation for what it is. They're paying attention. In that moment they have no need for dialect or the search for motive. At the moment of crisis, attention is everything.

Every moment is crisis.

How do men who can't read books, or who don't want to—how do such men lead honorable, generous and attentive lives? Isn't that really the big question for the race? It's said that Jesus said the poor will inherit the Earth. As a class, "the poor" doesn't read and never has.

The alarm rings at three-thirty. I get up to turn it off, then lay back on the bed again. I feel all right, I just don't want to kick up the typewriter yet. I can hear some men arguing down on the street but it doesn't sound very interesting so I don't pay any attention. Then I hear a gunshot. That's interesting. I sit up and draw back the bottom corner of the window drape. Three men are in a knot, struggling in the middle of the street. Then a young Hispanic breaks away and races toward the front entrance of the Nirvana Arms.

The two other men are still wrestling. There's another gunshot and I watch a Mexican throw a big black guy down on the pavement, turn, and with measured steps strut slowly back toward the Nirvana. The black guy lies across the white line on his back with his arms stretched out over his head. The shooter, older than the one who had run away, struts slowly up the walk and disappears slowly into the lobby below. He walks in a way that says the guy deserved it and I gave it to him and what are you going to do about it? Just before he disappears in the lobby below he looks up and our eyes meet. I've made a mistake.

I tiptoe to the telephone and dial the operator and say I want to report a murder.

"I can't hear you," the operator says.

"I want to report a murder."

"Well, where are you? Where are you?"

"Hollywood."

The police come on the line quickly. They want to know my name and address and apartment number and after a few minutes I watch a squad car pull up to the body, then four more squad cars arrive. The body begins to moan. I call the police back and say there are about ten officers standing around in the middle of the street while the shooters are inside the Nirvana Arms, where I am, and why don't a few of the officers come on in and have a look around?

I imagine how the shooter and his friend must be waiting until the police leave to come up here and have a chat with me because they know I know who they are. I think about all the times I've thought about buying a gun and haven't done it. I think about all the times I've run the Mexicans out of the hallway and off the fire escape. The largest weapon I have in the apartment is a kitchen paring knife. I feel like a big defenseless naked turkey. I put my pants on and look around for my shoes.

There isn't enough order in Hollywood so people say there should be more law. Law doesn't create order. What creates order is guns and love. If I had a gun for example maybe I'd go downstairs and look for the shooters. Maybe they didn't have a good reason to shoot the black guy and need to be remonstrated with. If everybody had guns everybody would have more respect for everybody else. The big issue is love but who can come up with it at a time like this? Guns are easy, so you get guns or you pay others to carry guns in your name. Everybody understands how that works. Everybody. You don't have to be a scholar. If someone makes trouble for you and you can't, if you absolutely cannot love him, you shoot him. That's the rule. We're only human. We know we're almost never going to love. We know that's something that's way out there. We've heard about love, sure, but we understand it's nearly always beyond us.

"When Cows Bark"

(1981)

The other night I dreamed about the number eighteen. At first there was only the number, then there was the understanding that I had eighteen minutes left to live. Eighteen minutes to prepare myself to die properly, with a little style. I knew that wasn't enough time, not for me. Then I realized it wasn't minutes, that I had eighteen hours to make the proper arrangements. But I knew I wouldn't be able to do it right in eighteen hours either because I'm just not ready, and when I woke up the body was swamped with fear.

The next day after work I parked the pickup in Mother's drive and went inside to have a chat and pick up my wash. In her front room she was in the wheelchair at the card table eating off the tray Alicia had prepared. The front of her dress was stained from breakfast and lunch. Her left hand was making involuntary movements from side to side. Sometimes she would press it down on her thigh, sometimes she would hold it with the other hand.

"Well," she said, "what did you get done today?"

"I worked on the Topanga Canyon job," I said. "It went pretty well."

"Are you going to have any money this week? We need a grocery marketing done around here."

"I'll be able to do a marketing. No sweat. Then I may take a little trip. I feel like I need a little adventure."

"What are you talking about?" Mother said. "Your adventuring days are over. Who do you know who's fifty years old and talks about having a little adventure?"

"You think it's all over with me, eh?"

"It's been all over with you for years." She looked at me sideways and laughed. There was food in her mouth. "You're so absent-minded you just haven't noticed. Anyway, don't talk to me about having a little adventure. Just do the marketing. Make yourself useful around here."

"All right, Ma."

"A little adventure. If you only knew how asinine that sounds."

In the dining room the paper bag was on the sewing machine with my wash that Alicia had folded neatly inside. There was some mail and I put that in the bag, said goodbye, locked the front door, turned off the porch light and walked down the hill toward my room.

I was taking off my boots when the telephone made the special ring. It was Jenny. After Pamela, Jenny had filled up my life. Not right away but after a while. We were together almost ten years. We had raised her two kids. It had been over for a year or so. That night we chatted about this and that and then she said, "Bradley, you know how Princess has all those allergies? The way she scratches and chews at herself all the time?"

"Yes."

"I'm afraid she just feels miserable all the time."

"She's so insouciant it's hard to tell how she really feels. But if I was a dog and I had to spend all my time scraping my belly across the asphalt in the alley I don't think I'd feel real good about my life."

"It's hard for me to say it," Jenny said, "but maybe it's time for Princess to go to dog heaven."

"I think you're right. She'll like it up there too."

"I don't feel comfortable saying it."

"I think her time has come. One day we're all going to have the same problem. She's no good the way she is and you're never going to be able to fix her."

"She's a good barker," Jenny said. "It's nice to know she's here at night, now that I'm alone."

"Well, she is a good barker. She's getting good at the biting too. The other day when I went over there to meet the washing machine repairman she'd already bitten him twice."

"Really?"

"Not that he minded all that much. He's Mexican, you know."

"Don't try to be outrageous, Bradley."

"All right."

"I'm really upset about this."

"All right."

"The problem for me is, I feel guilty about taking her to the pound."

"That's only cultural you know. It's not real. The Vietnamese, they have a different culture, so they eat the dogs. Have you noticed how few dogs are running loose in Hollywood these days and how sleek the Vietnamese look?"

"Is that true?"

"When you get Princess to the pound, pretend she's something to eat, something you feel you have the moral right to kill. Pretend she's a cow. You've always been fond of cows and you eat them too. If you pretend she's a cow you'll be able to off her and not have any real feelings about it."

"I see," Jenny said.

"Or you could give her to a Vietnamese child and make the kid promise he won't eat her. The kid will promise you. The Vietnamese are so polite they'll promise you anything and after he eats her you can say he promised and it isn't your fault."

Jenny said, "I feel like I need a dog that barks."

"Listen, I think I've got it. Take your cow to the pound and while you're there pick up a barking dog. If you get it home and it doesn't bark good you can take it back and trade it for one that works. This is something you don't want to be sentimental about."

"I feel bad just thinking about it. Bradley, will you take her to the pound for me?"

"Sure I will."

"Scratch that. This is something I should do for myself."

"All right. Here's the way to handle it. When you take one in, see it for the cow it is. When you take one out see it for the dog it is."

"Bradley, why are you talking so crazy?"

"The other way is to see the dog you take in to the pound as having reached the end of its suffering, while the dog you take out will discover an unexpected happiness living at your feet. That way you'll increase the level of dog happiness on Earth, on balance. In Los Angeles anyhow."

"All right, Bradley."

"Pretty good thinking, eh?"

"Thanks for your help, Brad."

"Sure. When you need help, it's always good policy to call a writer. Writers have answers for everything."

Jenny said: "Bye, Brad. It's been a pleasure." She said the words with such an effusion of charm that they almost knocked me over.

I undressed, got in the tub and pulled the shower curtain across it. It hadn't been a real conversation. Every real conversation I have with Jenny now is something of a tragedy. I stood under the shower and in my imagination I said, "Jenny, that's the difference between how a humane liberal talks and the way your typical Holocaust revisionist bigot talks. There's just no comparison."

I laughed a little thinking about it.

When the telephone made its special ring again it was Marrissa.

"Oh," she said, "I've been trying to get you for days. Where have you been? I call and call and you're never there."

"When I'm typing I pull the plug on the telephone and the rest of the time I'm working."

"But why haven't you called me? Do you know I'm leaving for school in a few days? I've been home all summer and you've hardly seen me."

"I thought you still had a couple weeks."

"Bradley, I'm leaving Wednesday night. I'm going to New York for a week, then I start school."

"I didn't think about you for a couple weeks, then just yesterday I made a note to call you."

"You didn't think about me for two weeks? You asshole."

Her voice turned away from the telephone. "Mommy," I heard her say, "Bradley says he didn't think about me for two whole weeks."

I heard Jenny's voice say, "Marrissa, I don't want you to talk to Bradley that way."

"Mommy says I shouldn't call you asshole."

"Marrissa," I heard Jenny say, "You're not being funny."

"I've only got until Tuesday," Marrissa said. "Then you won't be able to see me for months, maybe a whole year."

"I thought you had until Wednesday."

"I'm leaving Wednesday. Don't you understand? You have to see me before then."

"All right, kid. Name the hour."

"Tuesday morning. We can drive to the beach. I know a neat place to have breakfast. It's really nice at the beach in the mornings. You'll like it."

"Okay. Sold."

"You won't forget me, will you, Asshole?"

"Now, Marrissa," I heard Jenny say. "I mean it."

"I won't forget you."

"Call me before Tuesday."

"I'll call you."

"Don't forget."

"I won't."

"Psst."

"Yes?"

She was whispering and giggling. "Goodbye, Asshole."

"Now you just stop that," I heard Jenny say.

When I hung up the receiver there were tears in my eyes.

Monday afternoon I was in from the Canyon early when Marrissa called. She said, "Mommy wants us to take Princess to the pound."

"Us?"

"It's your responsibility. You're the one who brought her home in the first place."

"That was eight or nine years ago. Don't you ever forgive anyone anything?"

"Come on, Brad. I don't want to do it by myself. Please?"

I showered, walked to Mother's, got the pickup, drove over to Jenny's for Marrissa and Princess, and then headed across the Cahuenga pass toward the Valley.

Marrissa said, "I'm not sure if what we're doing is moral."

"We're only going to kill an animal. What could be more commonplace?"

"But I don't know if it's really right or not."

"I didn't know you were having those kinds of problems. Are you starting to think about things? Is that what those private schools do to girls?"

Marrissa said, "I've thought about things all my life."

"Yeah, I guess you have. When I was your age I didn't think about anything. One experiment you can make right now is in your imagination visualize all the animals that are being slaughtered in this city at this moment. So we can eat them. Thousands of cows, hogs, sheep, lambs, chickens, turkeys, ducks, quail. Animals we won't even be able to imagine on short notice. That's what Princess is, another little animal with scabby skin that can't imagine anything. Get rid of her."

"Those other animals, it doesn't feel the same as killing a dog."

"You've just put your finger on one primary philosophical methodology. Identify your feeling accurately, reflect on it, prepare to suffer a little anguish, and you won't go astray in your thinking. You may go astray in your ethics class but you won't go very far astray in your real life. Killing animals is similar to aborting fetuses. It's disgusting but it doesn't seem to matter much morally."

"I'd have an abortion if it was necessary."

"My little girl."

"I would."

"Well, it's the Christians who are transfixed by the horror of abortion. They think they've read someplace that God doesn't like it. If I were God there'd be a lot of things down here I wouldn't like. That's the difference between God and people. People are sensitive and caring. God just goes along doing whatever He wants, no matter how much disaster He trails out behind Him. I've never understood why people have such respect for God. They talk about God's love, but what they really respect is His power. What's power without sensibility? God's like a big animal. He does anything He wants because there's nobody to stop Him. It's the Christians who talk up morality all the time. God takes things as they come."

"Mommy says you're the most moral person she knows."

"Your mother has always been on my side." I felt a little uncomfortable. I fell silent. Marrissa was silent too, stroking Princess absentmindedly while the dog gazed up at her adoringly. I took the Sherman Way exit and headed west toward the pound.

"Bradley, are you going to do another issue of your paper?"

"I think so."

"Why do you want to publish something that makes people feel bad?"

"Did you feel bad about something you read in the paper?"

"I don't think of myself being Jewish. I just don't have those feelings at all. I feel like everybody else. Like an American."

"Did your mother feel bad about something I wrote?"

"I think she struggled with it. Mommy definitely feels Jewish."

"I feel an obligation to publish it. There's a lot of lying going on about the gas chamber stories. Straight out lying. I stumbled onto it. A lot of stuff is being covered up that shouldn't be covered up. People are being accused of crimes they didn't commit. I don't like it. I'm going to write about it and I'm going to go on publishing what I write. I don't know how far the lying goes but I think it goes right to the top. I don't know how important any of it is but I'm going to go straight ahead with it. I'm doing the right thing, within the context of my life."

"If you're not sure it's important, why would you go on writing things that hurt people's feelings?"

"Marrissa, do you mean why would I write things that might hurt Jewish feelings?"

"That's what you do, isn't it?"

"What if your mother was German rather than Jewish, and you were told all your life that she had done horrible things when she was young, then you discovered that some of the things you had been told were false but people went on saying them anyhow?"

Marrissa didn't say anything.

"What if you were told all your life that your German father had been a monster when he was young? What if it had been pounded into you year after year after year and then one day you found out that one, just one of the monstrous acts you had been taught to believe he had committed, he hadn't committed? You found out by accident, because you had always been a true believer in your father's monstrosity and guilt, but you found out? Do you think you'd let it slide?"

"I've never thought about how Germans feel."

"Think about it now. Put yourself in the place of a German girl. How would you feel?"

"I still think I wouldn't write something that made others feel bad."

"That's not fair, Marrissa. After all the war hate against the Germans you still see in the movies, on the television, that you read in the papers and in books and magazines. Has there ever been anything to compare with it? Have you ever heard of any society in history so obsessed with making a whole people feel bad?"

"I've never thought about Germans one way or the other."

"I can understand that. One of the things a writer does is look at the others in the same light that he uses to see himself. That's one of the things that separate artists from others. It's natural for a Jewish kid to grow up trusting Jews and being suspicious of Germans. When you get older the time comes to start seeing through the implications of all that. If you want to."

"I don't think I like what you're doing," Marrissa said. "I can't prove it's wrong, but I don't think I like it."

"Uh huh."

"Everybody says you're wrong about the Holocaust. Everybody."

"Not the Holocaust, Marrissa. The gas chambers. I am absolutely not wrong about the gas chambers because I'm only asking questions about them. I'm asking, is this piece of information about the gas chambers accurate? This particular gas chamber story, does it make sense? Is there any real evidence to support it, or am I supposed to take somebody's word for it? I'm told it's bad taste to ask questions about the gas chambers. I don't think so. Not bad taste, not good taste. Not moral, not immoral. I ask questions about the gas chambers to find out what's going on there. I'm not sneaking around about it either. You should look into your reasons for not liking it that I'm asking these particular questions when you've never thought that it was wrong to ask any of the other questions that I've gone around asking. Then you should look into the reasons your professors don't like it either. If you do, you'll get a whiff of what obsessive conformity and sniveling evasion are all about. You'll see professorial bowing and scraping before received opinion that'll turn your stomach. You'll discover…"

"Why are you getting mad?"

"That's not mad. That's intensity."

"I just don't know what to think," Marrissa said. "I don't have the information to say that you're wrong, or that you're right either."

"I understand that."

"I have this gut feeling though."

"Well, what do you think, Kid? Right or wrong?"

"Wrong, Asshole." She put one hand to her mouth and laughed until tears came from her eyes.

When I turned into the parking lot at the pound Marrissa said she didn't want to go right in. We walked along Sherman Way leading Princess with a piece of clothesline.

I said, "Your mother taught me something about dogs I've never forgotten. Now I'm going to pass it on to you, her only daughter."

"Thanks, Brad."

"One day in the kitchen Princess was pleading with Jenny to pet her, to show her a little attention, so Jenny went along with it. Petting dogs isn't her strong suit. But she petted Princess and looked into her eyes for a long moment. Then she said, 'When you look into a dog's eyes it's always the same. You just know there's nothing there.'"

"That's what she taught you about dogs?"

"That's it."

"It doesn't make me feel any better."

"That's not the point to understanding, to make you feel better. The purpose of understanding is understanding."

"Let's talk about something else," Marrissa said. "Will you go shopping with me after the pound?"

"After we have your dog killed? Sure. We'll kill the dog first, then we'll look around for something to buy."

"Thanks, Brad."

"Sure."

We walked along silently for a while. The afternoon traffic was heavy and the air was full of its exhaust. Princess took an interest in everything in her quick neurotic way.

"Want to hear a dream I had? All right? You'll love this one. I dreamed a decision had been made that I was to be burned at the stake. I think Mother was in on it. I accepted the decision as a matter of course. It wasn't something that was presented to me for my consideration. A decision had been made. The post was already in the ground, the wood was piled up around it and there was some way to light the fire. I climbed up on the wood and stood with my face to the post. There wasn't anyone there to tie me up or see to it that I didn't run away. It was the honor system. At first I did pretty well. The fire came up over my shoulders. It seared the left side of my face until the skin glistened, but when the smoke got too thick I turned my head to the side to get a little fresh air. I'd get a little air to the left, then I'd turn and get a little to the right. It was as if I were willing to be cooperative, to carry out the decision that had been made for me, but I didn't have enough character to see it through. I didn't have quite enough of the right stuff. Then the wood was all used up. The flames died out, the smoke drifted off, and there I was. I'd failed to finish what I'd started. But I still felt the obligation to carry it through, and that's when I woke up. I was awake but I could still see myself there in the dream. I was out under some trees gathering firewood."

"Oh, my God," Marrissa said. Then she said, "It sounds just like you."

"At first I saw the dream as a comic event. Now I see the pride and the self-indulgence in it."

"I wish I had dreams like that."

"What for?"

"I'm bored," she said.

In the pound there was a line of people waiting to destroy their animals or to save an animal. It was the same line. It was like something God would have thought up. When it was our turn I said we had an unwanted dog. That's the expression they use. A teenage girl was clerking behind the window.

"Shall we destroy her immediately?"

"Sure," I said. Just then Princess stood up and put her front paws on my thigh and licked my fingers. I felt the heart tug. Marrissa laughed nervously.

A young couple was standing in line behind us. They didn't have an animal with them so I supposed they wanted one. When the young man saw Princess licking my fingers he asked Marrissa, "What are you going to do with your dog?" There was an edge to his voice.

"We're destroying her," Marrissa said.

"Why are you doing that?" the young man said tensely.

Marrissa started making excuses and twisting from one foot to the other. The clerk handed me the destruction slip and told me to follow the yellow line through a glass door out to a courtyard. Marrissa pushed against my back to hurry me along.

"Did you hear what that guy asked me?" she said. "Why did he think I'm doing it to my dog?"

She imitated his tense masculine voice. "Why are you doing that to your dog, lady?"

"Oh, I really don't know," she answered in her own schoolgirl voice. "I just thought it'd be kinda kinky."

It was a tiny moment of unique theater just for us. It made me feel proud.

Author's Note

CHIP SMITH, my publisher, asks if I want to acknowledge some of those folk who helped me produce this book. I would like to. While nobody helped me write it, there were many who helped me live it. At the same time, anyone I might mention by name would run the risk of being insulted, humiliated and condemned for associating with me. I thought I understood very early on that, for myself, I had nothing to lose. I was wrong about that. Early on I was still thinking of career, money, public reputation. That much was true. Though at the time I had none of those things and no hope for them.

But I was not thinking of what really would matter. The loss of friends, some of great intimacy, was what was threatened, and what happened. There was nothing for it. What could I do? I could not give up on what my heart told me was the right thing to do. I'm not an intellectual; I don't depend on thought to guide my actions, but on awareness. For me, thought comes after the moment I recognize what it is I am seeing, or understanding. After that first moment I can go on to reflect on what I saw, judge its value, its good sense or the absence of it. Then I can use memory, my experience, to write about what I have in that moment become aware of.

Acknowledgements? I think I'll just stand alone here.

Bradley R. Smith
May, 2014

BRADLEY REED SMITH was born in South Central Los Angeles in 1930. He is a combat veteran of the Korean War (7th Cavalry) where he was twice wounded. He has served as a deputy sheriff in Los Angeles County. He has worked as a railway brakeman, as a merchant seaman, and in various construction trades. He was once a bullfighter in Mexico, and he was a freelance writer in Vietnam during the Tet Offensive. As a bookstore proprietor in Hollywood in the early 1960s, Smith was prosecuted – and convicted – for selling Henry Miller's *Tropic of Cancer*. He is the founding director of the Committee for Open Debate on the Holocaust (CODOH).

Bradley Smith has been described by the *Los Angeles Times* as an "anarchist libertarian" and by the Anti-Defamation League as one of the most dangerous "extremists" in America. He prefers to think of himself as "a simple writer." He currently makes his home in Baja, Mexico, where he lives with his wife of some forty years. They have two children and three grandchildren.

A Personal History of Moral Decay is his fourth book.

NineBandedBooks.com

Made in the USA
Charleston, SC
04 June 2014